NECESSARY GOODS

Studies in Social, Political, and Legal Philosophy

General Editor: James P. Sterba, University of Notre Dame

This series analyzes and evaluates critically the major political, social, and legal ideals, institutions, and practices of our time. The analysis may be historical or problem-centered; the evaluation may focus on theoretical underpinnings or practical implications. Among the recent titles in the series are:

Faces of Environmental Racism: Confronting Issues of Global Justice
    edited by Laura Westra, University of Windsor, and Peter S. Wenz,
    Sangamon State University
Plato Rediscovered: Human Value and Social Order
    by T. K. Seung, University of Texas at Austin
Liberty for the Twenty-first Century: Contemporary Libertarian Thought
    edited by Tibor R. Machan, Auburn University, and Douglas B. Rasmussen,
    St. John's University
In the Company of Others: Perspectives on Community, Family, and Culture
    edited by Nancy E. Snow, Marquette University
Perfect Equality: John Stuart Mill on Well-Constituted Communities
    by Maria H. Morales, Florida State University
Citizenship in a Fragile Word
    by Bernard P. Dauenhauer, University of Georgia
Critical Moral Liberalism: Theory and Practice
    by Jeffrey Reiman, American University
Nature as Subject: Human Obligation and Natural Community
    by Eric Katz, New Jersey Institute of Technology
Can Ethics Provide Answers? And Other Essays in Moral Philosophy
    by James Rachels, University of Alabama at Birmingham
Character and Culture
    by Lester H. Hunt, University of Wisconsin–Madison
Same Sex: Debating the Ethics, Science, and Culture of Homosexuality
    edited by John Corvino, University of Texas at Austin
Approximate Justice: Studies in Non-Ideal Theory
    by George Sher, Rice University
Living in Integrity: A Global Ethic to Restore a Fragmented Earth
    by Laura Westra, University of Windsor
Necessary Goods: Our Responsibilities to Meet Others' Needs
    edited by Gillian Brock, University of Auckland, New Zealand

NECESSARY GOODS

Our Responsibilities to Meet Others' Needs

Edited by Gillian Brock

ROWMAN & LITTLEFIELD PUBLISHERS, INC.
Lanham • Boulder • New York • Oxford

ROWMAN & LITTLEFIELD PUBLISHERS, INC.

Published in the United States of America
by Rowman & Littlefield Publishers, Inc.
4720 Boston Way, Lanham, Maryland 20706

12 Hid's Copse Road
Cumnor Hill, Oxford OX2 9JJ, England

British Library Cataloguing in Publication Information Available

Library of Congress Cataloging-in-Publication Data

Necessary goods : our responsibility to meet others' needs / [edited
by] Gillian Brock.
     p. cm. — (Studies in social, legal, and political
philosophy)
     Includes bibliographical references (p.   ) and index.
     ISBN 0–8476–8818–6 (cloth : alk. paper). — ISBN 0-8476-8819–4
(paper : alk. paper)
     1. Social ethics.   2. Social justice.   3. Need (Philosophy)
4. Basic needs.   I. Brock, Gillian.   II. Series.
HM216.N4   1998
303.3'72—dc21   97–45733
                                                                        CIP

ISBN 0–8476–8818–6 (cloth : alk. paper)
ISBN 0–8476–8819–4 (pbk. : alk. paper)

Printed in the United States of America

Contents

Preface

A great deal of contemporary discourse about moral and political matters invokes the language of rights, interests, or needs. Unlike the concepts of rights or interests, however, needs have received relatively little sustained philosophical attention. In an attempt to remedy this neglect, this anthology collects some of the best recent accounts of needs and arguments concerning the moral basis for responsibilities to meet needs. The anthology aims to give a comprehensive picture of how, when, and why our needs matter morally.

The focus for this collection is on these questions: What sort of moral or political importance do needs have? Which needs, if any, make defensible claims on anyone? What are the grounds for our responsibilities to meet others' needs, when we have such responsibilities?

Though authors identify the relevant categories of needs differently, there is surprising convergence among their positions about which needs are morally and politically salient. On the issue of why we have responsibilities to meet others' needs, several kinds of arguments are pressed from a variety of theoretical vantage points, including contractarian, Kantian, Aristotelian, rights-based, egalitarian, liberal, and libertarian perspectives. One might expect that the most severe opposition to our having any responsibilities to meet needs would come from libertarians. Several of the essays take on the libertarian, by exploring considerations she would find persuasive and showing why libertarians must acknowledge responsibilities to meet others' needs given their commitments and assumptions.

Altogether, then, in this anthology the authors present a range of arguments and so a compelling case for our having responsibilities to meet others' needs. Moreover, the arguments' resonance with current political concerns is particularly good: with global moves afoot to shrink the welfare state and cut welfare programs (for instance, in North America, Scandinavia, and New Zealand), the philosophical issues of just what responsibilities we have with respect to meeting needs deserve careful consideration.

I am indebted to several people for help with this anthology. Stephen Davies, Michael Ferejohn, and Geoffrey Sayre-McCord offered invaluable advice about the project. Robin Adler, Julie Kirsch, and Jennifer Ruark, from Rowman & Littlefield, and Cheryl Hoffman, from Hoffman-Paulson

Associates, were always exceptionally helpful. I am deeply grateful to Peta Bamber and Simone Rasmussen, who suffered much of the word-processing anguish with me, as we constantly discovered the limitations of our current package.

Acknowledgments

"Aristotelian Social Democracy" is reprinted from *Liberalism and the Good* edited by Bruce Douglas and Gerald Mara (New York and London: Routledge, 1990) by permission of the publisher.

"Equality, Justice, and the Basic Needs" is an abridged, reorganized, and partially rewritten descendant of "The Right to an Adequate Standard of Living: Justice, Autonomy, and the Basic Needs," which originally appeared in *Social Philosophy and Policy* 9 (1992): 231–61. Reprinted with the permission of Cambridge University Press.

"Is Redistribution to Help the Needy Unjust?" originally appeared in *Analysis* 55, no. 1 (January 1995): 50–60. It is reprinted here with permission.

"Necessity and Desire" was originally published in *Philosophy and Phenomenological Research* 45 (September 1984): 1–13. Permission to reprint the article has been received from both the journal and the author, who holds the copyright.

"Rights, Obligation, and Needs" was originally published in *Logos* 6 (1985): 29–47. Reprinted with permission of *Logos* and the author.

"A Theory of Human Need" has been adapted from *A Theory of Human Need* by Len Doyal and Ian Gough (London: Macmillan, and New York: Guilford, 1991) and is reprinted with the permission of the authors, Macmillan Press Ltd., and Guilford Publications Inc.

"Vulnerabilities and Responsibilities: An Ethical Defense of the Welfare State" was first published in *American Political Science Review* 79 (September 1985), 775–87. Permission to reprint has been granted by the American Political Science Association (which runs the journal and holds the copyright) and the author.

"What Is the Force of the Claim That One Needs Something?" is extracted from *Needs, Values, Truth: Essays in the Philosophy of Value* (Oxford: Blackwell, 1991). Reprinted with permission.

Introduction

Gillian Brock

Much contemporary discourse about moral and political matters employs the language of needs. We press claims using the language of needs all the time, and we often do this in a way that suggests that our needs claims deserve to be accorded moral force. But what moral force might needs defensibly have? Do any needs make *defensible* claims on anyone? If so, which needs and whose needs can do this? What are the *grounds* for our responsibilities to meet others' needs, if we have such responsibilities?

Indeed, just what are we saying when we make needs claims? Coherent statements of need have at least the following structure: x needs y in order to z. Statements of need may be true whether or not x is aware that she needs y in order to z or, indeed, even has a conception of y, or z, or anything else. For a coherent needs claim, we can always fill in a purpose or end-state, z, to be realized by x's having y, no matter how obvious or mundane the end-state might be. Statements of need are essentially instrumental claims. They express a relation that x's having y is needed to achieve some end, z. It is not necessarily the case that statements of need should have moral force. Tom may need an axe to be an axe-murderer. Mary may need golf clubs in order to play golf, but why should Mary's playing golf (typically) impose any moral responsibilities on others to provide golf clubs? Clearly, not all statements of need make defensible claims on others: some things may be needed to realize morally repugnant or even (relatively) trivial purposes. So, we will want to know, Are there any sorts of needs that do defensibly make claims on others? What sorts of claims of need are likely contenders for such moral importance? We will look at such questions shortly and notice that various authors have different, but importantly overlapping, ways of picking out these categories.

More generally, the articles in this anthology explore different aspects of the moral importance of needs. They tackle the following set of questions:

1

Q1. Which needs, or categories of needs, have moral or political significance?

Q2. What moral or political importance do various categories of needs have? What responsibilities do needs generate? What arguments can be marshaled for these claims?

Q3. Are opponents of the claims about needs' importance committed to accepting their force? What special considerations can be brought to bear to persuade those not disposed to the arguments that needs have moral or political importance?

Q4. What can be said to allay skepticism about needs and their capacity to do moral or political work?

Certainly, there are plenty of skeptical worries about needs and their being able to play a role in moral or political theory. Some of the most frequently pressed concerns involve perceived relativism about needs. What a person considers a need can be importantly affected by her beliefs, attitudes, conventions, and personal preferences. One person might claim to need a television set or air-conditioning, whereas others may believe that these are luxuries or matters of personal preference but certainly not needs of any morally important kind. Yet if needs are to play any substantive role in moral or political theory—if (say) there is to be state distribution according to need—it is thought that we will have to draw up standardized lists of what people need, or at least have some way of sorting real needs from mere pretenders. Can we draw up such lists that apply to everyone? Can we sort the real needs from the imposters? The amount of variation in what people claim to need would seem to suggest that we can do neither. Furthermore, if state officials are assigned the task of determining our "real" needs or drawing up such lists, there is fear that talk about needs might lend itself to authoritarianism, totalitarianism, or paternalism.

As we will see, the key to disarming all these objections is to show that the concept of needs does have limits and that these can be drawn in principled ways. In particular, it will be important to show that there is a clear criterion for determining the needs that are to be accorded moral or political significance. Most of the worries exaggerate the difficulties involved in determining what those needs are. As most of the authors argue, the concept of needs has a core area of application that is not so essentially contested as to be completely arbitrary, relative, or indeterminate.

I turn now to outline the authors' central claims, with particular attention to the set of questions Q1–Q4. Then in the subsequent section I examine what progress the authors make with respect to answering these questions.

The Central Claims and Arguments

Harry Frankfurt observes that the language of needs has a certain rhetorical potency over the language of desire. He notices, for instance, that people are

> widely disposed to accept the proposition that a need for something preempts a desire *for that thing*. This proposition, which I shall call the Principle of Precedence, attributes to needs only a quite minimal moral superiority over desires. It maintains no more than that when there is a competition between a desire and a need for the same thing, the need starts with a certain moral edge. That is, when A needs something that B wants but does not need, then meeting A's need is prima facie morally preferable to satisfying B's desire. (20)

Which needs enjoy the kind of status the Principle of Precedence would accord? Frankfurt goes on to observe that it is not the case that just any need deserves this sort of status. Suppose someone decides to complete a crossword puzzle, just on a whim, and suppose the person cannot do this without consulting a dictionary. Suppose he says he needs a dictionary. Such a claim to *need* a dictionary does not deserve more respect than another's claim to *want* a dictionary, which also arises just on a whim. Frankfurt correctly observes that the claim to need generated by one's whim does not deserve greater moral importance than a desire also generated by a whim. Needs are sometimes no more morally important than desires.

Frankfurt suggests two necessary conditions for a need to be morally important, and so to enjoy the protection of the Principle of Precedence. For Frankfurt, a need is morally important only if *harm will result* if the need is not met and that harm is *outside the person's voluntary control*.[1]

David Wiggins also sees harm arising from factors beyond one's control as crucial to why needs matter, when they do. To develop this idea, Wiggins introduces some terminology to reflect important differences. Wiggins draws a distinction between the badness, or gravity, of needs, their urgency, their basicness, their entrenchment, and their substitutability. These are all technical terms for him, but the following rough summary gets at the key points. For Wiggins, the badness, or gravity, of needs has to do with the quantity of harm that will ensue if the need is not satisfied. The urgency of a need refers to how soon harm will occur if the need is not satisfied. A need is basic if it results from a law of nature, an unalterable and invariable environmental fact, or a fact about human constitution. The entrenchment of a need has to do with how flexible the need itself is to modification. A need's substitutability is a measure of the flexibility with which the need can be satisfied.

For Wiggins, it is his category of "vital needs" or "vital interests" (and he seems to use these two terms interchangeably) that are especially morally important. Vital needs are defined in terms of the badness and substitutability of a need. He says that if someone "very badly needs at *t* to have *x* at *t,* and the need is also significantly entrenched as of *t* and scarcely substitutable at all, then his having *x* may be said to represent a vital interest of his. His having the need for *x* will then be the same as his having a vital interest in having *x*" (40).

According to Wiggins, the force of a claim of need depends on the aspect (or "phase") of justice under consideration. The main positive claims Wiggins makes about the importance of needs are these:

W1. The fact that something is a vital need is a ground for there being an abstract claim-right or entitlement to the needed thing. If one is denied what is needed, one has adequate reason to withdraw support for, and cooperation with, the society.

W2. If government intervenes in citizens' affairs, it should not interfere in such a way that vital needs are sacrificed to "mere" desires nor so that greater vital interests are sacrificed to lesser ones. He calls this "the Principle of Limitation." He argues that the Principle of Limitation is a prerequisite for any workable social morality.[2]

David Braybrooke is, arguably, the philosopher who has done the most to develop the details of how needs can assist in doing real political work. He shows how the concept of needs has much to offer not only to moral and political theory but also, and most importantly, to public policy. We need several key technical terms to understand his program. Here I introduce only the main ones (the names of which conveniently render the meanings transparent). A Policy-Making Population decides on policies dealing with matters of needs for a Reference Population. The first task for the Policy-Making Population is to decide on a List of Matters of Need and then to decide on the Minimum Standards of Provision for each Matter of Need. When members of the Policy-Making Population are deciding which needs should go on the List, they should have in mind a Criterion. He says: "Many people . . . would find persuasive a Criterion according to which something was a Matter of Need and provisions for it enough to meet the Minimum Standards of Provision if without having such provisions the persons in question would no longer be able to carry out fully four basic social roles: as citizens, workers, parents, and householders" (59).

Braybrooke's Census Notion tallies the number of needs being met by current arrangements for each Need on the List. The Census Notion can help us judge what progress is being made with respect to meeting needs by evaluating whether policies increase or decrease the numbers of Needs being met. There is much refinement that accompanies such evaluations; for instance, the Gains Preservation Principle seeks to protect advances that have been made with respect to needs that are met under current arrangements.

According to Braybrooke's Principle of Precedence, some people can be required to give up some goods that they do not require to meet their needs so that resources can be allocated to help others meet their basic needs. The Principle does not require people to give up what they need in favor of others having their needs met. Needs enjoy a certain "SL-lexicographical priority" according to the Principle. That is to say, "until every Minimum Standard of Provision for every person in the Reference Population and every Matter of Need has been reached, matters of preference, only a residual category not associated with Matters of Need on the List, have to wait in everybody's case" (61).

What arguments does Braybrooke offer for his Principle of Precedence? For Braybrooke, justice—even justice as defined by libertarian lights—will require as a necessary condition that needs be met. If people do not have their needs met, they are particularly vulnerable to having their rights violated, especially by the excessively wealthy, whose power can dictate economic and political policies. According to Braybrooke, even libertarians will want protections in place to ensure that people are not in danger of having their rights violated.[3]

In Braybrooke's view, utilitarianism has made little progress by cashing out utility in terms of preferences and in aggregating these. Providing for matters of need is a fairly reliable and underdeveloped way of fostering happiness and achieving the goals of utilitarianism. So, a better approach could well be to reform the principle of utility so that some priority is given to meeting needs. He believes utilitarianism might do better to recast itself as an ethics in two parts: one part that embraces SL-lexicographical priority for needs and a second part that attends to preference satisfaction, for, to be sure, at least some preference satisfaction should be included in stories about good lives.

Robert Goodin's defense of our responsibilities to meet needs also centers around the notion of vulnerabilities and how this generates responsibilities. Goodin prefers to talk of vulnerability rather than need, because "[s]aying merely that 'A is in need' leaves unspecified who should be responsible for meeting those needs. Saying that 'A is vulnerable to B' provides a ready answer to that question" (79), or so he argues.

On Goodin's view, "A is vulnerable to B if and only if B's actions and choices have a great impact on A's interests" (79). Responsibilities can vary with vulnerabilities: "[t]hose to whom one is relatively more vulnerable have relatively greater responsibilities" (79). He presents an argument that he believes can be used to analyze a broad range of social responsibilities. In outline, the argument is this: We have a number of special responsibilities to family members, friends, and others close to us. But the grounds of those responsibilities are not particularly special. It is the vulnerability of others that grounds these, not any voluntarily assumed obligations. There are many people who are vulnerable to our individual or collective actions, and so we have "strictly analogous (and, potentially, equally strong) responsibilities" to all these others too.

Someone might plausibly ask: What, actually, is supposed to be morally worrisome about vulnerability? After all, if there were no vulnerability, there could be no love, and a world without love would be a worse place. Goodin responds that it is not vulnerability as such that is bad. It is the asymmetry of the vulnerability. It is the vulnerability arising from unilateral dependence and asymmetrical power relations that is morally important, for these relationships make it possible for the strong to exploit the weak. Ensuring that provisions are in place for all to meet their basic needs goes some way toward protecting against such possibilities.

According to Goodin, his argument has all sorts of implications, including the following: state welfare services are a plausible way by which we can discharge our responsibilities to fellow citizens; affluent countries have strong international obligations to assist poor ones; and we should ensure that the effects of our actions on future generations, animals, and natural environments are not too onerous. How should we balance these competing obligations when they conflict, as they frequently do? Certainly, the nature of the interest at stake will be relevant, as will be the issue of whether we are the agents of last resort. Goodin suggests that, as a general rule, those relatively near to us both in space and time are likely to be more vulnerable to our actions, and we can therefore justify some bias for "our own kind"; "[c]harity may indeed begin at home, but morally it must not stop there" (85).

Onora O'Neill also sees vulnerabilities as central to the arguments for our having responsibilities to meet needs. She argues that the language of rights is inadequate to the task of accommodating needs; we should rather look to the more basic language of obligations if we want to take adequate account of needs.

In her view, prospects look dim for showing obligations to help the needy within a rights perspective. If we have a picture in which justice is "a matter of assignable, hence claimable, and potentially enforceable rights, which only the claimant can waive" (98) and beneficence is not similarly assignable and so is "unclaimable and unenforceable, "helping the needy becomes a voluntary matter left to the discretion of individuals or private organizations. According to this picture, "[o]thers' need, even their hunger and destitution, will be thought injustice only if we can either show that there is a universal right to be fed, to which a perfect obligation corresponds, or that each hungry person has a special right to have his or her material needs met" (99).

So are there any universal or special rights to have one's basic needs met? First, are there special obligations to assist the needy as compensation for past or present injustice? It can be argued that the plight of the needy in the under-developed world is due largely to the activities of individuals, nations, and multinational corporations of more developed countries, and so compensation is owed to the needy. Though plausible in some cases, these arguments are difficult to press in a wholesale way: some of those now most in need of help have hardly been touched by activities of the developed world, O'Neill argues.

Is there, perhaps, a universal right to have one's basic needs met? Typical arguments for this conclusion proceed from a recognition that if we are to take seriously liberty rights, and so the autonomy of agents, we must also concern ourselves with the material conditions for human agency, and having needs satisfied finds a place here. O'Neill does not believe such arguments are likely to succeed, because there is an important asymmetry between negative and positive rights: everyone can easily comply with the obligation not to kill, injure, assault, and so forth. By contrast, she thinks "it does not seem that 'welfare' claim rights can have as their counterpart universal obligations to make available an aliquot [fractional] amount of some good or to provide an aliquot service" (103). She correctly observes that once we start talking about enforcing these rights, the alleged distinction between positive and negative rights breaks down. She claims that an important difference nevertheless remains:

> Although it is true that the enforcement of a right not to be tortured demands positive action, just as enforcement of a right to food does, the difference between the two rights remains, whether or not there is enforcement. If, in the absence of enforcement, A tortures B, we are quite clear who has violated B's right; but if A does not provide B with food, or even with an aliquot morsel of food, we are not sure whether A has violated B's rights. There is nothing to show that it is *against* A that B's claim to food should be lodged, rather than against others, or to show that it is a legitimate claim. (103–4)

Unless assignable obligations are attached to rights claims, O'Neill believes that the rights claims amount only to manifesto rights. So she believes that if we start with obligations, we will do better in having needs incorporated into ethical discussion.

Because she believes the discourse of obligations is more appropriate when considering action-oriented ethical reasoning, she thinks the "Kantian ethical enterprise" might be a particularly good way to proceed here. According to Kant, we should refrain from acting in ways that are not universalizable (in relevant ways), and so we can identify several principles of justice. Importantly, one of these is a principle that prohibits coercion. According to O'Neill, Kant emphasizes that his principles of obligation are principles for actual, finite, rational beings. In order to see whether actual, finite, rational beings are being coerced, we will have to take account of their circumstances, for what constitutes a threat will sometimes depend significantly on relative power and vulnerability. Of course, a very basic form of vulnerability is that of those who are needy "to those who have the power to grant or refuse them the means of life, whether directly by help or hindrance or indirectly by the mediation of social institutions" (108). It is widely thought that "[w]hen we are in great need, others do not have to threaten much for compliance to be as ready as it would be, under other circumstances, to a pointed gun" (108). So if the needy are not to be coerced, we will have to ensure that they are not totally vulnerable to the actions of the powerful, and this means, at the very least, that we must ensure that institutional arrangements are in place to take care of their basic needs.

In direct contrast to O'Neill, who believes that we cannot find room for responsibilities to meet needs within a rights framework, David Copp argues that we can. Copp argues that there is a right to be enabled to meet one's needs. He calls this "The Right." The Right is held against the state (rather than individuals) and is conditional on one's society's being in favorable circumstances. Copp attempts to clarify what is entailed and what is not entailed by The Right. For instance, it is not the case that The Right entails that very costly needs must be satisfied, especially if this leaves many others unable to satisfy their needs. The Right is limited by a "stop-loss provision," so that the state is not obligated to go past a certain specified limit to enable any particular person to meet her basic needs. Also, perhaps after a person has enjoyed a normal life span, the state is not unjust if it then limits the resources it allocates to enabling her to meet her needs. Costly needs and other difficult cases must be balanced against the interests of all citizens in continuing to meet their needs.

For Copp, the basic human needs are roughly the requirements of rational autonomy. He says that "the basic needs are the things that, at some time in the course of life, are indispensable in some form and quantity to a rational and autonomous life for a human, given the 'laws of nature, unalterable and invariable environmental facts, or facts about human constitution'" (125).

What argument does he offer as to why this right exists? Clearly, many moral views suggest that good societies should foster the rational agency of their members, and he points to Kantian, Aristotelian, and Utilitarian theories as evidence of this.

> There is reason, moreover, to think that society has a *duty* to bring this about. For if meeting one's basic needs is necessary to avoid harm, then any theory that implies a duty to help people avoid harm would imply a duty to help people meet their basic needs. And since one particularly important kind of harm threatened by failure to meet one's basic needs is damage to one's rational autonomy, any theory that implies a duty to promote the rational autonomy of others as well as of oneself would imply a duty to help people meet their basic needs. (128)

Moreover, Copp argues that other rights against the state are grounded crucially in their protecting autonomy and "[i]t is a small additional step to claim that . . . the state ought to give priority to enabling the citizen to preserve and promote her rational autonomy" (129). Copp believes that a good case can be made that the needs of citizens give them rights against the state. If the state has a moral duty, then citizens have a duty to support it in discharging that duty, so citizens must pay their share of the cost of programs designed to enable people to meet their needs.

Martha Nussbaum also believes that meeting needs is a fundamental state duty. She offers an Aristotelian defense for the view. Aristotle saw that the task of political planning is to "make available to each and every citizen the material, institutional, and educational circumstances in which good human functioning may be chosen: to move each and every one of them across a threshold of capability into circumstances in which they may choose to live and function well" (135). Nussbaum fleshes out a picture of good human functioning that she calls "the thick vague conception" of a good human life, showing at crucial points how her Aristotelian conception contrasts with the liberal view. (In particular, her thick conception is meant to contrast sharply with thin liberal theories that try to be as neutral as possible about what constitutes a good human life.)

For Aristotle, wealth, income, possessions, and so forth are not goods in themselves; they are useful for doing something. So it is more important to have a view of what is good human functioning—what it is to live a good human life—and then to ask what resources enable such a life than to focus on distribution of resources in the abstract. Nussbaum's "thick vague conception" of what it is to live a good human life is supposed to apply to all human lives. She believes that there are many cross-cultural, common elements to myths and stories that deal with the human condition and the structure of human life. By examining these, we can come to a partial list of those common features and thus can construct a list of basic human functional capabilities. Her long list includes being able to have good health; being adequately nourished; having adequate shelter; having opportunities for sexual satisfaction; being able to have attachments to things and persons outside ourselves; being able to love those who love and care for us; being able to engage in critical reflection about the planning of one's own life; being able to engage in various forms of familial and social interaction; being able to laugh, to play, and to enjoy recreational activities. The task of Aristotelian politics is to ensure that

> [w]ith respect to each of the functionings mentioned in the thick vague conception, citizens are to receive the institutional, material, and educational support that is required if they are to become capable of functioning in that sphere according to their own practical reason—and functioning not just minimally, but well, insofar as natural circumstances permit. . . . Both the design of institutions and the distribution of resources by institutions are done with a view to citizens' capabilities. (151)

Clearly, the Aristotelian view has high expectations of what politics can and should do for individuals' lives. Len Doyal also offers a lush view of the task of government and of the obligations of each of us to one another. For Doyal, basic needs are "universalizable preconditions that enable nonimpaired participation both in the form of life in which individuals find themselves and in any other form of life that they might subsequently choose if they get the chance" (158). Doyal goes on to explore what some of the preconditions for nonimpaired participation in a form of life might be. "For individuals to act and to be responsible, they must have both the physical and the mental capacity to do so—at the very least *a body that is alive* and that is governed by all of the relevant causal processes and the *mental competence to deliberate and to choose*" (158). In order to act, individuals must physically survive and have sufficient personal autonomy. These preconditions generate others. For instance, simply surviving is not enough to enable participation in a form of life; rather, physical health is what is required. Similarly, three key variables affect levels of individual autonomy: the level of understanding of the agent; her psychological capacities to formulate options; and the objective opportunities for action. Agents should also have the capacity for "critical autonomy," that is, the ability to reflect critically at high levels and opportunities to express both freedom of agency and political freedom.

What arguments does Doyal offer as to why we might have responsibilities to meet needs? He argues that we have duties to help those in our community meet their needs because we expect all members of our community to behave in certain ways, and since they will need their basic needs met in order to perform any actions, our expectations of them generate a duty for us, collectively, to meet their basic needs. But we also have responsibilities to meet strangers' needs (that is, the needs of non–community members). He invites us to consider a situation in which many on a beach see a child drowning in the surf. Who is responsible for helping the drowning child? Those who have special responsibilities, for instance, lifeguards and parents, might have primary responsibility here. But if those charged with primary responsibility do not act, others must. If strangers' needs are being ignored by those who have special responsibilities to meet those needs, others are obligated to step in. When it comes to satisfying strangers' needs, collectives rather than individuals are primarily responsible. Individuals must discharge their responsibilities to satisfy the needs of strangers by supporting relevant institutional agencies.

It can be expected that libertarians would eschew these lush views (embraced by, for instance, Goodin, Nussbaum, and Doyal) of our responsibilities to one another and of the requirement for a high level of state involvement in enabling us to meet needs. Libertarians hold that the only kinds of obligations we have to one another are ones of not interfering with one another's liberties or rights. It is all very well if citizens volunteer to help meet the needs of others; however, to tax people for this purpose would be to interfere with their liberties and rights, and so taxation for welfare purposes is unjust. I argue against the libertarian view that redistribution to help the needy is unjust because such redistribution violates rights. I claim that, even if we are sympathetic to libertarians' points of departure, we cannot reach their desired conclusion. I show in particular how others' needs crucially affect the defensibility of property rights by examining how such rights are justified by libertarians.

The main argument has three key premises. First, for an account of property acquisition to be defensible, there must be some constraints on what counts as permissible acquisition. No defensible account of initial acquisition can endorse unconditional taking of unowned stuff. Second, whether or not an initial acquisition is justified depends importantly on the scarcity of resources relative to those who need them. A determination of what one may defensibly appropriate must take into account the effects the appropriation will have on others. The number of people who might also need access to vital resources significantly alters whether initial acquisitions are justified. Third, constraints on initial acquisition permanently track the property right; that is, constraints on initial acquisition must continue to be met if the property right is to retain its defensibility. Should those conditions no longer be met, the defensibility of the property right can be called into question. From these premises, it follows that property rights must be permanently sensitive to others' needs if they are to retain their defensibility. I show that libertarians actually accept each of the key premises, in one form or another. But more importantly, I show that they are committed to accepting these premises if they want to lay claim to a defensible account of initial acquisition and property rights, more generally.

For which needs is redistribution permissible, then? One gloss on the central argument goes like this: taking resources may be defensible so long as you leave enough for others to make their own way in meeting their needs. I suggest that this is unproblematically equivalent to saying that property rights may be justified (initially and more permanently) only so long as you leave enough for others to make their own way in meeting their own needs, or supply the necessary conditions for others to do this, and the second disjunct is now the relevant one dictating action. The emphasis is on enabling people to meet their own needs themselves, ensuring the necessary conditions for this to be possible; thus, ensuring the necessary conditions for human agency must surely deserve priority here.[4]

James Sterba also takes on libertarians at their own game. He offers two main arguments targeted at two different kinds of libertarians. Libertarians are concerned to promote an ideal of liberty. This ideal may be interpreted in two ways. Following Herbert Spencer, some libertarians take the right to liberty as basic. Other libertarians, following John Locke, take a set of rights, such as a right to life and a right to property, as basic and define liberty as the absence of constraints in the exercise of these rights. Sterba argues that both strands of libertarianism are committed to welfare rights.

Spencerian libertarians hold that a right to liberty—a negative right to non-interference—is primary. As discussed, the apparatus of the welfare state requires contributions from citizens, and libertarians claim that taxing citizens to support the welfare state interferes unjustly with their liberty. Sterba argues that libertarians fail to appreciate that the liberties of the poor are also at stake here: "[w]hat is at stake is the liberty of the poor not to be interfered with in taking from the surplus possessions of the rich what is necessary to satisfy their basic needs" (188). He writes:

> When the conflict between the rich and the poor is viewed as a conflict of liberties, either we can say that the rich should have the liberty not to be interfered with in using their surplus goods and resources for luxury purposes or we can say that the poor should have the liberty not to be interfered with in taking from the rich what they require to meet their basic needs. If we choose one liberty, we must reject the other. What needs to be determined, therefore, is which liberty is morally preferable: the liberty of the rich or the liberty of the poor. (188)

He argues that it would clearly be unreasonable to require that the poor sacrifice the liberty to meet their basic needs so that the rich can have the liberty to meet their need for luxuries. The poor cannot be morally required to "sit back and starve to death." It would be unreasonable for the poor to make such a sacrifice in comparison with *the size of the sacrifice* the rich could be asked to make in giving up consumption of luxury goods.

How does the argument go for Lockean libertarians? Lockean libertarians believe that a set of rights is basic—and this set typically includes a right to life and a right to property—and that liberty consists in persons not constraining one from doing what one has a right to do. Sterba argues that if the rich prevent the poor from taking what they require to satisfy their basic needs, the rich, in effect, are killing the poor (whether intentionally or unintentionally) and so violating their right to life. Sterba also defends his view against a number of libertarian objections.

John Baker and Charles Jones can also be interpreted as taking a cherished libertarian ideal seriously and showing why the libertarian cannot escape responsibilities to meet needs. They take up the popular idea of individualizing responsibility for meeting needs—the view that each person should satisfy her own needs—and show why it is untenable: some people are quite incapable of meeting their own needs (such as young children), some needs are intrinsically social (such as the need for companionship), and some needs are for services that no one can seriously be expected to provide for herself (such as education and health care). Furthermore, every act of need satisfaction occurs within a socially constructed and maintained structure of choice. The social structures within which people find themselves sometimes allow people no real opportunities to meet their needs.

One response to these objections is to formulate a more sophisticated principle that preserves the original thought. Such a principle might be something like this:

> A. Social structures should be organized to ensure as far as possible that individuals have an equal and real opportunity to satisfy their own basic needs; that is, they are equally enabled to satisfy these needs.
> B. Insofar as people do have such an opportunity/ability, they should be responsible for satisfying their own needs.
> C. Such responsibility for satisfying basic needs as it remains impossible to devolve onto individuals should be shouldered by people attached to them by kinship, religion, ethnicity, nationality, or other forms of communal attachment, not by strangers. (221)

Baker and Jones show that part A of the principle entails considerable collective responsibilities. Insofar as we want to hold people responsible for meeting their own needs, there is a collective responsibility to ensure that the framework is in place to make this possible. Part A will have a number of practical implications. For instance, since the major way in which people are able to satisfy their own needs is through employment, we must be committed to a policy of full employment and of adequate wages for meeting needs at market prices.

Baker and Jones show that part B has several limitations. In some cases, a policy of strict personal responsibility can be counterproductive. In others, coordinated, collective action leads to better outcomes for all than does uncoordinated, individual action. Furthermore, because collective action generates certain needs, this collective action entails some responsibility for helping to satisfy the needs it generates. For instance, the need to be literate and numerate to function in developed countries generates a need for certain kinds of education, and our collective action in generating the first may mean we now have collective responsibilities to assist in the satisfaction of the second. There is room for individual responsibility, but its scope should not be exaggerated.

Baker and Jones argue against the plausibility of part C on several grounds, some of which parallel the arguments against individual responsibility. Endorsing a policy of strict local responsibility (rather than global responsibility) can be counterproductive and inefficient. Moreover, "apart from family and friends, those with whom we share various sorts of group membership are strangers, and therefore the ethical appeal of closeness in relationships does not support special concern for fellow nationals or compatriots" (229).

Though they argue that, ultimately, there are global responsibilities for need satisfaction, Baker and Jones do not see this as ruling out the devolution of some responsibilities to local communities. Indeed, in many cases, this would be preferable for reasons of efficiency and to avoid domination by others. All things considered, it is best if people are empowered to define and meet their own needs themselves.

Taking Stock: A Progress Report on Some Answers to the Crucial Questions

I turn now to see what progress has been made with answering the set of questions Q1–Q4. First, Q1.

We have seen a variety of views on how to pick out the morally relevant categories of needs. For Frankfurt, a need is morally important only if *harm will result* if the need is not met and that harm is *outside the person's voluntary control*. These two features are echoed in all the other accounts. Indeed, we might see many of the other authors as elaborating on the kind of harm that is likely to ensue if the crucial needs are not met and the ways in which averting the harm could be beyond our control. For Copp, the crucial harm occurs when our ability to live a rational and autonomous human life is undermined, and the indispensability of the need is dictated by the laws of nature, unalterable and invariable environmental facts, or facts about human constitution. For Wiggins, it is the graveness of harm and the entrenchment and nonsubstitutability of what would satisfy the need that are crucial. Nussbaum, Braybrooke, and Doyal all stress that morally relevant needs are those that are important in being able to function minimally: if the needs are not met, harm that derives from the constraints of human functioning occurs. For Doyal, basic needs are universalizable preconditions that enable nonimpaired participation in any form of life. Nussbaum introduces a list of basic human functional capabilities to give content to the idea of minimal human functioning. Braybrooke tries to expand on the idea of minimal human functioning by examining what humans basically do. For Braybrooke, if one does not have basic needs met, one would be unable to carry out fully four fundamental social roles, namely, the roles of citizen, worker, parent, and householder.

Several common elements emerge. As the authors emphasize, the needs that matter morally are bounded by the idea of the necessary, the essential, the indispensable, or the inescapable. Furthermore, if the needs are not met, we are unable to do anything much at all and certainly are unable to lead a recognizably human life. Meeting the morally relevant needs is central to our abilities to function as human agents. So, while the authors may pick out the category of relevant needs in different ways, their identifications share several features, so the apparently different categorizations have key ingredients in common.

Different principles are introduced to help capture the importance of needs. Frankfurt offers us his Principle of Precedence, according to which, when A needs something that B wants but does not need, meeting A's need is prima facie morally preferable to satisfying B's desire (20). According to Braybrooke's Principle of Precedence, some people can be required to give up some goods that they do not require to meet their needs so that resources can be allocated to help all meet their basic needs; needs enjoy a certain lexicographical priority. Wiggins offers us his Principle of Limitation: If government intervenes in citizens' affairs, it should not interfere in such a way that vital needs are sacrificed to "mere" desires nor so that greater vital interests are sacrificed to lesser ones. He argues that the Principle of Limitation is a prerequisite for any workable social morality, as is recognition that vital needs can generate an abstract claim-right or entitlement to the needed thing. If one is denied what is needed, one has adequate reason to withdraw support for, and cooperation with, the society.

Might Wiggins be right to think that the Principle of Limitation is a requirement for all workable social moralities? Is Braybrooke's Principle of Precedence plausible? Can strong cases be made for these principles' having standing in moral or political theory? These questions are best answered in tandem with more general questions about the moral and political importance of needs. So then, what moral or political importance do needs have? What kinds of responsibilities do needs generate, and what arguments can be marshaled in defense of these claims? Furthermore, what special considerations do the authors bring to bear to persuade those opposed to the idea that we have responsibilities to meet needs? That is, what can be said in response to questions Q2 and Q3?

Several sorts of arguments about responsibilities to meet needs are pressed. One common strategy is to show the centrality of needs as necessary preconditions for autonomy, human agency, or good human functioning and then to argue that these necessary conditions should be protected and underwritten by communities. Wiggins, for instance, argues that we must secure the necessary preconditions for agency if we are to maintain a workable social morality or if there is to be a community of cooperators. Insofar as we care about the benefits of cooperation, we have reasons to protect its bases. Such considerations are likely to have some bearing with everyone, including libertarians.

Another common strategy, one employed by Goodin, O'Neill, and Braybrooke, is to point out how people are especially vulnerable to coercion, or to having their rights violated, if they do not have their needs met. Neediness, coupled with circumstances such as severely asymmetrical power relations and unilateral dependence, can create opportunities for coercion. Insofar as we expect the state, through its agency, the government, to protect us from rights violations and coercion, it could be argued that governments have responsibilities to meet needs that remove our vulnerabilities to force and injustice.

A further common strategy, one that is more general, examines the task of government. What is it that government is supposed to do? According to Wiggins, quite minimally, governments should protect the vital interests of citizens, but this might mean guaranteeing, protecting, or underwriting some of the necessary conditions for agency, which, in turn, requires that certain needs be met. Others believe government should be expected to go well beyond merely protecting the vital interests of citizens. According to the lush Aristotelian view, government's task is to ensure and facilitate the flourishing of citizens, and so meeting needs would be one among many issues that government should attend to in ensuring that citizens thrive. According to libertarians, by contrast, the job of government is more minimal. It is to ensure that liberties are not infringed nor rights violated. It is to act only as a nightwatchman. But, as replies to the libertarian, there are the arguments of Sterba and myself. These show that cherished libertarian beliefs and ideals commit one to meeting needs, given the nature of the rights and liberties at issue, and if there are to be no liberty infringements or rights violations. Also, a common libertarian ideal of self-reliance—that of strict individual responsibilities with respect to needs satisfaction—entails collective responsibilities to meet needs. The necessary conditions for individualizing responsibilities for need satisfaction, when clarified, show that a number of collective responsibilities are generated, as Baker and Jones explain.

It is also plausible to suggest that another part of government's job is to act in some cases as coordinator of our moral responsibilities. If we all have moral responsibilities (individually or collectively) to help others with their needs, an efficient way for us to coordinate and discharge these responsibilities is via the apparatus of a welfare state, set up and managed by government. Furthermore, as several authors point out, it is likely that, if we have obligations to help the needy in other countries, these are collective responsibilities. The best way to discharge such responsibilities is in a coordinated fashion.[5]

And finally Q4: what do the authors say that can allay skeptical fears about needs? Certainly, there can be real concerns about the cultural, historical, and individual relativities of needs. What is considered a need can be in large measure determined by cultural or other beliefs, attitudes, conventions, and personal preferences. The authors stress that, despite all these relativities, the concept of needs does have limits and its boundaries can be drawn in principled ways. In particular, they each argue that there is a clear criterion for determining the needs that are to be accorded moral or political importance, and they argue why the needs picked out deserve such consideration. Significantly, as I have emphasized, the proposed criteria share common ingredients, which make them importantly overlapping if not coextensive. Patching together some common ingredients, we might get to the following account of basic needs: a need is basic if satisfying it is a necessary condition for human agency. Examining the prerequisites of human agency, of what it is to function as a human agent, can get us to a list of common ingredients. The basic needs themselves would then be constrained by the nature of human agency and thus would not be radically relative to culture, beliefs, and so forth, though, clearly, the ways in which basic needs can be satisfied might be relative to just such things. Indeed, this brings us to a further common strategy for allaying concerns about relativism. This strategy distinguishes between morally relevant needs and what would satisfy them and is inflexible about the first issue but not about the second. Basic or vital needs are universal, the authors emphasize, but those things that satisfy these needs—the "satisfiers"—may be culturally variable. Provisions to meet basic needs can take a variety of forms, though the crucial needs themselves are universal, dictated by the constraints of human agency.

Does talk about needs lead dangerously to excessive state intervention, authoritarianism, or paternalism? Not necessarily. Paternalism, totalitarianism, and so on are not inevitable consequences of talk about needs or distribution according to needs but are rather a function of the decision-making procedure for arriving at policies concerning needs. Why assume that the individuals whose needs are at issue will not participate in formulating policies about their own needs (for example, about what might satisfy them)? Indeed, an acceptable decision procedure for policymaking about needs must allow just such participation. That those in power can abuse talk of needs is not incriminating evidence against the concept of needs, but rather evidence that people should not be given the kind of power that offers many opportunities for abuse. One way to prevent abuse is not to allow any one person or group to have a monopoly on decisions about needs. Furthermore, we are not guilty of paternalism if we make available real opportunities for people to meet their needs (in accordance with their self-articulated conceptions of their needs) but leave to them final choices about whether they will take up these opportunities. The authors say a good deal, then, to allay suspicion about needs' doing moral and political work.

In the articles collected here, the authors make significant progress in answering the crucial questions, Q1–Q4. The articles give a comprehensive picture of how, why, and when our needs matter. If it is still to be maintained that others' needs do not place responsibilities on the rest of us, new arguments will have to be found. In particular, libertarian arguments, if there are to be any, will need quite some reworking.

Notes

1. In "Morally Important Needs" (*Philosophia,* in press), I discuss how we should further develop these two conditions.

2. See my "Justice and Needs," *Dialogue: Canadian Philosophical Review* 35, no. 1 (Winter 1996): 81–86, for some criticisms of these arguments.

3. See my "Justice and Needs" for discussion of some of the weaknesses in this argument.

4. Such necessary conditions may well include publicly provided systems of education, legal aid, and basic health care.

5. The mere fact that something is recognized as a morally or politically important need (in virtue of being basic or vital, say) does not necessarily entail that there are moral or political responsibilities to provide the needed good or service directly. On plausible views of what counts as a basic need, something like companionship, love, or at least nonadversarial relations with some others is going to turn out to be a basic or vital need. It is far from obvious that everyone has a moral responsibility to befriend, love, or care for those who have unmet needs of these kinds. What is clearer is that we could have responsibilities as a society not to thwart such needs, say, by promoting institutional arrangements that have this effect.

1

Necessity and Desire

Harry G. Frankfurt

"Need" versus "Desire"

The language of *need* is used extensively in the representation of our personal and social lives. Its role in political and moral discourse is especially conspicuous and powerful. People commonly attribute needs to themselves and to others in order to support demands, or to establish entitlements, or to influence the ordering of priorities; and we are often inclined to respond to such attributions with a rather special respect and concern. In particular, an assertion that something is *needed* tends to create an impression of an altogether different quality, and to have a substantially greater moral impact, than an assertion that something is *desired*. Claims based upon what a person needs frequently have a distinctive poignancy. They are likely to arouse a more compelling sense of obligation, and to be treated with greater urgency, than claims based merely upon what someone wants.

Care must be taken, however, to avoid exaggerating the inherent superiority of claims grounded in needs over claims grounded in desires. It is surely not the case that the moral force of needs is unconditionally greater than that of desires in the sense that every need, without exception, is properly to be accorded unqualified priority over any desire. There are many occasions when it makes perfectly good sense for a person to sacrifice something he needs, even something he needs very badly, for the sake of something he desires but for which he has no need at all. For example, it might be quite sensible for a seriously ill person to use his limited financial resources for the pleasure cruise he has long wanted to take rather than for the surgery he needs to prolong his life. Decisions to enjoy life more at the cost of not taking care of ourselves as well as we might—to enhance the quality of life at the expense of its quantity—are neither uncommon nor invariably unjustifiable.

Perhaps this is insufficient to show that a claim based upon desire can ever compete successfully on *moral* grounds against a claim supported by need. In fact, however, needs may be no more compelling than desires even so far as strictly moral considerations are concerned. Consider a person who feels like completing a crossword puzzle and who is unable to do so without looking things up. He needs a dictionary, but the moral importance of this need is altogether negligible. It would hardly be difficult to find numerous desires with at least as much moral importance.

But now it seems that if a need may be utterly inconsequential, then attributions of need really have no inherent moral weight after all. This result appears to be decisively confirmed, moreover, by elementary theoretical considerations. Nothing is needed except for the sake of an end for which it is indispensable. The moral importance of meeting or of not meeting a need must therefore be wholly derivative from the importance of the end that gives rise to it. Whatever the importance of attaining the end, it will be exactly that important to meet the need. If the moral significance of the need for a dictionary is negligible, it is just because the goal from which the need derives is of no moral consequence. Thus it seems that the satisfaction of needs cannot be entitled to any systematic moral priority over the gratification of desires. The mere fact that something is needed, considered in isolation from the value of what it is needed for, has no independent justificatory force.

However, we must be as careful to avoid claiming too little for needs as to avoid claiming too much for them. Even apart from other considerations, the view that there is no special moral significance in the fact that a person needs something is difficult to reconcile with the manifest rhetorical potency of certain loosely manipulative uses to which the language of need is often put. These typically involve blurring the distinction between needing something and wanting it, with the obvious intention of attracting for some desire the same degree of moral consideration that tends to be accorded particularly to needs.[1]

Maneuvers of this sort would be pointless unless people were widely disposed to accept the proposition that a need for something preempts a desire *for that thing*. This proposition, which I shall call the Principle of Precedence, attributes to needs only a quite minimal moral superiority over desires. It maintains no more than that when there is a competition between a desire and a need for the same thing, the need starts with a certain moral edge. That is, when A needs something that B wants but does not need, then meeting A's need is prima facie morally preferable to satisfying B's desire. If needs do not enjoy at least *this* much precedence over desires, then it must certainly be an error to attribute *any* particular moral significance to them. In any case, the principle appears to be eminently reasonable. Other things being equal, it seems clearly preferable to allocate a resource to someone who needs it rather than to someone who wants it but who has no need for it at all.

Yet there are exceptions to the Principle of Precedence. Suppose someone undertakes a certain project just on an unreflective whim. The fact that he thereupon needs whatever is indispensable for completing the project has no more justificatory force than a casual or impulsive desire for the same thing would have. The claim of a person who needs a dictionary merely to gratify his whim to finish a puzzle is no weightier than the claim of someone who has no specific need for a dictionary but whose desire it is, for no particular reason, to possess one. Giving precedence here to the need would arbitrarily assign greater moral importance to one whim than to another.

The moral significance of a need is not, then, necessarily greater than that of its corresponding desire. Therefore we cannot unequivocally accept the doctrine that it is morally preferable to allocate resources to those who need them rather than to those who only desire them. We must distinguish between the kinds of needs that do merit precedence over the desires that correspond to them and the kinds of needs that do not.

Free Volitional Needs Lack Moral Interest

At the heart of the concept of need is the notion that there are things one cannot do without. When something is needed, it must therefore always be possible to specify what it is needed *for* or to explain *what* one cannot do without it. If a person needs surgery in order to survive, then what he cannot do without the surgery is to go on living. All necessities are in this respect conditional: nothing is needed except in virtue of being an indispensable condition for the attainment of a certain end.[2]

In many cases, a person needs something because he actively desires a certain end for the attainment of which that thing is indispensable.[3] Thus the person in my example needs a dictionary because he wants to finish the puzzle. In fact, he needs the dictionary *only* because he wants to finish the puzzle; he would not need it except for that desire. But of course a person may need certain things for more than one reason or in more than one way. When something is needed because there is something else that a person *wants*, then to that extent the need depends upon the person's *will*. I shall refer to needs of this kind as "volitional needs."

Having a volitional need is not necessarily a voluntary matter. This is because a person's will is not invariably under his voluntary control. That is, it may not be up to him whether he has the desire upon which his volitional need depends. Many of a person's desires are indeed voluntary, since they derive simply from his own decisions. Someone typically acquires the desire to see a certain movie, for example, just by making up his mind what movie to see. Desires of this sort are not aroused in us; they are formed or constructed by acts of will that we ourselves perform, often quite apart from any emotional or affective state. However, there are also occasions when what a person wants is not up to him at all but is rather a matter of feelings or inclinations that arise and persist independently of any choice of his own.

Now suppose that with respect to a certain desire, it is up to the person whether or not he has it. Then it is also up to him whether or not he has a volitional need for whatever is indispensable for the satisfaction of that desire. On the other hand, if he has no control over what he wants, then he also has no control over whether or not he has volitional needs for those things without which the desire in question cannot be satisfied. I shall refer to volitional needs that depend upon voluntary desires as "free" and to those that depend upon involuntary desires as "constrained."

Free volitional needs are not, as such, morally interesting in the sense specified by the Principle of Precedence. In other words, they do not merit priority over the desires corresponding to them. From the fact that a person needs M because it is indispensable for E, which he wants, we cannot conclude that the consideration to which his need for M is entitled is greater than the consideration that would be merited by a mere desire for M. There is no reason to think that his claim for M receives more powerful support from his desire for E than another person's claim for M would receive just from that person's desire for M itself. Why should the latter desire convey a lesser claim, after all, than the former? The fact that one person desires M while another person has a free volitional need for it leaves it entirely open which person's claim for M is better.

If free volitional needs are as such morally unimportant, it is not because the desires from which they derive are uniformly of no consequence. The fact that a desire is voluntary implies nothing whatever concerning its significance. A person may decide of his own free will not merely that he wants to finish a crossword puzzle but also far more portentous matters: that he wants to become a musician, that he wants to renounce his obligations and devote himself ruthlessly to the pursuit of his material interests, that he wants to die, and so on. The desires upon which a person's free volitional needs depend may make a very considerable difference to his life.

Other things being equal, the desirability of meeting a free volitional need depends wholly upon how desirable it is to satisfy the pertinent voluntary desire. To whatever extent it is desirable to satisfy someone's desire for a certain end, it will be desirable to the same extent to meet the needs generated by that desire. Thus the desirability of a person's end may justify his claim for what he needs in order to attain it. But insofar as his desire for the end is voluntary, the desirability of satisfying it cannot endow his claim with the *distinctive* moral quality that is specific to claims warranted by need.

This is because free volitional needs have too little necessity in them. There are two related considerations here, which illuminate the moral precedence over desires that needs of certain kinds enjoy. In the first place, since the desire from which a free volitional need derives may be for anything whatever, it may be neither important nor necessary for the desire to be satisfied; hence, it cannot be assumed that needs of this kind *need to be met*. Second, from the fact that the desire that generates a free volitional need is voluntary, it follows that the person who has such a need does not *need to need* what he needs. In order to be morally interesting, by contrast, a need must be radically distinct from a desire. It must be what I shall call "categorical"— that is, characterized by both of the necessities just considered: (1) the need must be one that the person not only wants to meet but needs to meet; and (2) what the person needs must be something that he cannot help needing. I shall discuss these two conditions in turn.

Moral Interest: The Harm Connection

The reason free volitional needs do not as such need to be met is that the desires upon which they depend may be for things that are not needed. In such a case the person *wants* his need to be met so that he may enjoy what he desires, but he does not *need* it to be met any more than he needs the desired thing itself. Suppose it should turn out that he cannot meet his free volitional need and that consequently he cannot have what he wants. Then he may well both be disappointed and have grounds for being resentful. But, given that what he wants is not something he needs, *no harm will have been done*. He will have failed to obtain a benefit of greater or of lesser value, but he will not have been harmed.

It is the linkage to harm that differentiates needs that satisfy the Principle of Precedence, and that are therefore morally interesting, from others. A person's need has moral interest only if it will be a consequence of his failure to meet the need that he incurs or continues to suffer some harm. This condition may be met, of course, even if the person has no desire for the needed object. Insofar as the link to harm does not depend upon a desire, the need is a nonvolitional one. Free volitional needs have no inherent moral interest because the mere fact that a person has a certain desire indicates at most that he expects what he desires to be in some way of benefit to him. It does not entail that he will suffer any harm if he does not obtain it.

It is not clear how to distinguish systematically between circumstances in virtue of which a person is harmed and those in virtue of which he merely fails to obtain a benefit; nor is it apparent how to define those special conditions under which someone who fails to obtain a benefit actually does thereby also incur a harm. One way to deal with the latter problem would be to maintain that failing to obtain a benefit is tantamount to incurring a harm, just in case the benefit is something the person in question needs. This is plausible but, for obvious reasons, not very helpful in the present context. Instead of attempting to formulate a more satisfactory account of the matter, I shall limit myself to three elementary observations pertinent to the relationship between benefits and harms.

First, being harmed has to do with becoming worse off than one was, while failing to obtain a benefit is more a matter of not becoming better off than before. Second, there is sometimes no way to prevent a situation from becoming worse except by making it better. In cases of that kind failure to obtain the pertinent benefit is tantamount to being harmed. Third, the life of a person whose condition is bad becomes worse and worse as long as his condition does not improve, simply because more of a bad thing is worse than less of it. Someone may be harmed, therefore, even when in a certain sense his condition does not deteriorate. This makes it possible to endorse the commonsense judgment that a chronically ill person has a morally relevant need for whatever treatment is essential to the alleviation of his illness, for it implies that even though the state of his health remained very much what it was before, he would not only fail to obtain a valuable benefit if he did not obtain the treatment but would actually be harmed.

These observations suggest why meeting needs merits priority over satisfying desires. It is because making things better is, from a moral point of view, less important (measure for measure) than keeping them from getting worse. We usually expect that when something is entrusted to a person's care, he will make a reasonable effort to protect it from damage or harm; but we do not ordinarily suppose that he has any comparable obligation to enhance its condition. With respect more generally to that part of the world that comes under a person's care—that is, for which he has responsibility—his obligation to keep it from getting worse is more compelling than his obligation (if any) to improve it. This is why allocating resources to meeting needs takes precedence over allocating them to fulfilling mere desires. The former aims at avoiding harm, while the latter aims only at providing unneeded benefits.

A person's morally interesting needs need to be met, then, because harm will ensue if they are not. But in addition, the link to harm must be of such a nature that whether or not the harm ensues is outside the person's voluntary control. This is the second respect in which free volitional needs have too little necessity in them. Not only do they derive from desires, which means that there may be no harm done even if they are not met, but furthermore the desires from which they derive are voluntary, which means that the person need not have the needs at all.

Suppose it is just in virtue of his own decision concerning what he wants that a person has the desire from which a certain need derives. This hardly puts him in the grip of necessity. The grip in which he is held is merely his own, from which he can free himself as he likes. It is no wonder that needs of this kind do not as such elicit any particular moral concern. Even when the person will in fact suffer some harm if he fails to get the object he needs, this consequence is one that he imposes upon himself and to which he continues to be exposed only as long as he is willing to be exposed to it. He does need the object, since it is indispensable to an end that he desires. But his need for it is his own concoction. The object's indispensability to the end touches him only insofar as he wants it to do so. It does not affect him unless, by his own free choice, he adopts the pertinent desire.

Unsatisfied Desire, Frustration, and Harm

Neither desires nor free volitional needs are inescapably linked to harm. This is why they are morally indistinguishable from each other and why each differs morally from categorical needs. In fact, not only do free volitional needs fail to merit precedence over the desires corresponding to them, but also there is no basis for according them as such any moral interest at all. That is, we cannot even suppose that meeting needs of this sort is inherently desirable or preferable to not meeting them.

Meeting free volitional needs would be inherently desirable only if it were inherently desirable to satisfy desires. Only in that case could the desirability of meeting any given free volitional need be presumed. Now, some philosophers do maintain that it is necessarily desirable for a desire to be fulfilled. Thus William James writes: "Take any demand, however slight, which any creature, however weak, may make. Ought it not, for its own sole sake, to be satisfied? . . . Any desire is imperative to the extent of its amount; it *makes* itself valid by the fact that it exists at all."[4] James would of course acknowledge that the desirability of satisfying a desire may be overridden by other considerations. But in his opinion the fact that a person wants something is always a reason in itself for preferring that he have it.

In my view, on the other hand, the mere fact that a person wants something provides no support for a claim that his having it is preferable to his not having it. I do not mean to deny that it is better for some of a person's desires to be satisfied than for none to be satisfied. Perhaps, other things being equal, it is necessarily better that a life include some satisfied desires than that all the desires it includes be unsatisfied. But it does not follow from this that, with respect to each of a person's desires, it is better that he have what he wants than that he not have it. What follows is only that a person's having some of the things he wants is better than his having none of them.

So far as I know, the only argument available for the position to which James adheres runs more or less as follows. An unsatisfied desire inevitably involves frustration, which is unpleasant. Hence there is always at least the same consideration in favor of satisfying a given desire as there is in favor of minimizing unpleasantness. Now in fact there is a presumption in favor of minimizing unpleasantness. Therefore, there is always a prima facie case for satisfying a given desire in preference to not satisfying it. A desire is "imperative to the extent of its amount," as James puts it, because the unpleasantness consequent to frustration will be more or less severe, and thus more or less undesirable, according to how strong the frustrated desire is.

However, the most that can validly be inferred from the premises of this argument is that there is a prima facie case against the desirability of any state of affairs in which someone has an unsatisfied desire. The only presumption warranted is, in other words, merely that satisfied desires are preferable to frustrated ones.[5] This differs substantially from a presumption in favor of the satisfaction of desire, because a satisfied desire is not the only possible alternative to a frustrated one. After all, a person also avoids frustration when—through being persuaded or in some other way—he gives up or loses his desire without satisfying it. Some of the methods that may be effective in eliminating a person's desires without satisfying them are, to be sure, quite objectionable. But this is equally true of some of the methods by which desires may be satisfied.

James's thesis undermines the conceptual distance between need and desire by linking desire to harm and thus by implying that wanting something entails needing it. If it were inevitable for a desire that is not satisfied to be frustrated, then a person could not avoid unpleasantness unless he got what he wanted. Now it is plausible to suppose that suffering unpleasantness amounts to being harmed and that everyone wants to avoid it, so that everyone both nonvolitionally and volitionally needs whatever is indispensable for avoiding unpleasantness. It is precisely because an object of desire may actually *not* be indispensable for someone else's achievement of this goal that wanting something does not entail needing it. Since a desire may be given up or lost, a person may be able to avoid frustration without getting what he wants. Thus the satisfaction of a desire is not necessarily necessary for avoiding harm.

Gratuitous or Perverse Needs

With respect to some of the things a person wants, however, it may not be possible for him either to bring himself or to be brought to stop wanting them. This is not because the desires in question are especially intense or difficult to control. Even desires that are quite unobtrusive and easily managed may nonetheless be ineradicably persistent. Needs generated by desires of this sort, which must be either satisfied or frustrated, are what I have called "constrained volitional needs." It is clear that they involve more necessity than free volitional needs do. A person whose constrained volitional need is not met will unavoidably, no matter what he voluntarily chooses or does, suffer some harm—namely, frustration. This suffices to make such needs categorical and to warrant gratifying them in preference to gratifying the desires that correspond to them.

All constrained volitional needs satisfy the Principle of Precedence. However, some of them appear worthy only of a rather qualified or equivocal concern. What distinguishes these is not that the harms to which they are linked are relatively minor, for the harms may actually be very severe. Rather, it is that the needs seem somehow to be gratuitous or even perverse. For example, suppose a man is seized by the idée fixe that his life will be worthless unless he has a certain sports car; and suppose the frustration of his desire for the car would be so deep that it would indeed ruin his life. The man cannot help wanting the car, and he wants it so badly that he will suffer sustained and crippling misery unless he obtains it. Since there is a link here to substantial harm, which is not under the man's voluntary control, his need for the sports car is both categorical and severe. What is the basis, then, for our uneasiness concerning it? Why are we inclined to be less than wholehearted in acknowledging that the claim it makes is truly legitimate?

Our reaction to the man's need for the car is likely to be the outcome of a variety of considerations. The one to which I want to call particular attention has nothing to do with any judgments concerning the paltriness of his ambition or the shallowness of his character. No doubt our respect for the man is significantly impaired by our feeling that the object of his desire is unworthy of the enormous importance it has for him. But our response to his need is also affected by a feature that need shares with others whose objects are far more worthy of desire and concern than sports cars: namely, the man's need has less to do with the specific characteristics of its object than with the nature of his desire for that object.

It is not directly because of the car's speed or beauty, or even because of its snob value, that the man will suffer if he does not get it. Presumably, it is in virtue of these characteristics that he wants the car; but they do not account for the fact that he needs it. One might even suggest that what he really needs is not the car as such at all but the gratification of his desire for it. His need is inescapably linked to harm only in virtue of his desire and not in virtue of the consequences to him that doing without the car would otherwise entail. If he did not want the sports car as he does, he would in fact have no morally significant need for it. In other words, he has no nonvolitional need to which his desire for the car corresponds.

The point may be illuminated by distinguishing needs of this kind from needs due to addiction. The latter commonly have constrained volitional needs associated with them, but they are not themselves essentially volitional. The heroin addict does typically have an involuntary desire for heroin; but it is more likely that this desire arises on account of his need for the drug than that the need derives from the desire. In any event, being addicted to something is not a matter of being unable to avoid wanting it. The characteristic suffering to which heroin addicts are subject is not the pain of frustrated desire. It is a more specific condition, which is caused just by the lack of heroin. It occurs independently of what the addict—who may not know what he is addicted to, or even that there is something to which he is addicted—wants or does not want.

There are two types of situations involving constrained volitional needs. In situations of one type, a person has a nonvolitional need as well as a constrained volitional need for a certain object; he would therefore need the object even if he did not desire it. In situations of the other type, the person's need is exclusively volitional; that is, he needs a certain object only because he desires it.

Because he has a nonvolitional need for heroin, the addict's involuntary desire for the drug serves a useful purpose. It moves him to obtain something that he needs and that he cannot help needing independently of his desire for it. On the other hand, no such purpose is served by the desire (e.g., for a sports car) upon which a person's constrained volitional need depends when the person has no nonvolitional need corresponding to the desire. In that case, there is no need and no liability to harm apart from the desire. The desire does not respond to or reflect a need; it creates one. Now, this creation of a liability to harm in no way enhances either the inherent value of the desired object or its availability. Thus it subjects a person to additional burdens and risks without endowing him with any compensatory benefits. It is in this respect that needs of the kind in question are gratuitous or perverse.

"True" and "False" Needs

The range and severity of a person's needs are contingent upon what he wants, upon how he wants it, and upon those nonvolitional aspects of his situation that determine what will harm him and what will protect him from harm. This means that needs may be generated, altered, or eliminated by changes in the environment and by the natural course of human life. Moreover, needs of each of the three types I have considered may be affected by deliberate or by unintentional human action.

Many social critics maintain that one of the ways in which exploitative societies injure their members is by causing them to incur various needs that the critics characterize as "false" or "inauthentic" or to which they refer in some other manner suggestive of undesirability or defect. One might ask, perhaps, whether it is desirable to have any categorical needs at all. The question hangs upon whether we would be better off if we were not vulnerable to harm or whether it is somehow a good thing for us that we are in this respect less than omnipotent. In any case those who condemn the creation of false or inauthentic needs do not intend to object against any increase whatever in the burden of need that people bear. Their complaint is against increases of a more particular sort. What they consider objectionable in the creation of a false need is not that an additional need has been created but that the need that has been created is a false one.

I suggest that a criterion that captures at least an important element of what is objectionable in certain needs—needs that it is plausible to consider false—may be grounded in the difference between those constrained volitional needs that coincide with nonvolitional needs and those that do not. By this criterion a person's need for a certain object is "true" or "authentic" only if the person needs the object regardless of whether or not he wants it. A need is false or inauthentic, on the other hand, if the person needs the object only because he desires it. Volitional needs are true or authentic, in other words, only insofar as they reflect needs that are nonvolitional.

This account cuts across the distinction between needs that are natural and needs that are socially imposed. What makes a need false is not that it has causes of a certain kind. Needs may be authentic or true even when they are not only artificial in the sense of being produced by human contrivance but also when the contrivance is malicious or unjust. The falsity of a need is not a matter of its origination in the machinations or the negligence of the reactionary or the wicked but of its being gratuitous or perverse in a way that has already been indicated. False needs are those in which there is no necessity except what is created by desire. Their defect is analogous to that of Protagoras's truths, which—according to the representation of his doctrine in the *Theaetetus*—are created wholly out of beliefs. Just as belief cannot correctly be construed as the measure of truth, so desire cannot properly be regarded as the measure of need.

There is a difference between our response to needs that arise exclusively from constrained volition and our response to needs that are not volitional at all. This difference remains even when, as in a case of self-induced addiction, someone's nonvolitional need is the result of his own voluntary behavior. The necessities that nature imposes upon a person (even when it is his doing that brings this about) incline us to a more sympathetic and empathic concern than those that derive immediately from the person's own free will (even when he has no control over what he wants). Our feeling that it is incumbent upon us to assist a person in need tends to become somewhat attenuated when the need is essentially derivative from that person's desire.

This may be because the hardening of desire into necessity strikes us as an analogue of "bad faith," so that we suspect the person in question of being unable to control his desire only because he does not really want to do so. In that case we do not regard the need as fully constrained, and hence we do not construe it as being genuinely categorical. It is possible that there is another reason as well. In seeking to avoid the harm to which a constrained volitional need exposes him, a person is contending not so much against nature as against himself. Perhaps this diminishes our sense of comradeship with him. If he were struggling against nature, which is our common enemy, our instinct to ally ourselves with him would be more compelling.

Notes

1. Jean-Paul Sartre and Fidel Castro collaborate in the following conversation to produce an egregious instance: "'Man's need is his fundamental right over all others,' said Castro. 'And if they ask you for the moon?' asked Sartre. '[I]t would be because someone needed it,' was Castro's reply." Quoted by George Lichtheim in *The Concept of Ideology and Other Essays* (New York: Random House, 1967), 282.

Now, from the fact that someone asks for something, it follows at most, of course, that he wants it. This sort of confusion between what is wanted and what is needed is rather common among Marxists. Thus, although it seems obvious that some commodities may satisfy only desires, Marx himself defines a commodity as "a thing that by its properties satisfies human needs of some sort or another" (*Capital* [Moscow: Foreign Languages Publishing House, 1961], 1:35). I shall take it for granted that wanting something does not entail needing it, and vice versa: a person may desire to undergo surgery but not actually need an operation, or need surgery without wanting it. This does not entail, by the way, that the concepts of need and desire are logically independent. They would be logically independent if, and only if, something could be desired without anything being needed and something could be needed without anything being desired. What the example shows is only that someone may have a need without having a desire *for what he needs* and that he may have a desire without having a need *for what he wants*.

2. It appears to be implicit in the concept of need that what something is needed

for must be other than itself. That is why it is somewhat dissonant to suggest that life and happiness are among the things people need. Circumstances may occur in which it actually does serve a special purpose for some person to go on living or to be happy; and in some cases of that kind it may be appropriate to say that the person needs to live or to be happy. But we do not suppose that the value of life, or of happiness, derives in general from the value of something else.

3.   Joseph Raz has pointed out to me that a person may want something and yet not need certain things that are indispensable for its attainment, because it is clear that he would be unable to attain it even if he got them. If he recognizes that he cannot satisfy any set of sufficient conditions for the attainment of what he wants, then he does not need to satisfy the necessary conditions. Similar considerations apply if for some reason other than unattainability—for example, very low priority—the person does not expect or intend even to attempt to satisfy his desire. By speaking of what a person "actively desires," I mean to exclude desires that he has no expectation or intention of trying to satisfy. In what follows I shall assume, without explicitly specifying them as such, that the desires upon which needs are said to depend are in this sense active.

4.   William James, "The Moral Philosopher and the Moral Life," in *Essays in Pragmatism by William James*, ed. Alburey Castell (New York: Hafner, 1948), 73.

5.   Cf. Gary Watson, "Free Agency," *Journal of Philosophy* 72 (1975): 210–11.

2

What Is the Force of the Claim
That One Needs Something?

David Wiggins

1. The Search for a Connection

It has been felt for a long time that there must be some intimate connection between the needs of human beings and their abstract rights. H. L. A. Hart was giving voice to a strong and widespread intuition when he wrote:

> A concept of legal rights limited to those cases where the law . . . respects the choice of individuals would be too narrow. For there is a form of the moral criticism of law which . . . is inspired by regard for the needs of individuals for certain fundamental freedoms and protections or benefits. Criticism of the law for its failure to provide for such individual needs is distinct from, and sometimes at war with, the criticism with which Bentham was perhaps too exclusively concerned, that the law often fails to maximize aggregate utility.[1]

In practice, the connection between needs and rights has proved elusive. Of course it ought not to have been expected that a linkage of this kind would be simple or hard-and-fast or that it would provide the one missing clue to everything that still puzzles us in the idea of justice. But if the connection is not only complicated but important too, and if what validates it is there to be discovered among the sentiments that actually sustain our various ideas about justice, it will be a great shame if the failure to be simple or hard-and-fast continues to stand in the way of our trying to understand the special force and political impact of a claim of serious need. To postpone the problem is to postpone the day when we attempt to get ourselves an account of justice that is based on as many distinct ideas as justice itself may prove to contain within itself.

In advance of questions of justice and entitlement, however, where I have been happy to work within a framework rather similar to J. L. Mackie's, not presupposing the welfare state but reasoning positively and point by point about the kind of entitlement that needing creates,[2] it will be necessary to attend for its own sake and at some length to the question of what needing is— a precaution disregarded almost equally by champions and by critics of the idea that there is something serious to be made of this notion in political philosophy. One can hardly explain the special force of a claim when one will not first determine what exactly one who makes it says, or in what contexts it seems particularly natural to make it, or what conceptions and misconceptions these contexts especially lend themselves to.

2. Need and Purpose

Something that has been insisted upon in most analytical accounts of needing is that needing is by its nature needing for a purpose[3] and that statements of need that do not mention relevant purposes (or "end-states" as Alan White calls them) are elliptical—some will say dishonestly elliptical—for sentences that do mention them.[4] One thing seems right with this claim, and another seems wrong.

The thing that seems right concerns what may be called purely instrumental needing. Someone may say, "I now need to have £200 to buy a suit," or, speaking elliptically, "I need £200." If he can't get the suit he has in mind for less than £200, then it is true, on an instrumental reading of his claim, that he needs £200. All that has to hold for this to be the case is something of the form:

> It is necessary (relative to time t and relative to the t circumstances c) that if (.... at t'') then (__ at t').[5]

In the present case, the antecedent of the conditional relates to the man's having the suit and the consequent to his having £200.

So far so good. If something like this is correct, then it makes excellent sense of the claim that certain uses of "I need to have x" are elliptical (e.g., the claim "I need £200" as made by this man); and one whole class of non-elliptical *need* sentences receives a plausible treatment. But there is something else the elucidation fails to make sense of. This is the fact that, if we have already been through everything this man can say about his need, still we can properly and pointedly respond to his claim with: "You need £200 to buy that suit, but you don't need £200—because you don't need to buy that suit." The ellipse theory suggests that he ought then to insist that there is an end of his for which the suit is necessary. But it is plain that without deliberate misunderstanding of what we are now saying, he cannot make this retort. If he did respond in this way, then it would be open to us, meaning our remark to him in the only way we could mean it, to declare that he was missing the point. What he has to show, if he wants to make more than the instrumental claim, is that *he cannot get on without that suit*, that *his life will be blighted without it*, or some such thing.

What is suggested by the existence of this extra, more problematical requirement? It suggests that, although there is an instrumental sense of "need" where we can ask for some purpose to be specified in a nonelliptical version of the "needs" claim and there are no limits on what purpose this is (except the limits of what can be of any conceivable concern to anyone), there is another sense of "need" by which the purpose is already fixed, and fixed in virtue of the meaning of the word.

3. The Instrumental and the Absolute Senses of Needs

We have to assign at least two senses to "need," it seems, if we are to assign the right significance to the sorts of things people use the word to say or to understand the special argumentative force of needs claims. But of course there is a connection between the purely instrumental and the not purely instrumental sense, or what we may call (simply for the sake of a name, not to exclude the relativities to be set out later) the absolute or categorical sense of the word. Thus:

> I need [absolutely] to have x
> if and only if
> I need [instrumentally] to have x if I am to avoid being harmed
> if and only if
> It is necessary, things being what they actually are, that if I avoid being harmed then I have x.

What distinguishes the second sense of "need," so defined by reference to the first, is that it is in virtue of what is carried along by this second sense of the word "need," not in virtue of context (whatever part context plays in determining that this is the sense intended), that appeal is made to the necessary conditions of harm's being avoided. If so, the identity of the antecedent "...." of the conditional "Necessarily, since circumstances are what they are, if ...., then ___" is fixed by the presence of the word "need" taken in this absolute sense.[6] It must follow that there is then no question of ellipse in this case. (One does not have to supply again what is already, however latently, there.)[7]

4. Relativeness of Needs

Normativeness apart, there are at least three distinct ways in which needs statements of the simple singular variety we have elucidated must appear to be relative (notwithstanding the other respect, in which they are absolute).

First, the suggested elucidation in terms of harm exposes a certain parameter that is always there to be discovered within claims of absolute needing. This is the idea, not innocent of the metaphysics of personhood, of well-being or flourishing, by reference to which we make judgments of harm.

What follows from this relativeness? Not too much. Relativeness to something else is no obstacle in itself to the most extreme or perfect kind of objectivity. Indeed, making such relativeness fully explicit sometimes has the effect of revealing the subject matter in question as a candidate for unqualified or absolute truth.[8]

The first relativeness was only a matter of *need*'s involving a parameter. The second and different way in which need sentences may appear to be relative qualifies some of the hopes that might be inspired by this account of the first. What constitutes suffering or wretchedness or harm is an essentially contestable matter and is to some extent relative to a culture, even to some extent relative to people's conceptions of suffering, wretchedness, and harm. Obviously, there is much more to be said about that (even if it is doubtful how much of it involves the idea of "relative deprivation"—a relativity that we have ventured to omit altogether from the argument). But rather than go into that, let us hurry on, simply insisting that, even when the instability is conceded of some of the opinions that have been reached within our culture about absolute needs, many need claims are so far from being indeterminate or seriously contestable that they are more or less decidable. We shall return briefly to this point after making mention of a third relativity.

The third relativity is relativity to the particular circumstances of the time or times associated with the need and to the background of (in part normative) assumptions associated with those circumstances. When we make a claim of the form *Necessarily at t if such-and-such then so-and-so*, where *t* is a moment for which this "necessarily" is temporally indexed, we thereby confine our consideration to all alternative futures from *t* onwards, and what we are saying is equivalent to the claim that every alternative in which such-and-such holds is one in which so-and-so holds. If pure historical necessity at t, $\Box t$, were our concern, then a future would count as an alternative for times $> t$ only if it could coherently be described and every correct description of it was compatible with the conjunction of (1) the state of the world that actually obtained at t and (2) all true laws of nature. Thus $\Box t$ (p) is true if and only if p is true in every alternative world whose history is indistinguishable from the history of the actual world up to the moment *t*, natural laws being counted as part of the history of the world and fixed as of *t*.[9] But where needing is concerned, it seems that the definition of alternativeness must be modified to restrict the class of alternative futures to futures $> t$ that (1) are economically or technologically realistically conceivable, given the actual state of things at *t*; and (2) do not involve us in morally (or otherwise) unacceptable acts[10] or interventions in the arrangements of particular human lives or society or whatever; and (3) can be envisaged without our envisaging ourselves tolerating what we do not have to tolerate.

This relativity to circumstance imports one more feature that deserves special comment. The fixed antecedent of the whole conditional that is governed by the modal operator "necessarily relative to the circumstances *c* obtaining at *t*" speaks of avoidance of harm. This is not obscure, but it will not determine the sense that some cases of absolute needing demand, unless some associated standard is thought of as supplied by which harm is judged according to context. Such a standard will import the idea of *some however minimal level of flourishing that is actually attainable in this context*. Avoidance of harm can then be understood always by reference to a norm of flourishing that is relative to *c*, and this in its turn can import the entailment or implicature that, if *y* noninstrumentally needs *x* at *t* under circumstances *c*, then there *exists* some alternative future in which *y* does flourish to some however minimal extent.[11] (When I am utterly doomed however the future is realistically envisaged, then I can begin to lose some of my ordinary needs, even as I acquire often very special short-term needs.)

For noninstrumental or categorical needing, this third species of relativity furnishes more of what was already furnished by the second. It is not just that the idea of harm, or the norm of flourishing by reference to which harm is judged, is historically conditioned and essentially contestable. It is also circumstantially *conditioned as of some time t* what futures are to count as realistic, morally acceptable alternatives, how long a forward view we have to take of flourishing in considering what counts as harm, and what the relevant standard of harm ought to be with respect to the time span that is agreed to be the right one to apply in the given case. It may even be contestable—before we consider how much the present constrains the future—what exactly the circumstances are that prevail at *t*. The second and third sorts of relativity interact.

There is plenty here for an ardent objectivist to face up to. And yet, in spite of the real and manifold contestability of most of these things, some may be tempted to conclude (as I do) that the agreement that can be reached about the truth or falsity of a wide variety of needs claims (when they are seriously and correctly construed as making the contextually constrained but very strong claims that they do make) is really far more striking than the disagreement that some others will arouse. The temptation exists to claim that objectivity is a matter of degree and that some significant degree of it can coexist even with the second of the three kinds of relativity we have distinguished.

5. Essential Questions

The thought we have now arrived at is that a person needs x [absolutely] if and only if, whatever morally and socially acceptable variation it is (economically, technologically, politically, historically. . . , etc.) possible to envisage occurring within the relevant time span, he will be harmed if he goes without x. A proper development of this that enabled us to try to measure the relative public weights of various claims of need would have to make room for certain obvious and essential refinements. And it would have to prepare the ground for these by distinguishing certain distinct questions.

There is the question of the *badness* or *gravity* of needs. How much harm or suffering would be occasioned by going without the thing in question? And there is a consequential question of *urgency*: given that some not inconsiderable harm or suffering would be occasioned by going without the thing in question, how soon must this thing be supplied? And then there is the question of the *basicness*, the *entrenchment*, and the *substitutability* of needs. Being technical terms, however, these categorizations all require more elaborate introduction.

When we attempt to survey the class of alternative possible futures and then, restricting this to envisageable acceptable futures, we ask whether every future in which person y is not harmed is one in which he has x, we shall often discover that it is a matter of degree how difficult it is to envisage realistically some alternative in which y will escape harm without having x, or how morally acceptable it would be to propose—or to acquiesce in—that alternative's being deliberately brought about. Often we resolve such difficulties by imposing a threshold on what departures from the familiar we are to regard as realistically envisageable, as morally acceptable, or as practical politics. The lower such thresholds are set, the more futures then count as real alternatives, and the harder it then becomes for a need statement to count as true. Seeing the effects of lower settings of the thresholds but being reluctant to deny that y really needs x at all, we shall often have to choose between (1) again raising the threshold of moral and social possibility; (2) quite differently, lowering (relaxing) the standard by which the harm to y is judged, allowing more things to count as harm; and (3) keeping the lower threshold of moral and political possibility, together with the more exigent truth-condition it imports, but disjoining having x with having some slightly inferior potential substitute for x.

In light of all this, it will be a useful stipulation to say that y's need for x is entrenched if the question of whether y can remain unharmed without having x is rather insensitive to the placing of the aforementioned threshold of realistic envisageability-cum-political-and-moral-acceptability of alternative futures. When we are concerned with the problem of arbitration between general needs claims or arbitration between general needs claims and other claims, it will then be important to distinguish between entrenchment with respect to the shorter term (where extant arrangements create definite requirements that cannot be escaped immediately but may in due course be escaped) and entrenchment with respect to the longer term. Some desirable disruptions of the established order that would enable people to escape harm without having x cannot be envisaged happening as it were overnight; but in many cases the change can be coherently and easily described and can be quite realistically envisaged taking place gradually and by stages.

Developing a special case of entrenchment, one might then stipulate that y's need for x is basic only if what excludes futures in which y remains unharmed despite his not having x are laws of nature, unalterable and invariable environmental facts, or facts about human constitution.[12] And within the basic, one might try to discriminate between (1) that which is owed to unchangeable tendencies of things to turn out in one rather than another specifiable kind of way (either in general or given the particular place, time, or culture) and (2) that which is owed to something nonnegotiable in the various ideas about human harm and flourishing that condition our sense of the socially possible (as well as our sense of what y must have).

Finally, we may find it useful to be able to say that y's need for x is *substitutable with respect to x* if some slight lowering of the standard by which y's harm is judged permits us to weaken claims of need by disjoining y's having x with his having u or v or w or whatever.

It should be obvious that these labels correspond to overlapping but independent categorizations. A need for x can be not very bad but basic, for instance; or bad and also urgent yet substitutable with respect to x; or bad in the extreme and highly entrenched insofar as it is urgent but, insofar as it is not urgent, relatively superficially entrenched in the mid term and not entrenched at all in the long term. It should be equally obvious how important it is to be clear whether the need we are talking about stems from a judgment about a particular human being, or about all human beings in specified kinds of circumstances, or (making the truth-condition most exigent of all) all human beings under all actual variations of circumstance.

6. Needs, Desires, and Interests

How then are needs and desires and needs and interests related? Perhaps we had better see needs themselves (contrast things needed) as *states of dependency (in respect of not being harmed)*, which have as their proper objects things needed (or, more strictly, *having* or *using . . . these things*). In that case our categorization in the preceding section is a categorization of states of dependency. Such states often find expression in desire or striving (or avoidance or whatever), and often the propositional object of the desire or striving will be the same as that which we find in some correct statement of the need. But even in this special case it is not perfectly obvious that the desire ought to be simply identified with the need. A more plausible identification is between someone's having a certain need and his having a certain interest. If a person needs *x,* then he has an interest in *x*'s being or becoming available to him. And if he very badly needs at *t* to have *x* at *t,* and the need is also significantly entrenched as of *t* and scarcely substitutable at all, then his having *x* may be said to represent a *vital interest* of his. His having the need for *x* will then be the same as his having a vital interest in having *x.* This is a good ruling, or so I believe, but only if we use the word "interest" to mean what it means in English, where its connection with "want" or "desire" is complicated and indirect (cf. White, *Modal Thinking,* 120), and if the proposed equivalence is without prejudice in favor of any general alignment between needs and interests.

7. The Challenge of Alternatives

Having grasped the complexity and stringency of the truth-condition, we must start to see any statement of the form *"y* needs *x* [absolutely]*"* as tantamount to the challenge to imagine an alternative future in which *y* escapes harm or damage without having *x,* or an alternative future where *y*'s vital interests are better adjusted to others' vital interests than they would be if *x* were what he had. We must proceed like this, not because to be concerned with needs is to take up an attitude of stinginess or meanness, but because, if we do not, some vital needs and interests may not be properly determined or may go unheeded. It is without prejudice one way or the other to the satisfaction of desires for things that are not needed.

Sometimes (as we have noticed) this sort of challenge to the imagination will lead not to outright rejection of a statement but to a weakening of the specification of the thing said to be needed: "He will get by if he has *x* or *w* or *v.*" This is a very familiar move, and the elucidation of needing given here explains why that is. Overspecificity in a "needs" sentence makes it false.[13] But the thing our elucidation equally predicts is that often whatever survives the weakening (the introduction of disjunctions, etc.) will still be a very strong statement—most especially where the particular judgment of y's noninstrumental need results from a process in which the actuality of y's concrete situation and the constraints that this puts upon the future are fully apprehended (taking into account the real, however hypothetical, intentions of all relevant other persons or groups of persons), a process that clarifies both the worst and the best that can befall y and y's vital interests. (This will prompt us to climb down from "y needs x," where x is the best but most expensive remedy, well out of y's reach unless he forgoes everything else, to "what y really needs [given the circumstances] is w," where absence of w will blight even that minimal level of well-being that is the best real possibility for y.) It seems certain that, even when claims of need are scrutinized in this way, we shall be left with much more than a tiny handful of needs statements.

8. Three Phases of Justice

What then, if it is irreducible or sui generis, is the distinctive political force of a statement of a serious need? The positive answer to be offered to that question here will depend on a threefold division of justice corresponding to a hypothetical reconstruction of the genesis of the conception of justice that we have inherited and that we seek now to apply within the social morality that animates our thoughts about the political sphere.

In this scheme, phase 1 justice will be justice as the guardian of rights as narrowly and strictly construed. Phase 2 justice will be justice as the definer of the limits of aggregative reasoning in the public sphere and the vigilant arbitrator between rights and certain other claims (to be called counterrights) that are not themselves rights. Phase 3 justice will be justice as the custodian and distributor of public goods—justice, as I am apt to think, outgrowing its own size. On the view taken in the article from which this chapter is an extract, phase 3 justice ought to operate only within the area allowed to it by the principles of phase 2 justice, which limit stringently the operation of aggregative reasoning. This division looks forward to my eventual conclusions.

We must begin, however, by excogitating the prerequisites of something's counting as a possible social morality. In this way, let us try to identify the role that such a social morality must give (at phase or level 1) to the idea of a right. Deploying this idea, we shall find that needs come to appear as special candidates to make abstract claim-rights (claim-rights that ought to be recognized and realized concretely); and certain others that do not attain to this status will nevertheless appear at the second phase or level as candidates to represent abstract *counterclaims*. (Such counterclaims will lie well within the province of justice, however strictly it is conceived, and will rest upon the same sort of foundation that abstract rights rest upon.)

There are two necessary preliminaries to this approach. First, even though need statements, when they weigh with us at all, do always weigh at least in part *as* statements of need, yet we must note that their public force is highly variable. (It is variable even when their truth is not being questioned.) Certainly this force is not always proportional to the need's admitted seriousness. Any account of these matters must explain or allow for this variability and leave room for the influence or countervailing influence of factors other than need itself. Second, it is still worth insisting, against one kind of positivist, that the moral force of a claim of need cannot be identified with its being acknowledged to have this force or with society's acting upon it or having regard to it in practice—just as the social morality that a claim of need depends on for its force ought to be clearly distinguished both from the actual norms of reciprocity and cooperation that the morality makes possible and from the extant laws and social institutions that regulate these norms.

9. Needs and Social Morality

These preliminaries being noted, I suggest that, for the purposes of a social morality S that is actually lived and proposes to agents shared concerns that they can make their own, there is *an abstract claim-right or entitlement to x under conditions C just where x is something the denial or removal of which under conditions C gives (and can be seen as giving)*[14] *the person denied or deprived part or all of a reason, and a reason that is avowable and publicly sustainable within S, to reconsider his adherence to the norms of reciprocity and cooperation sustained by S.* This is to say that, if in such a case the victim who is deprived of *x* disappoints us in some spoken or previously unspoken expectation of cooperation, then that counts as something morally intelligible within the shared sensibility that depends on this expectation.[15]

In order to grasp the full import of this very exigent condition for the existence of a right, it will assist to state the assumption it rests upon. This is the assumption that unless there existed *some* condition under which withdrawal of consensus was found intelligible and natural *even within S*—that is, some condition under which S itself allowed someone party to S to think of himself as having been unjustly (even unjustifiably) sacrificed—S could scarcely count as a social morality at all. For a social morality, as conceived for these purposes, is not just any old set of abstract principles. It is something that exists only as realized or embodied (or as capable of being realized or embodied) in a shared sensibility and in the historically given mores and institutions that are themselves perpetuated by it. It is only by virtue of participating in this sort of thing, and seeing one another as participating in it, that ordinary human beings are able, as actually constituted, to embrace common concerns and common goals that can take on a life of their own or be perceived as enshrining values that possess what Hume sometimes called "moral beauty." A social morality cannot, of course, give any particular person a guaranteed title to wealth, health, happiness, or security from ordinary misfortune. On the other hand, it must not be such as to threaten anyone who is to be bound by it that it will bring down upon him or any other individual participant, as if gratuitously, the misfortune of having his vital interests sacrificed simply for the sake of some larger public good.[16] What sustains and regulates or adjusts a social morality and what rebuts objections to it must be something intelligible to all its individual participants, in human (never mind archangelic or ideal observer) terms.[17] It must engage with the passions of those who are to live by it—or at least not disengage from those passions.

10. The Requirements of Social Morality

It is a small step from requiring that a social morality lack this license to requiring, more positively and definitely, (1) that it should place explicit limitations on the social goals it promotes or tolerates, on the burdens individuals can normally be asked to endure in the common pursuit of this or that kind of public goal, and on the scope and ambit of the modes of aggregative reasoning it countenances; (2) that it should sustain rights under a rule of law, securing individuals from arbitrary arrest, imprisonment, or punishment and assuring them of other civic and legal protections; and (3) that it should uphold the right of individuals to make certain sorts of agreements with other individuals, to buy the necessities of life, to sell the product of one's labor, and not to be dispossessed of that which one has appropriated or mixed one's labor with in ways seen as worthy of being accorded legal recognition.

Items that find a place in this enumeration will not find it *simply* because they are needed. But as Hart anticipated, the idea of need plays its own distinctive and recognizable role in helping to generate and constrain the enumeration. What is more, its presence helps to render the idea of an abstract claim-right unmysterious. Certainly the derivation is not obliged to represent itself as a priori or as premoral or as resting upon natural law (a concept it needs neither to invoke nor to denounce). In a very general way it is a posteriori. No doubt the a posteriority of the question of what social moralities have to be like in order to be possible will appear to many philosophers of some temperaments to disqualify the entire approach. But a posteriority is what we ought to have predicted if we expected morality to have the hold upon motive and action that Hume argued that it must. Morality must have this hold intelligibly, by virtue of the content of the judgments it delivers, and by virtue of the possibility that the values and concerns that it proposes to agents will become for them nothing less than ends in themselves, furnishing them with reasons they can see as good for being concerned or affected in certain ways.[18]

This whole view of rights may provoke the accusation that I say that there is a right wherever there is an opportunity for blackmail or that I submit morality itself to what Nietzsche called "the trading mentality" and might equally well, with almost equal moral ugliness, have called "the contracting mentality." But, wherever else this accusation may be appropriate, it does not belong here. The view of rights that I am defending is consistent with a morality's *not* being something whose force, nature, or content is supplied, directly or indirectly, from any kind of prudence. The view does not merely respect the fact that we do not opt or contract into a social morality; no weight at all has been attached to the possibility (which I discount) of reconstructing the reasons that we would or might, as presocially conceived, have had for so opting or contracting. A social morality, as here conceived, is not even something that *it is as if* we have opted or contracted into.[19] It is simply the sort of thing that we find ourselves in the midst of. By virtue of being what it is, having the content it has, and deserving to command the consensus of those who live within it, such a morality normally withholds from its adherents all decently avowable reasons to *opt out of it*. It is neither here nor there if there are all sorts of other moralities that pass this test or that we might have found ourselves in the midst of. Our attachment does not depend on that's not being so, still less on our satisfying ourselves that there is no other social morality that might have offered someone in our position a better package of rights.

11. Rights and Needs

Principles 1, 2, and 3 are concerned with great goods. They presuppose an enormous charge on the state. But consideration of what it takes to ensure the persistence of these goods in the real world is certain to lend color to an independent demand for certain much more specifically political rights, as well as for publicly provided systems of education, legal aid, and basic health care. These things are intelligible extensions in what it is still just possible to recognize as the same spirit. The reason that I should say that these things were at most one step beyond the rights whose nonrealization will give someone good reason for disaffection from society is that (1), (2), (3), and their proper extensions are little more than the preconditions of someone's securing his own material survival in his own way, or in the best way relative to his circumstances, by his own efforts. Someone who demands such rights as these asks for scarcely any strictly first-order good—only for the conditions on which to get his own, within a community that recognizes him as a participant with this right and that he in his turn recognizes as conferring, guaranteeing, and limiting that right and recognizes as presupposed, in some condition or other, to any life that he can fully value. Still less does he ask for an equal title to an equal share of first-order goods.

However familiar or unfamiliar our general method of justification may have appeared, the embryo rights that it generates are familiar enough. What will be noted, however, is that, despite the fact that some needs have now turned up as generating rights and/or liberties with a protective fence of claim-rights, we still have no *general* vindication of the force of serious needs claims taken simply as claims of need. It is true of course that some who set store by rights are apt to insist on more numerous and stronger rights than any afforded under (1), (2), and (3). It is also true and important that, in practice, many extant social moralities will recognize, and impress upon the institutions and laws that they sustain, more rights than the abstract things that one can demonstrate by the general method we have sketched.[20] But that would not be enough for our purposes. For, having rejected the idea of a social contract and what one is *owed* for one's accord in this, because we rejected the idea of a reconstruction of any however hypothetical, prudence-based reasons for opting into morality, we *dare* not see first-order benefits that go too far beyond (1), (2), (3), or all needs simply as such, under the aspect of moral rights or abstract entitlements—lest they appear under the guise of a sort of quid pro quo for the retention of participative adherence or consensus. No idea could more quickly subvert a social morality, or more effectively despoil the achievement that it represents.

There is a second reason not to find rights, or what have sometimes been called "claim-rights in the making" or "manifesto rights," wherever there happen to be some serious needs. This reason will hold good even for cases where certain needs are far harder to ignore than some unproblematical, acknowledged rights are. If we hold onto the conception of rights introduced in section 9, then it will be natural to suppose that a categorical abstract claim-right exists only where there could in principle be some institutional obligation upon someone or something to arrange for people to have the chance to take official or legal action against some specific defendant or legal entity in order to require some specific performance of him or it.[21] However we rearrange society and its processes, there will always be claims of dire need that fail this test.

If we use the idea of right to prevent these from falling into oblivion, then we run the risk of losing all sharpness in the idea of a right.[22]

At this point there will be a temptation to try to see needs that are not good candidates to be simple rights as having a force somehow comparable to a claim-right and as requiring that whoever has this or that serious need should be recognized as owed *special consideration* when the mass of claims that bear upon any particular matter is reviewed. But, even though this is correct enough for certain kinds of claims of needing, it is too vague. What is far worse, it still leaves everything unexplained. Why *should* these kinds of needing deserve special public consideration?

The general form of the answer that I shall offer to this question, in what I shall number the second phase of the explanation promised in section 8, is that serious noninstrumental needs that do not constitute rights or entitlements can sometimes stand in a certain counterpoise relation, first, with straightforward rights actually recognized and then (in a potentially contrasting way) with the ends of concerted public action. Especially, vital needs (as defined in section 7) can do so.

12. Entrenched Rights versus Vital Needs

Principles 1, 2, and 3 of section 10 start life as scarcely more than the preconditions of human beings' securing their own survival in their own way, or in the best way relative to their circumstances. But the principles have a tendency to outgrow their beginnings. And according to our a posteriori cum consensual approach, the strength and status of class 3 rights and entitlements to property, inheritance, etc. are not fixed exactly or for all places and times. What *is* determined about them, given the finitude of the world's natural resources, the long-term impossibility of each person's appropriation from natural resources leaving behind as much and as good for the next, and the accumulation of power that has inevitably accrued in a finite social space to those who stand at the end of long chains of inheritance of property and influence, is only that the stronger the support and confirmation that a given social morality provides for entrenched entitlements, and the greater the legal and political protection accordingly extended to those exercising a large number of class 3 rights, the greater must be the state's and its servants' moral duty to respect in all legal and political deliberation the needs and vital interests of the people there will always be who have not got themselves into a position to acquire or exercise very many such rights and entitlements. And the readier the state must then be, having recognized property and other entitlements, to diminish the extent to which such entrenched rights can countervail against true claims of vital need that must otherwise go unsatisfied. Surely needs must offset property rights *at least* to the extent that the appropriations and transfers of the centuries render ineffective all present efforts to command the resources that one requires to live by one's own efforts.[23] But one ought to go further. The stronger the property rights that are politically recognized and legally enforced, and the greater the efficacy of the social morality in sustaining the institutions that protect these rights, the more self-conscious society must then become (at least in the more populated, civilized, and economically exploited parts of the earth) about the *inflexibility* and *possible failure* of the systems of entitlement relations that govern possession and use,[24] and the readier it must be to give practical expression to this self-consciousness by regulating commerce, by ministering directly to unsatisfied vital needs, or (much better) by ensuring that wealth should be created closer to the point where there are vital interests that will otherwise go unsatisfied. Society must cultivate this self-consciousness—on pain of being seen precisely as worsening the plight of those who have least and who might otherwise have combined to take by force what they needed for self-sufficiency,[25] or on pain of the state's finding itself forced to subdue these people by methods that will in the end subvert morality itself.

13. The Risk of Going Too Far

With counterclaims and everything they involve, one enters immediately into an area of conflict, of revolution even. One half of the difficulty is that rights like those of class 3 give rise to expectations, legitimate expectations, about the character and extent of the interventions against historical contingency and luck that society will undertake in the name of justice. Not only are rights like those in class 3 founded in a special way in a human need, but also it is a deep human need to be *able* to frame such long-term expectations of tenure and security. (To remove the possibility of these is to abandon one of the most distinctive advantages of the very civilization that almost everyone aspires to enjoy who looks to ordinary politics for the redress of injustice.) The other half of the difficulty is, of course, that in certain cases the situation of those whom a certain system of rights impedes from living by their own efforts may be nothing short of desperate.

Sticking to what our approach suggests ought to be least controversial, I would urge:

1. The clearest case, both for rights falling within classes 1, 2, and 3 and for counterclaims, reposes upon vital needs that human beings will not otherwise be able to satisfy by their own efforts.

2. However strong the case in need for however stringent an abridgment of rights of acquisition or tenure, the correction or redistribution ought to be gradual and nonretrospective, lest considerations that purport to represent social justice invade and annihilate the very idea of a right.

3. When the satisfaction of counterclaims makes it necessary to abridge rights—for example, by raising taxes above levels that were justified by the expense of providing and protecting rights and benefits falling within categories 1, 2, and 3—this should be done in a manner that is (a) perspicuous in intention; (b) generally consistent with a person's original title to what he or she earns;[26] (c) such as to force upon us the question whether enough (or too much) is being attempted, and whether in the right way.[27] Otherwise we lose sight of the terms of the original conflict between the accumulated entitlements of some and the vital interests of others, and we blur the distinction between that issue and other issues that arise at a later phase of the evolution of social justice (namely, phase 3).

4. Finally, I note that the more complicated and diverse the admissible counterclaims that can appear under the aspect of claims in justice, and the more complicated and diverse the response to them that is attempted in society's name, the more likely this public response is to get muddled up with different kinds of public projects whose rationale is not vital-need-based at all but founded in much more contestable ideas (such as the idea of everyone's equal entitlement to an equal share in everything worth having and the ideas that bear the marks of class hatred).

Justice mediates between rights and counterrights on the principle that, when the rights system leaves insufficient room for everyone to satisfy vital needs, rights may have to be abridged on a principle of equal concern for anyone's and everyone's vital need. But at this point let us be as serious as possible about what a vital need is and not deceive ourselves into thinking that the defense of vital interests or needs is any foundation or justification for collective reasoning directed at other shared objectives—for example, an increase in the overall sum of opportunities. That last may be a good. But it is not the same as (and may even threaten) the scrupulous protection of vital interests.

14. The Principle of Limitation

We need a limitative principle that will regulate both rights/counterrights arbitration and collective reasoning that is conducted in pursuit of public goods. Perhaps it is this: Even if there is nothing unjust in actions of the state or its agencies making one person poorer in a way that makes another person less poor than he was (in kind or money)—and even if there need be no injustice as such (whatever pause it suggests for thought) when among those who lose are to be found people who are already the least fortunate of all the parties involved—*it is pro tanto unjust* if the state or an agency of the state intervenes against contingency, or changes its policy, or confounds citizens' sensible expectations in a way that sacrifices anyone's strictly vital interests to the mere desires of however many others. More speculatively, one should perhaps think that *it is pro tanto unjust* if, among vital interests actually affected by such interventions, the greater strictly vital need of anyone is sacrificed in the name of the lesser needs of however many others.

Such limitative principles—which must be based, as always, in the connection between justice, consensus, and citizens' sense of the legitimacy of government—are still in the spirit of the arguments of section 11, for a society that allows type 3 rights to outgrow their proper rationale does precisely threaten vital interests. And the same applies to a society that is uncritical of the counterclaims it finds valid, even if it mouths slogans of equal entitlement. In fact, actual societies' perception of the duty of governments to intervene in the name of counterclaims has usually coincided with (or even been preceded by) the perception of quite different reasons for public intervention. Governments may want to solve coordination problems or provide various benefits that coordination problems prevent the market from providing. It is hard to show any objection in principle to this, even where the resulting projects are not vital-needs-based. But experience suggests that, as society's public actions become more heterogeneous, as lower incomes begin to be taxed, and as public projects impinge more and more severely upon the environment, displacing citizens for public works such as schools, hospitals, parks, the defense of the realm, or public-road building (the last having an understandable tendency always to seek out the areas of lowest ratable value), those who stand in the direst need of the Principle of Limitation are almost never the rich or the fortunate. I would add that the more it then begins to seem proper for the state to undertake, the smaller will be the probability that the consensually requisite protections of every individual's vital interests will be available already, in the shape of effective, recognized legal and/or constitutional rights, such as those falling in our classes 1, 2, and 3, and the smaller the probability that there will be remedies that can be opposed to the actual or prospective, direct or indirect effects of public action.

Notes

This essay is an edited extract from *Needs, Values, Truth: Essays in the Philosophy of Value* (Oxford: Blackwell, 1991). Some sections of this essay first appeared in a tribute to John Mackie, *Morality and Objectivity*, ed. Ted Honderich (London: Routledge & Kegan Paul, 1985). Some sections are adapted from work on needs that appears elsewhere and in another form in "Needs, Need, and Needing" (*Journal of Medical Ethics* 13 [1987]: 61–68), under joint authorship with Sira Dermen. The author is grateful for advice and suggestions about the original essay given by Bernard Williams, Ronald Dworkin, Jennifer Hornsby, Susan Hurley, Robert Gay, Michael Smith, Margery Eagle, Roger Scruton, and Anthony Price. The extract was prepared by the editor with the approval of the author.

1. H. L. A. Hart, "Bentham on Legal Rights," in *Oxford Essays in Jurisprudence*, ed. Alfred W. B. Simpson (Oxford: Clarendon Press, 1973), 2: 200.

2. J. L. Mackie, "Can There Be a Rights-Based Moral Theory?" *Midwest Studies in Philosophy* 3 (1978): 350–59; J. A. Mackie, "Rights, Utility, and Universalization," in *Utility and Rights*, ed. Raymond G. Frey (Oxford: Blackwell, 1984).

3. The exceptions are (1) G. E. M. Anscombe, "Modern Moral Philosophy," *Philosophy* 33 (1958): 7: "To say that [an organism] needs that environment is not to say, e.g. that you want it to have that environment, but that it won't flourish unless it has it. Certainly, it all depends whether you *want* it to flourish! as Hume would say. But what 'all depends' on whether you want it to flourish is whether the fact that it needs that environment, or won't flourish without it, has the slightest influence on your actions"; (2) Joel Feinberg, *Social Philosophy* (Englewood Cliffs, N.J.: Prentice-Hall, 1973), 111: "In a general sense to say that *S* needs *X* is to say simply that if he doesn't have *X* he will be harmed." (Cf. David Miller, *Social Justice* [Oxford: Clarendon Press, 1976], 130; David Richards, *A Theory of Reasons for Action* [Oxford: Oxford University Press, 1970], 37–38; A. M. Honoré, "Social Justice," in *Essays in Legal Philosophy*, ed. R. S. Summers [Oxford: Blackwell, 1970], 78.) The main difference between these analyses or elucidations and the one we shall propose consists in the fact that we propose to see *need* as an explicitly modal notion that leads us to insist that Anscombe's conditional be governed by "necessarily." For other works that appear to be under the direct or indirect influence of Anscombe's formulation, see David Wiggins, *Sameness and Substance* (Oxford: Blackwell, 1980), 183; and J. Finnis, *Natural Law and Natural Rights* (Oxford: Clarendon Press, 1980), passim.

4. This is the common point in the otherwise very different (and differently modulated) accounts of Anthony Flew, Alan White, and Brian Barry. See Anthony Flew, *Politics of Procrustes* (London: Temple Smith, 1981), 120: "If I say that I need something, it is never inapt to ask what for. . . . There is always something hypothetically imperative about my need"; Alan White, *Modal Thinking* (Oxford: Blackwell, 1971), 105–6: "To say that A needs to V is elliptical for saying that A needs to V in order to F [where to F is the end-state], . . . a failure to notice the elliptical nature of statements about what A needs leads to arguments at cross purposes. . . . 'Does A need X?' is an

elliptical not a normative question"; Brian Barry, *Political Argument* (London: Routledge & Kegan Paul, 1965), chap. 3, sec. 5a.

5. Strictly speaking, we have to add something here entailing that whatever "...." holds a place for is a *matter of concern*. But very shortly, when we come to the noninstrumental needs, which are our real interest, the addition will be superfluous, because we shall supplant the "...." in the antecedent by a sentence representing something the person cannot help being concerned with. I draw attention to this, nevertheless, because, even if there is a usage according to which the antecedent need not endorse some end as a matter of concern ("to do something totally pointless knowing that it is totally pointless you need a lot of patience"—can one truly say that?), the common elliptical usage discussed in the next paragraph is available only when the suppressed antecedent does relate to something that is a matter of concern.

The three time variables t, t', t'' are all needed in the full form of the "need" sentence as given without any ellipse or abbreviation (even though, evidently, they do not vary entirely independently). t'' need not be t', because the goal mentioned in the antecedent may be achieved later than the prerequisite mentioned in the consequent. t need not be t', because the end-state—a child's having good second teeth, for instance—may create an earlier necessity that certain measures be taken. And t need not be t either, because it may be necessary *now* (t) that certain measures be taken next year (t') for the subsequent (t'') good of the second teeth—even though it was not necessary last year (before t) that these measures be taken at t'. Before t there was a chance of dispensing with these t' measures, e.g., by taking proper or better care of the first teeth. It is well beyond my present scope to trace the relationship of the time indicators in this sort of elucidation to the tenses that appear in the various natural language forms that it seeks to elucidate.

6. What might possibly confuse one is that if someone says that he needs something [absolutely], then he may perfectly well explain himself (as our equivalences indeed suggest) by reference to what he needs [instrumentally] to stay alive or avoid harm.

7. The feeling that this proposal imports a semantical singularity of some sort may be substantially reduced by reference to a certain more familiar and uncontroversial example of ambiguity, where there is a similar nesting of one sense of a word in the account of another sense of the same word: where "V" holds a place for a verb or verb-phrase, and "iff" abbreviates "if and only if,"

> z has a [liberty] right to V iff z has no duty not to V; z has a [claim] right to V iff z has a [liberty] right to V and some person or agency has no [liberty] right not to secure to z the opportunity and ability to exercise his [liberty] right to V.

Cf. Joel Feinberg, *Social Philosophy*, 58: "One can have a liberty which is not also a [claim] right but one cannot have a [claim] right which is not also a liberty."

8. For instance, relativizing length, duration, and motion and reformulating Newton's laws to render them relative to the reference frame of the observer and all reference frames in uniform motion with respect to him, and then qualifying the laws in

certain ways suggested by the Special Theory of Relativity, made of a theory that was not previously unqualifiedly true a theory that may yet prove to be absolutely true.

9. Cf. David Wiggins, "Towards a Reasonable Libertarianism," essay 8 in *Needs, Values, Truth* (Oxford: Blackwell, 1987).

10. Note that we have already had implicit recourse to this thought in the discussion of the instrumental sense insofar as we allowed that N needed £200 to buy a suit. The fact that there is a future in which he has a suit without paying £200, because he steals one, was not allowed to count against this claim.

11. Thus for our conditional in section 3 governed by the specially indexed modality, the problem simply does not arise that the impossibility of the antecedent will make the conditional true vacuously.

12. "Basic" will be here, as in all the schemes we have encountered in other writers, a technical term to be grasped in the first instance by the definition of the category and in the second instance by reference to the *point* of setting up such a category. In particular, we would remark that our basic category is not the same in definition or point as the category of *survival needs*, or biological needs as Benn and Peters call them (Stanley Benn and Richard S. Peters, *Social Principles and the Democratic State* [London: Allen & Unwin, 1959], 144–46; see also Stanley Rosen's criticisms in *Mind* 86 [1977]: 88). Nor is it the same in definition or point as Benn and Peters's own category of *basic needs*, which simply concerns a decent standard of living; or the same as the modern Marxist category of *really human needs*, or *one's needs as a human being*, which are usually introduced to make a contrast with *false needs* (a contrast we have partially, but only partially, absorbed by bringing out the full exigency of the truth-conditions of statements of need).

13. A good example of this is provided by modern transport planners' ingrained habit of speaking of "mobility" (by car) as a standing need of Western civilization. There is no doubt that, with present tendencies towards concentration of facilities, closure of smaller shops and offices, and more dispersed patterns of development, such mobility approximates to a short- or medium-term need with a considerable and rising degree of entrenchment. But, if alternative tendencies can be envisaged, we shall get a fairer view of all the available options if we realize that the right name for the standing, invariable need (the need that underlies the shorter-term need) is not "mobility" but, more plastically and indefinitely, "access [to facilities that are frequently needed]."

14. Note that the *nonavailability of x* is not sufficient. The condition is limited to the denial or deprivation or removal of *x*.

15. In connection with this whole approach, compare, e.g., J. L. Mackie, "Rights, Utility, and Universalisation"; J. L. Mackie, *Ethics* (Harmondsworth, England: Penguin, 1977); Bernard Williams, *Moral Luck,* x and passim, e.g., "Internal and External Reasons," 101–13. Insofar as my treatment differs from Mackie's and Williams's, it is mainly in respect of the crucial importance I should attach in these matters of motivation to judgments of value being what they seem to be, viz., statements about features of reality, albeit essentially anthropocentrically categorized, that are discovered to us by our interest in them. Cf. Wiggins, *Needs, Values, Truth,* essays 3, 5. For certain aspects of social morality equally neglected by Williams, Mackie, and myself, see

A. M. Honoré, "Groups, Law, and Obedience," in *Oxford Essays in Jurisprudence*, vol. 2, ed. Simpson.

16. Cf. Mackie, "Can There Be a Rights Based Moral Theory?" 352–54: "A central embarrassment for the best known goal-based theories, the various forms of utilitarianism, is that the well being of one individual should be sacrificed without limits, for the well being of others. . . . Why should it not be a *fundamental* moral principle that the well being of one person cannot be simply replaced by that of another? There is no proof of purely aggregative consequentialism at any level."

17. States go to war, and in fighting wars they have exacted the sacrifice of millions of lives. But states that deserve the loyalty of their subjects do not go to war "to maximize the public good"—rather, they do so to avoid invasion or national humiliation or subjugation or to defend vital interests that subjects can identify with.

18. A posteriority is again what we ought to predict if we will allow that the relation between social morality and its embodying social institutions needs to be a reciprocal one. It needs to be reciprocal if the morality is to take up from mores and institutions the distinctive coloration and distinctive emphases that will characterize the communal ends and socially conditioned individual ends that the morality recognizes as intelligible ends of human endeavor and concern. (In fact, both logically and historically speaking, social morality and social institutions must come into being simultaneously.) To reject a posteriority here is to reject the idea that values and shared concerns need to have a historical aspect. But without a historical aspect most values and concerns that go beyond simple human survival are simply arbitrary and, in every relevant sense of the phrase, rationally unintelligible.

19. If we suppose that it is even a bit like something to opt into, then we immediately find ourselves forced to think that it ought to be possible to reconstruct the reasons (it is now as if) we once had for the choice that (it is now as if) we once made when we opted into it. But surely, if such reasons had to be found, none could possibly be provided. How could any candidate to be such a reason both show, as it would need to show, that this was the morality we would have been most *prudent* or *rational* to adhere to and also respect the status as a morality of what it is as if we should have chosen? Any consideration at all that promised to be suitable to count as a reason of the required sort would *either* employ a notion of rationality and prudence that begged the question (this, I insist, is the innocent, fruitful way with the matter in all other connections) *or* depend on a conception of rationality that would have us as choosing virtue or justice not for what it is in itself but in the expectation of a return of another sort.

20. Historically some have recognized rather fewer. But the reader will have guessed that I shall claim this does not matter. What people will put up with is an a posteriori question, one dependent on factors of human psychology and awareness that change gradually but constantly through time. These changes are for the most part irreversible. As in all matters of awareness, a kind of ratchet mechanism operates. What people will acquiesce in is to some degree a moral question, for what people can acquiesce in depends on what they think is fair to them. And what they think fair must depend, however indirectly or minimally, on what *is* fair. If our explanations in these sections were intended as reductive or eliminative, this would be fatal to them. But our

aim here is only to exhibit the *interconnections* of the concepts *claim-right, need, participants' consensus, social justice.* . . .

21. On claim-rights, see also Alan Ryan, "Overriding Interests," *Times Literary Supplement*, 22 April 1983, 411.

22. Cf. also the question put by Charles Fried, *Right and Wrong* (Cambridge: Harvard University Press, 1978), 122:

> The major objection to a theory of rights based on needs [is that] though needs and their satisfaction have an objective quality, the fact is that any commitment, via the recognition of positive rights, to meet need also makes us hostages to vastly varied and voracious needs. . . . How to contain this voraciousness? If needs create rights to their satisfaction, how are we to prevent them from claiming so much that there is no energy left to pursue other goals?

Having given an account of rights that answers Fried's question, let me refer to a complementary and no doubt better account of rights, which I did not know when I formulated mine, namely, Joseph Raz's version of the so-called beneficiary theory of rights as given in his "On the Nature of Rights," *Mind* 93 (1984): 192–214. The careful adherent of a position like Raz's may certainly hold that to say a person has a right is to say that some interest of that person's is a sufficient reason for holding another person or body to be subject to some duty that serves the interest. But not just any old interest will count, nor just any old ground. Everything depends on what kind of interest, with what provenance, and (if the interest passes that test) what protection, if any, is not only stably and foreseeably beneficial to the right-holder in society but also nearly invariably indispensable to the protection and enjoyment of that interest. What the Aristotelian account explains is how needs can be important enough in *certain classes of cases* to be indispensable to the justification for imposing such duties, not how needs automatically generate rights *wherever* needs ought to impinge as needs on the determination of public policy.

23. Cf. Mackie, *Ethics*, 175–76; and Mackie, "Rights, Utility, and Universalization." And for a relatively ancient statement of the relevant (still neglected) platitude, see J. von Neumann, *Collected Works* (New York: Pergamon Press, 1961), 6: 505: "Literally and figuratively we are running out of room. At long last, we begin to feel the effects of the finite actual size of the earth in a critical way."

24. I am indebted in this formulation to important general ideas expounded by Amartya Sen in his *Poverty and Famines* (New York: Oxford University Press, 1983) and, later, to his contention that what famine dramatizes is not so much the power of natural disaster as the failure or weakness of systems of entitlement relations.

25. I say "otherwise." But, of course, they may do this anyway. And they may do it in a way that goes well beyond taking by force what they need. What is being urged here without prejudice to any of those questions is simply the weakest claim: that, if under these circumstances human beings combine to take by force what they need, then moral justification may be available for that, whatever condemnation may also be possible for whatever else they do.

26. A citizen is taxed, surely, on what he has earned and made his own. He ought not to be deemed not even to have earned the portion he gives up. He cannot give *back* to society what is never his.

27. Consider, for instance, subsidized, publicly owned housing. Is this a better solution to the problem than subsidizing rents of those of low income in a flourishing, properly regulated private sector? For a powerful but wholly neglected argument that public or special housing is not the only solution to the problem, see Jane Jacobs, *Death and Life of the Great American City* (London: Jonathan Cape, 1962), 323–27. And *why* in any case (we must always ask) are the incomes of some hardworking, industrious persons doing essential work too low for them to be able to afford adequate housing?

3

The Concept of Needs, with a Heartwarming Offer of Aid to Utilitarianism

David Braybrooke

My assigned task is to set forth a brief reprise of my account of the concept of needs. I shall carry that task out, but in the course of doing so, I shall introduce some nuances to increase the flexibility of the account. I shall also give a prominent place to the ways in which the concept of needs, on such an account, can assist in making good the project of utilitarianism.

Bentham's original impulse, to hold social policies accountable to effective evidence of their impacts on human welfare, has enabled utilitarianism to survive the long-standing embarrassment of not being able to make anything effective of the felicific calculus. It has even survived the more recent embarrassments that come from redefining utility as simply a matter of realizing preferences and of having projects of aggregating personal preferences founder in the self-stultifying renunciations of welfare economics and in the paradoxes of social choice theory. For utilitarianism keeps in view an indispensable project, even if it does so in a form not realized and, for practical purposes, of doubtful realization forever. What alternative is there, in ethics or in ethics applied to politics, to the project of utilitarianism (in some sense, broad if not narrow) about having impacts of policies on human welfare considered? And how (though philosophers and economists have made it a puzzle just how) can such impacts not be considered (whatever else is) in evaluating social policies? Utilitarianism with its project thus stands in the right place to look to for a principle to guide policy evaluation.

If utilitarianism is to be more than an unfinished project in the right place, it has to be recast; and the most promising way of recasting it is to make use of the concept of needs. Utilitarianism can make at least three substantial uses of the concept of needs:

1. to explain how, by operating through surrogate concepts like the concept of needs, utilitarianism or tendencies of thought congenial to

utilitarianism have had practical effects on policy evaluation and policy choice while the calculus has remained unfinished and unapplied

2. to provide a means of recasting the principle of utility so that it gives something like lexicographical priority to meeting needs (and thereby escapes, by and large, both the embarrassment of not having an applicable calculus in hand and the embarrassments of social choice theory)

3. to show how, even if it is not so recast, the principle of utility can be safeguarded from common objections about unjustified personal sacrifices in the same way as comparisons respecting meeting needs

To be really useful in any of these connections, however, the concept of needs has to be, if not itself recast, at least extricated from the incessant confusion with which it is commonly used. Not everything that people intensely want—invisibility, the power of unaided flight, fame, another life, death—is something that they in every case, or sometimes in any, need even adventitiously for some goal both optional and feasible. What within human powers (even powers carried as far as we could expect research to go) can give them invisibility without their being annihilated, another life, or the power of unaided flight? What further goal is to be achieved in all the cases in which they intensely want fame or death? Not everything that people do need to reach adventitious goals is something that they need without qualification. They may need jewelry or a limousine to impress neighbors or customers, or a set of golf clubs to play golf; on the other hand, they would cease to need these things if they ceased to pursue the goals at stake. They cannot cease, during the whole course of their lives, to need food, shelter, clothing, safety, companionship.

The claims made under the concept of needs, however, often do not in practice heed the cautions just mentioned. The way to make sure that they are heeded, and that the concept can be used effectively to evaluate policies, is to seize upon certain features of familiar usage that can be exhibited in a systematic construction.

The construction begins by assuming that there is a Reference Population whose needs are under consideration and something that may not be identical with the Reference Population, a Policy-Making Population,[1] whose understanding of the concept of needs will be decisive for the policies adopted for the Reference Population. The simplest case is one in which the Reference Population is identical with the Policy-Making Population, and that is the case that will be treated here; but the case in which the two populations are wholly separate is important for policies affecting the economic development of the Third World.

The construction leads to a schema with a number of dimensions in which agreement will in practice almost always come about (if it comes about at all) only after protracted discussion, which should be open to general participation by the Population (in both its Reference and its Policy-Making capacities). For expository convenience, I shall postpone dealing with the complications that the multiple dimensions create for discussion. The Policy-Making Population, let us suppose, has to agree on two things: first, the needs to be met in that population; then, once that issue has been fully defined and settled, the arrangements, that is to say the policies, to meet them.

What is the issue now about defining needs? It, too, can be taken to have two parts: first, fixing upon a List of Matters of Need; then, fixing upon the Minimum Standards of Provision for each Matter of Need on the List. The List on which discussion settles may vary; perhaps everyone will agree to have food, shelter, and clothing on the list, but (considering that the List is to guide social policies) not everyone would perhaps agree to have sexual activity on the List, or recreation. The Minimum Standards of Provision will vary with discussion even more: in respect to persons provided for—one person will need more food daily than others; in respect to generosity of provisions; in respect to differences in culture. Even were the List of Matters of Need— food, clothing, shelter, and other things—to remain the same, variation in the kinds of resources, religion, and other factors will make some provisions eligible under the conventions of one culture that are not eligible at all in another. It will be no help to offer pork as provisions in an Islamic culture. In the present paper, to be sure, we are dealing in the simplest case with one population and one culture. However, it removes a lot of the uneasiness about the fluidity of the concept of needs to recognize that Matters of Need can remain the same while provisions, and hence Minimum Standards of Provision, vary with conventions.

Conventional variation does not prevent us from making the definition both of Matters of Need and of Minimum Standards of Provision answer to a Criterion. Any of a family of Criteria having to do with life and death and, short of these things, with social functioning might do. Many people, however, would find persuasive a Criterion according to which something was a Matter of Need and provisions for it enough to meet the Minimum Standards of Provision if, without having such provisions, the persons in question would no longer be able to carry out fully four basic social roles: as citizens, workers, parents, and householders. Even here some disagreement is to be expected; and what provisions are required is something often settled by settling in accordance with prevailing views upon minimal packets of provisions, with ingredients not strictly defensible as necessary by the Criterion. However, if the List and the Minimum Standards of Provision become uncomfortably inflated, the Schema of the List and the Minimum Standards can always be contracted, and the ingredients of the packets reduced in variety or quantity, until effective agreement is reached. Or the Schema can be expanded, on evidence that the ingredients of current packets do not suffice to prevent observable impairment of the functioning of the people provided for.

How is it told whether the needs of the Population are being met, or met better under one set of policies than under another? The basic form for telling and for making comparisons is given by the Census Notion, and this is to be understood, insofar as it is looked to for guidance in adopting policies, as something used in conjunction with a Principle of Precedence, a Revisionary Process, and a Gains-Preservation Principle.[2] (I shall explain what these amount to as they are introduced, one by one, below.)

The Census Notion requires observations that (unlike measurements of utility) are philosophically unproblematical and well within the compass of familiar everyday practice. Suppose that inquiry is to be made into the extent to which shelter as a Matter of Need has been provided for in the Reference Population. The Minimum Standard of Provision is set after discussion as having a place to sleep that is dry, well ventilated, and in the winter heated to sixty-eight degrees Fahrenheit. Then, after observations have been made, everyone in the Population (or everyone in a statistically valid sample) will have been assigned to one category or another in a table like the following, which assumes a Population of one hundred or a sample of that size from a larger Population:

With shelter	70
Without shelter	30

Someone proposes a new policy for shelter that promises to increase provisions to cover half the number of people now without shelter. A comparative census table taking into account both the present policy and the new policy would take the form

Status Quo		New Policy	
With shelter	70	With shelter	85
Without shelter	30	Without shelter	15

Other things being equal, the new policy would bring in a clear improvement in respect to meeting the need for shelter.

At this point, the Principle of Precedence may come into play. Moving to the new policy may be possible only if some of the people who have shelter in the status quo give up some goods. The Principle of Precedence requires them to give up goods that they themselves do not require to meet their needs under the Minimum Standards of Provision applicable, if only in this way can the Minimum Standards of Provision be met for some members of the Reference Population. We can think of the Principle of Precedence as something that members of the Policy-Making Population accept along with accepting responsibility for meeting the Minimum Standards of Provision for a List of Matters of Need with respect to a certain Reference Population.

Other things being equal, the Principle of Precedence, invoked with a rigor that for descriptive purposes will have to be relaxed later, calls here for the new policy to be adopted, even if it reduces for some people (say, ten of the seventy under the Status Quo policy) provisions over and above what they require to meet their needs. They might prefer to keep these provisions, but the Principle of Precedence overrides such preferences (and thus defies the Pareto Welfare Principle, which licenses only moves that heed more peoples' preferences without running counter to the preferences of anybody). On the other hand, the Principle of Precedence does not require people to give up meeting their own needs to meet the needs of others, or to give other people's mere preferences more weight than their own.

The Principle of Precedence will call for advances in provision up and down the List of Matters of Need, and continue to call for them, falling silent only when for all the people in the Reference Population all the Matters of Need on the List have been met at the Minimum Standards of Provision. This goal is thus treated as a lexicographical priority, strictly speaking, a priority that is lexicographical only up to a satiation limit that is the conjunction of the satiation limits for all the Matters of Need. The goal is the conjunction; the conjuncts are the Minimum Standards of Provision (a range of minima, varying from person to person, for each Matter of Need).

"Satiation" is the correct technical term, borrowed from economics; but the technical use clashes incongruously on the present topic with the connotation of its ordinary use. To make the clash unobtrusive, I shall refer to "SL-lexicographical" rather than to "satiation limit–lexicographical" priority.With SL-lexicographical priority, until every Minimum Standard of Provision for every person in the Reference Population and every Matter of Need has been reached, matters of preference only, a residual category not associated with Matters of Need on the List, may be called on to give way in everybody's case.

Is this practical? Waiving for the moment the point that people may not be ready to conform with such rigor to the Principle of Precedence, it is practical so long as the resources available to the Policy-Making Population, here identical with the Reference Population, allow it under suitable arrangements to meet all Matters of Need at the Minimum Standards of Provision and still leave a surplus, if only a vanishingly little surplus, for other purposes. It may take some time to find the most suitable arrangements; the market may prove effective in some connections and not others, and arrangements to supplement the market without impairing its effectiveness, so far as it is effective, are notoriously controversial. Nonetheless, SL-lexicographical priority for Matters of Need will turn out to be practical if it can be honored within the limits of the resources that can be made available to honor it. Moreover, any worry about having room to work within such limits seems to be based on a very far-fetched hypothesis: Citing estimates by the World Bank, Partha Dasgupta says, "The financial requirement for a broadly based human resource development strategy designed to meet basic needs would total approximately 5.5% of GNP" even in countries in sub-Saharan Africa (where military expenditures have been running at 4.2 percent of GNP).[3] That would leave a considerable surplus after needs have been met, which unfortunately does not guarantee meeting them.

The Revisionary Process operates in conjunction with the Gains-Preservation Principle. This prescribes that none of the seventy people now provided for in respect of shelter should cease being provided for. How often will there be clear improvements in view, straightforwardly satisfying both the Principle of Precedence and the Gains-Preservation Principle? In comparisons confined to one Matter of Need, perhaps quite often. The List of Matters of Need, however, presents more than one Matter of Need to be provided for; and combinations of policies that would bring in clear improvements in respect of one Matter of Need may actually worsen provisions for another, or at least bring the provisions for some people whose needs are now being met below the Minimum Standards of Provision for them. The Census Notion, as a basis for guiding policies, might be defeated again and again in this way.

The operation of the Revisionary Process, however, transcends this limitation. In the Process, I mean to include any forms of taking into account suggestions from any source of revisions in existing options or suggestions of new policy proposals that, like the revisions, offer ways of avoiding difficulties with the existing options. Suppose the new policy for providing shelter would make an advance in meeting the need for shelter but reduce below the Minimum Standards of Provision the provisions for a number of people in respect to education (say, by diverting funds that would have been used to repair schools) or just leave many people without such provisions (because new schools will not be built). People concerned to apply the Principle of Precedence will turn to the Revisionary Process to find a combination of policies that will increase provisions for shelter without having an adverse effect on provisions for education.

In the face of such mixed effects from a combination of policies as having more provisions for shelter for some people at the expense of reducing below the Minimum Standards the provision for some of education, the Gains-

Preservation Principle prescribes at least maintaining the present distribution of provisions for education if the advances in provisions for shelter are to be seized. Preservation is in order, moreover, whether or not the people whose provisions for education would be jeopardized if the Revisionary Process does not produce another combination of policies are among the people whose provisions for shelter are to be increased. But again, this is something in either case different from applying the Pareto Welfare Principle, since as the Principle of Precedence demands, consistently with the Gains-Preservation Principle, resources may be transferred from people who have more than enough to meet all their needs, whether or not their preferences would have it otherwise.

For all its reliance on familiar ideas and familiar sorts of observations, how realistic would it be to claim that the construction just described can be made to work in everyday politics? Some features of the construction are realistic enough. The Criterion, for example, resting as it does on familiar social roles, invites ready assent at least to the most basic items on the List of Matters of Need: food, shelter, clothing, safety. If I were more interested in making a connection between the concept of needs and the philosophical literature on autonomy, I might follow Gillian Brock in making explicit room for personal autonomy in the criterion for Matters of Need, along with other aspects of human agency that may not be covered transparently by the four social roles that I mention. I would accept a variant criterion of this kind as belonging to the same family of criteria.[4] I am so intently concerned, however, to demonstrate what can be made of the concept of needs as a practical and effective alternative to anything that the utility industry in philosophy and economics has made of the concept of utility that I prefer a Criterion the ingredients of which everyone understands. Do even philosophers understand the concept of autonomy?

Moreover, I think that a Criterion resting on familiar social roles does markedly better in fixing for effective political use ideas about Minimum Standards of Provision. We may expect much more disagreement on the Minimum Standards than upon the basic List of Matters of Need. In both cases, however, we have the advantage of letting the basic schema (List of Matters of Need taken together with Minimum Standards of Provision) contract or expand according to the extent to which ready agreement on the content to be ascribed to it can be achieved in a given Policy-Making Population. The arguments for contraction or expansion would continually appeal to the Criterion, which anchors the construction in firm if narrow ground in matters of fact.

What extent of agreement should we seek to achieve? It would help to show that the basic schema could be completely fixed for a time for use in a variety of applications to argue that given a contracted schema for this purpose, a consensus embracing pretty much the whole of a Policy-Making Population is not out of reach, especially if, as discussion ends for the time being, we set aside the irreducible disagreement of an intransigent minority of 5 percent or 10 percent. Arguments aiming at consensus upon the contracted schema might invoke, sardonically, the Matters of Need and the Minimum Standards of Provision that would be appropriate for people being kept in prison. Should not the population out of prison, too, have provisions at least at this level? It might be said that the provisions should not be given them; they should in every case do work to get them. But this is not a question about what should be on the List and what the Minimum Standards of Provisions should be, in other words, not a question of principle to be settled by fixing the Criterion and appealing to it. What is to be in the schema is one issue; what arrangements are to be made to give it effect is another (though no doubt people adjust their positions on one to accord with their positions on the other). The best arrangements for giving the schema effect logically might be arrangements encouraging self-sufficiency (entailing in some places agrarian reform) or arrangements leaving everything to the market.

I do not think, given this point, that widespread disinclination to accept the Principle of Precedence would stand in the way of an agreement fixing the schema and guiding its use. The very people who might be most disinclined to make sacrifices to conform to the principle may be people who think that the sacrifices will never come home to them—the best arrangements for self-sufficiency will make any sacrifices unnecessary. Moreover, there is a lot of room in the process of expanding or contracting the schema for discussion, in which people ready to make some sacrifices but anxious not to make too many[5] will be able to call for a shorter List of Matters of Need or less generous Minimum Standards of Provision. At the same time, if the discussion is open and free, people who would lose by the contraction can argue against it. Others can argue for expansion. Keeping to a List and Minimum Standards accepted for prisoners would not, after all, do more than provide for the bare beginnings of a commodious life for the general Population.

What will, much more often than not, make it difficult to fix upon one persistent, agreed-on schema is that contracting and expanding it will not go smoothly. Contracting the List, people may differ on which Matters to strike off in which order; they may differ also in being readier to accept more generous Minimum Standards of Provision for some needs than others—some, for example, will be more generous respecting provisions for safety, some more generous respecting provisions for education. Moreover, some people may be ready to subscribe to a longer List with less generous Minimum Standards of Provisions for all the Matters on it, while others would be more generous about Minimum Standards of Provision for the Matters, fewer in number, that they would take into account. In the face of considerations like these, advanced by Gillian Brock as criticisms of my account in *Meeting Needs*,[6] I think the best course to take is not to take a stand on the combination of strong conditions that, by limiting variations in attitudes in the Policy-Making Population, would guarantee smooth contraction or expansion of the schema. The best course is to treat the schema and the other features of the construction as offering various dimensions calling for discussion before any comprehensive use of the concept of needs giving SL-lexicographical priority to all Matters of Need taken together could be made sure of. For example, there will be discussion about which Matters of Need are to be included in the List and how each Matter of Need is to be defined and discussion about what range of Minimum Standards of Provision is to be accepted under the head of any given Matter of Need.

Is this allowance enough for discussion and variation in interpretation? It is consistent with the allowance, and indeed it is a point that I would insist upon, that we can predict from the familiar use of the concept of needs some Matters of Need that will be settled upon very quickly and some Minimum Standards of Provision below which discussion will not descend without becoming absurd. I would resist making so loose an allowance for discussion and interpretation as would risk losing the distinctive moral force of the concept of needs. The moral force depends in part, not just on there being some received agreement, extending across differences in social and economic position as well as in political beliefs, on the dimensions of discussion exhibited in the schema, but also on there being some received agreement, likewise extended, on how to begin filling the schema in. Food will be one of the Matters of Need, and more food than a thimbleful of rice will be required every week by every member of the Reference Population under the Minimum Standards of Provision for food.

Too much fashionable flapdoodle about the politics of interpretation in which the concept is no doubt involved will obscure the possibility of capitalizing on this agreement to bring about at least modest reforms. It will also be to a degree self-defeating. If you wish to convince people that facilities should be provided for battered wives to enable them to live apart from their husbands, should you omit making the point that in their present households their needs for bodily, mental, and emotional security, including freedom from terror, are going starkly unmet? Even if you would prefer to make the case in terms of rights, you might think twice before disregarding the possibility of founding the women's rights on the narrow but firm ground of their minimal needs.

The force of the concept of needs can be carried beyond the bare minima where the force is strongest, and in many cases, I would hope, even in the present circumstances of politics, to more generous standards of provision than are now commonly adhered to. However, I think the concept should not be expanded so far as to risk making an approach to meeting needs indistinguishable from an approach to achieving all the good things in life that feminists, environmentalists, and activists for other causes seek, even when it is perfectly reasonable for them to seek these things. If it is to keep its distinctive force, the concept of needs, in my view, can go only part of the way to defining the common good and making sure of a commodious life, though it is a vital initial part of the way. Tragically, many people do not benefit from application of the concept even in respect to the bare beginnings where the concept is firmest and its force least deniable.

In practice, we should almost certainly not think of getting widespread agreement on all dimensions of the schema. So we should not think, in practice, of getting consensus on the schema fixed at some level of contraction or expansion for persistent use applied to the whole variety of Matters of Need. We should expect to be getting consensus only for a moment on one or two Matters of Need that have become salient issues and (equally transiently) on the associated Minimum Standards of Provision. Furthermore, the consensus may not be firm beyond a policymaking community (relevant bureaucrats, experts, lobbyists, and legislators); and even within the policymaking community, consensus may be undermined by a division of opinion about suitable arrangements. This picture goes hand-in-hand with a picture of fitful attention to policy questions about needs and fitful commitment to the Principle of Precedence. Matters of Need do make themselves felt in politics: people worry from time to time about safety of children in the central cities, about homelessness, about the proliferation of food banks, about the adequacy of public provisions for education. Seldom, however, do any of these Matters get enough sustained attention to dispose of them by making sure of adequate provisions. Much further away from characterizing real politics is anything like systematic combined use of the Principle of Precedence, the Census Notion, and the Revisionary Process (together with the Gains-Preservation Principle). But this is not (as is the case with the concept of utility) because people would not understand how to apply the schema of needs making systematic use of these things. It is because of the complications of politics—lots of issues, many of them not about needs, arising without coordination, distracting attention as they arise, and aggravating the distraction already present with the multiplicity of issues already present; lots of competing interests, some of them cherished more by the people who have them than any effective commitment that they might have to meeting the needs of other people.

In *Meeting Needs*, when I came to consider what it was realistic to expect in the way of applying the concept of needs in the complex democratic politics of a populous industrial society, I moved from SL-lexicographical priority for the Principle of Precedence, which only a thoroughly conscientious Policy-Making Population could be expected to press home, to what I called Role-Relative Precautionary Priority. This allows for people being more attached to priority for Matters of Need when they are charged with working out policy proposals than they are when as citizens they must choose between the proposals; and more attached in their role as citizens (coming together to make decisions for the Common Good) than they are as consumers. Recognizing how addiction to tobacco runs counter to people's meeting their needs, the proponents of policy may seek to eliminate the tobacco industry; but as citizens they will divide on how long elimination should be put off, given the unsettling economic effects that eliminating the industry would have for many people; and as consumers (some of them, in their capacities as proponents and citizens, strong adversaries of the tobacco industry) they will go on using tobacco so long as the industry feeds their habit. Yet even in such a situation the concept of needs counts for something; with the Principle of Precedence, it leads to agitation about the tobacco industry and to proposals that sooner or later, bit by bit, check its activities.

A relaxed priority is unlikely to count for enough to do as much justice as the concept of needs calls for. Having some people comfortably provided for while others are desperate for provisions to meet their needs is a spectacle that has always, for people with sensitive consciences, raised questions about justice. It at least seems to require some explanation as to why justice would not call for removing the discrepancy. A familiar explanation is that the discrepancy results from some people being more industrious and productive than others; so the people who are not comfortable have no complaint; they should have worked harder and more productively. But this explanation does not seem relevant in situations (most situations) where the greater comforts of the comfortable classes originate in large part in riches accumulated by their ancestors. (Then the lesson to be drawn is perhaps that the people who are not comfortable should have chosen ancestors who worked harder or more productively, or at least that the ancestors that they do have should have worked harder or more productively.) However, a philosopher famous for being willing to accept the result of honest industry and lawful transactions for generations on end has led the way in concluding that the appeal to the occurrence of these things in previous generations cannot justify present discrepancies. He is quite clear in his mind about how property is legitimately appropriated and transmitted, but he also feels compelled to admit that the pedigrees of present property holdings are tainted—significantly, though in ways that cannot in many cases be accurately specified—by past deviations from legitimate appropriation and transmittal. He recommends dealing with present discrepancies between the comfortable and the desperate by using the Difference Principle to give at least a rough measure of justice.[7] Then the people on top will be able to keep only so many comforts as are required to enable them to make a maximum contribution to the standard of living of the people on the bottom. In fortunate enough circumstances, this will assure the latter of meeting their needs.

The connection between needs and justice that I want to emphasize most here, however, is an indirect one. It goes by way of rights and the jeopardy that arises for some people holding and exercising those rights when other people accumulate extraordinary amounts of wealth and, with it, inordinate power both in economic relations and in political ones. Money talks in both connections. The power can be used in disregard of, and in violation of, the rights of poorer people. The rights so violated might be rights directly to having their needs met. Dasgupta, for one, talks as much about rights to have needs met as he does about the needs themselves, framing his discussion by a distinction between "positive rights," of which he takes rights to basic provisions to be examples, and "negative rights."[8] Yet even people ready to recognize such rights if they are useful may find direct resort to the Principle of Precedence and comparative uses of the Census Notion more economical conceptually and more efficient in practice.

Furthermore, not everyone will be ready to recognize the rights. Libertarians, for example, may incline to think that it suffices to meet needs for people to have a right to personal liberty and rights to property acquired by honest industry and lawful transactions. How can it suffice to have those rights? For some people, in some circumstances, both rights are liable to disregard and violation by other people who have overweening power based on extraordinary wealth. Especially vulnerable are people whose needs will not be met, even transiently, if they do not give up their rights in submission to the designs of the extraordinarily wealthy. The pressure for submission may simply take the form of making the right holders' positions economically untenable: desperate to meet their needs, they sell out at a nominal price, when, if they could have bargained on equal terms, they need not have sold at all. Or— as has been very frequent in history—the wealthy arrange to override the rights in question.

It may be said that if those designs infringe some people's rights, they are morally objectionable and should be vigorously proceeded against as unlawful. But where is the vigorous proceeding to come from, when the police, the prosecutors, the judges, and the legislators have been corrupted? Overweening wealth had its way in reinstituting serfdom in Poland in the sixteenth century; it had its way in the Highland Clearances; it is having its way at this very moment as smallholders are pushed out of the way during the clearance of the Brazilian jungle. Justice, even justice on a libertarian definition, will not survive in practice if some people's provisions for their needs are put in jeopardy by an adverse distribution of wealth. And so justice requires as a necessary condition—not in logic, but in practice—at least as much approach to equality of income as assures everyone of provisions for needs.[9]

If it were not rights to liberty and property but the principle of utility, as now commonly understood, that is to be invoked to safeguard meeting needs expectably important to everybody's utility, one might fear that to get optimal overall results in meeting needs one would sometimes sacrifice meeting some people's needs to meeting others. Might this not mean introducing some injustices just to ward off others? But the schema for needs opens up no room for such injustices. The Principle of Precedence is not an optimizing notion; it is, to use Herbert Simon's term, a satisficing one. It falls silent when all the needs on the List have been met at the appropriate Minimum Standards of Provision for everyone in the Reference Population. Questions about what to do with resources not required to accomplish this will of course remain; but though they may have to do with a much larger quantity of resources, they will not be so urgent morally, because the neglect of them will not be so morally grievous as shortfalls in meeting needs.

During the advance to fulfilling the Principle of Precedence, the Gains-Preservation Principle stands against stopping or reducing (below the Minimum Standards) the provisions going to some to make sure of getting provisions to others. The Census Notion itself stands against discarding anyone in the group surveyed in order to improve results. A policy that meets the needs of a greater proportion of a population because some people have been eliminated (who are present under the policy to be superseded) is not supported by a statistically relevant comparison. To compare the condition of a given group under one policy with its condition under another requires, as a basic consideration in statistics that is at the same time a basic consideration of justice, that the comparison not be rigged by tampering with the population.

I am not sure that we can attribute the Gains-Preservation Principle to the teachings of the great figures in the history of utilitarianism—Bentham, Mill, Edgeworth, and Sidgwick—though I expect that they would give it a sympathetic hearing. I am tolerably sure that we can attribute to them the presupposition that a population to which the principle of utility is to be given comparative application is to remain the same for any comparative assertions about the happiness of that population.[10] To be sure, very early in the historical career of utilitarianism, thinking in terms of the felicific calculus seems to have moved on from thinking of the happiness of the people in a group to thinking sometimes of the aggregate, sometimes of the average happiness of the group. This led Sidgwick, a judicious thinker elsewhere, to license increasing the population of the earth until the marginal net increment of happiness attainable by adding yet another person to the population vanishes, though the appearance of this person diminishes by crowding and other ill effects the happiness of everyone else.[11] But it did not lead him, or any of the others, to suggest that to get a higher aggregate happiness score, some people might be done away with. The closest any of them come to such a suggestion is Edgeworth's idea that especially morose people might be encouraged to emigrate,[12] but he was supposing that while the people at home would be happier for their absence, the morose people would be no less happy living abroad than before. He stopped there.

In their extended reviews of objections to utilitarianism, neither Mill nor Sidgwick considered defending, because they did not dream of having to defend, utilitarianism against being ready to tamper with a population to get better overall scores. Thus utilitarianism, if it is not ready to be recast as an ethics giving SL-lexicographical priority to needs, and not content to operate with the concept of needs as a surrogate and source of surrogates, can at the very least make explicit the same safeguard against sacrificing people's lives as comes with the schema for needs—a safeguard that rests on a basic statistical consideration logically prior to using either the calculus or the Census Notion to marshal statistics. It can also, to its great advantage, adopt the Gains-Preservation Principle. This will be more conservative in operation applied to happiness, unbounded in any individual case, than it is applied to needs, where it can license transfers of resources above and beyond what individual persons require to meet their needs. It would still not be so conservative as the Pareto Welfare Principle, if it were not taken to imply (as it need not be) that people could be happy only with the combination of goods that they happen now to prefer.

It might be best for utilitarianism to abandon utility, though given the intellectual investment in the utility industry this will not be easy to bring about. Utilitarianism could recast itself as an ethics in two parts, the first part of which frankly champions, ultimately, SL-lexicographical priority for needs settled upon after due discussion under the schema for basic needs, and the second part of which deals with the pursuit and mutual accommodation of preferences that do not express needs but that still must be heeded to have commodious lives. Should utility be brought back for service in this part? I don't think so. No one has yet drawn up a preference map or utility map for even one person, let alone the millions of people who compose in each case most current societies. No one ever will. It would be much more fruitful to think directly of seeking, alongside the operation of a market in private goods, goods public relative to one or another public and making institutional arrangements to minimize conflicts about which of these goods to have. But it is not my business here to work out how utilitarianism can dispense with utility even when it goes on from needs to matters of preference only.

Finally, the light that making the concept of needs clear throws upon the theory of utilitarianism recast as the theory of a needs-based ethics extends to showing how the theory, even unrecast, has had some effect on the choice of policies in spite of offering a principle incapable of direct application. It has not required direct application to be effective. For, one could assume, at least in a rough practical way, that providing for this or that Matter of Need would foster happiness. The need for sanitary housing, met by introducing a modern system of sewers, was a good, intelligible surrogate for utility or happiness. As Chadwick saw, London tenements with courts ankle-deep in human excrement generated diseases that stood in the way of fulfilling anything like the principle of utility, were one to find a way of applying it.

Notes

Gillian Brock and Tara Smith have commented on drafts of this paper, and I am grateful to them for their helpful suggestions.

1. In *Meeting Needs* (Princeton, N.J.: Princeton University Press, 1987), I called the Policy-Making Population a Selfgovliset—a self-governing subset of people with a common language—to make a philosophical point about the empirical linguistic basis for the construction.

2. All of these were present in the account given in *Meeting Needs*, but the Gains-Preservation Principle was not given a name there.

3. Partha Dasgupta, "National Performance Gaps," in *The Progress of Nations: 1996 UNICEF Report* (New York: UNICEF House, 1996), 33–34. This is one of a series of annual reports by the United Nations Children's Fund that rank with the annual reports of the United Nations Human Development Program in pressing forward for public policy purposes social indicators unequivocally related to basic human needs.

4. Indeed, in the chapter in *Meeting Needs* entitled "The Expansion of Needs," I endorse amending the Criterion to embrace "the full development of human personality," a notion that should make room for autonomy.

5. "Thou shalt not strive officiously to keep alive."

6. Gillian Brock, "Braybrooke on Needs," *Ethics* 104, no. 4 (July 1994): 811–23.

7. Robert Nozick, *Anarchy, State, and Utopia* (New York: Basic Books, 1974), 231. The Difference Principle, of course, is advanced by John Rawls in *A Theory of Justice* (Cambridge: Harvard University Press, 1971) and as an example of an "end-result principle" is one of the principal objects of attack earlier in Nozick's book.

8. See the essay cited above for the *1996 UNICEF Report*.

9. In *Meeting Needs*, I went on to generalize the argument away from the vulnerability that having needs imposes on people with less power and contend that assignments of resources under any system of justice are liable to be undermined by accumulations of wealth that gave people some power to disregard it. But the argument is

most poignant when we consider departures from a system of justice under which everyone is to begin with equally provided for in respect to needs; and the argument is most dramatic when we consider departures from a system of justice, founded on property rights, that does not anticipate having to provide for meeting needs equally. Making a distinction between several such arguments seems to me the best way to respond to Gillian Brock's comments in "Justice and Needs," *Dialogue* 35 (1996): 81–86.

10.   An essay that will appear in a book, *Moral Objectives, Rules, and the Forms of Social Change,* collecting selected essays of mine (Toronto: University of Toronto Press, 1998) elaborates the attribution.

11.   Henry Sidgwick, *The Methods of Ethics,* 7th ed. (1907; reprint, London: Macmillan, 1963), 415–16.

12.   F. Y. Edgeworth, *Mathematical Psychics* (London: Kegan Paul, 1881), 71–75; cf. 65.

4

Vulnerabilities and Responsibilities: An Ethical Defense of the Welfare State

Robert E. Goodin

The aim of this chapter is to broaden our sense of social responsibility. It is first and foremost an argument in favor of state welfare services. The basic strategy is to try to put them morally on a par with the services we render—and which we firmly believe we *should* render—to family and friends. The method of discharging these other responsibilities differs, but, I will argue, their moral basis is the same. A parallel argument, which here I have space only to sketch baldly, generates analogous international and intergenerational responsibilities and responsibilities for protecting animals and natural environments. Thus this approach promises to provide a unified analysis of a great many of our moral responsibilities.

The argument employs the method of the "reflective equilibrium," in which the goal is to bring our general moral principles and our "settled intuitions" about what is right and wrong in any particular case into line with one another, striving all the while for coherence within our set of general principles and for concordance between those principles and our various other "background theories."[1]

In such a procedure, we must always be prepared to reject some of the moral duties and responsibilities that untutored intuition lays upon us. By the same token, the reflective equilibrium can also carry us well beyond ordinary moral instincts by showing us that we have moral duties and responsibilities that intuitively we might deny having. This is the side of the reflective equilibrium that interests me here.

The moral theory that best explains those intuitions that we do have will, typically, also commit us to moral judgments about what we should do in situations that are strictly analogous but about which we have no strong intuitions. By showing us what lies hidden within our ordinary moral sentiments, the reflective equilibrium can thus drive us to acknowledge commitments that we would preanalytically have shunned.

Special Responsibilities

My argument starts from what I take to be one of our firmest moral intuitions, one that we would be loath to sacrifice in this process of reflective equilibrium. That is the intuition that we have especially strong responsibilities toward our families, friends, clients, and compatriots. Charity, we seem strongly to believe, not only does but *should* begin at home. Our primary responsibilities are toward those who stand in some special relationship to us. Strangers get, and are ordinarily thought to deserve, only what (if anything) is left over.

An example from Bernard Williams effectively evokes this intuition. Suppose you were in a fiery air crash and able to pull out only one other victim before the entire plane exploded. On one side of you is a distinguished surgeon, black bag at hand, who could save the lives of several other passengers thrown clear of the airplane when it went down. On the other side is your son. It would, according to the intuition Williams shares with so many others, be morally reprehensible for you to save the surgeon in preference to your own son.[2]

Now, of course, such favoritism would be perfectly understandable from any number of perspectives. Both psychologically and sociologically, it is easy to see why our affections should extend principally to those "of our own kind" rather than to the unknown strangers the surgeon might save. Sociobiologists would point out that saving your son increases the chances of your own genes surviving in the next generation. There is no shortage of adequate explanations for why you would, in fact, favor your own flesh and blood. The question is whether morally you should.

A long tradition in moral theory says firmly that you should not. Indeed, any universalistic theory—be it Kantian or utilitarian—would take just that stand. But that, say many philosophers and even more laypersons, is precisely what is wrong with all universalistic ethics. Sir David Ross insists that "the essential defect of the . . . utilitarian theory is that it ignores . . . the highly personal character of duty";[3] he is outraged that, for example, act-utilitarians are incapable of distinguishing between my giving ten dollars to my benefactor and my giving the same sum to someone who needs it just as badly but "to whom I stand in no special relation." In a continuing stream of articles, Williams has been arguing for the moral importance of respecting people, which entails among other things respecting their "projects," including their special commitments to their families and friends.[4] For Parfit "commonsense morality largely consists" in "special obligations" owed to "the people to whom we stand in certain relations—such as our children, parents, pupils, patients, members of our own trade union, or those whom we represent."[5] Or, for a final example, a central theme in Walzer's *Spheres of Justice* is that "[t]he idea of distributive justice presupposes a bounded world, a community within which distributions take place, a group of people committed to dividing, exchanging and sharing, first of all, among themselves."[6]

Our firm moral intuitions go further still. Not only do we feel that we have these special duties to family and friends, alongside our other, more general moral duties. We also feel that "carrying out these obligations has priority over helping strangers," as Parfit goes on to say.[7] Perhaps those special obligations are not quite strong enough to override negative duties not to harm others. It would be thought wrong for us to commit murder, even if that were necessary for us to feed our own children. But apparently those special duties are quite strong enough to override any duties we might have to render positive assistance to others in general. In *Bleak House,* Dickens ridicules Mrs. Jellyby's "telescopic philanthropy," that is, her tendency to aid distant Africans while neglecting her own family. No doubt most of us are intuitively inclined to say that it is right to satisfy our own children before giving food to needy neighbors. The consequence of acting on such intuitions, however, is that our duties to those with whom we enjoy some special relationship ride roughshod over our duties to help others at large. That, obviously, is an outcome that any theory of social justice, or even of simple humanity, would dearly hope to avoid.

In what follows, I shall not be arguing that we lack any such responsibilities toward family and friends. Neither shall I be denying the strength of such claims. What I shall be arguing is that there is nothing *special* about those responsibilities. There are many others with precisely the same basis—and, depending on circumstances, perhaps even the same strength—as those responsibilities that we have always regarded as particularly binding. The upshot of this argument, if it is successful, is that we are not justified in our present practice of serving one set of claimants systematically to the exclusion of the other.

Alternative Bases of Special Responsibilities

The theory ordinarily offered to account for the moral importance of these intuitively appealing special responsibilities deals in terms of self-assumed obligations. That analysis figures most famously in H. L. A. Hart's classic essay, "Are There Any Natural Rights?" which first introduced the concepts of special rights and duties into modern moral philosophy. "I think it is true of all special duties," Hart wrote, "that they arise from previous voluntary acts."[8] Hart's own discussion is characteristically cagey, abounding with qualifications, exceptions, and ambiguities. His general principle, however, has passed into the philosophical conventional wisdom pretty well shorn of equivocation. Thomson, for example, asserts quite baldly, "Surely we do not have any . . .

'special responsibility' for a person unless we have assumed it, explicitly or implicitly."[9]

The great appeal of the model of self-assumed obligations is that it explains so neatly what is "special" about our special rights, duties, obligations, and responsibilities. Special obligations are distinguished from general ones in two ways. First, whereas everyone has the same general duties, special obligations vary from person to person: I have special responsibilities that you do not. Second, whereas general duties are owed to everyone equally, special obligations are owed to specific others: I have different responsibilities to different people. The analysis of special obligations as self-assumed obligations accounts beautifully for both features. According to that analysis, I have some obligations that others do not because I have assumed them and others have not; my obligations vary because I have assumed obligations with respect to some people but not others.

The paradigm case of a special obligation is, for Hart as for all advocates of this model, a promissory or contractual obligation.[10] A promissor, through a voluntary act of will, imposes upon himself an obligation that is peculiarly his own, not shared by the world at large, and his obligation is owed to a specific individual, the promisee, rather than to the world at large. Various other special responsibilities—of businessmen to their customers and employees, of professionals to their clients, of all of us to our families and friends—are, within this model, seen as more-or-less attenuated instances of this same basic promissory pattern.[11]

Perhaps the most important practical consequence of analyzing special responsibilities as self-assumed obligations is to reinforce our intuitions about their restricted scope. After all, most of us voluntarily assume responsibility in any way whatsoever for only a very limited number of people. On this account, we have no special responsibilities (but only, at most, much weaker general responsibilities) that have not been voluntarily self-assumed.

The model I want to counterpose to that traditional one traces our special responsibilities to the peculiar vulnerabilities of specific others to our actions and choices. It is their vulnerability, not our promises or any other voluntary act of will on our part, that imposes upon us special responsibilities with respect to them. The promissory obligations that figure so centrally in the traditional account are, on this analysis, just a special case of vulnerability. If I promised and others are depending on me in consequence, then I am obliged to do as I promised—not because I promised, but merely because they are depending on (i.e., are vulnerable to) me.[12]

Whereas the paradigm of self-assumed special obligations is the promise or contract, the paradigm for the vulnerability model is family responsibilities. Hart himself admits the difficulty of assimilating these rights and duties to his model of self-assumed obligations.[13] And well he should. You do not enter into families voluntarily. You do not ask to be born; you do not choose your parents or siblings. In the first instance, anyway, you make them no promises and extract none from them.

Even areas of family life that appear on first brush to be contractual turn out not to be completely so. The standard "marriage contract," for example, deviates crucially from the legal ideal of a contract. The authors of the *Second Restatement of the Law of Contracts* are at pains to emphasize that fact: "Although marriage is sometimes loosely referred to as a 'contract,' the marital relationship has not been regarded by the common law as contractual in the usual sense" because "many terms of the relationship are seen as largely fixed by the state and beyond the power of the parties to modify."[14] Even if marriage partners were to write their own contract, certain duties (such as the duty of support) would be regarded legally as "essential features" of the marital relationship and the two parties involved would be legally unable to alter them, even by mutual consent. That, of course, violates a fundamental precept of contracting.[15]

To see how completely ill suited a model built around contractual or quasi-contractual notions of reciprocity is to the analysis of family responsibilities, consider just two of its more absurd conclusions. First, on that account, a child who lived at home until age twenty-one would have incurred a debt to his parents 16.6 percent greater than that of his sister who left home at eighteen. But surely the children's obligations to aid their ill and aged mother depend merely on her present needs and their relative capacities to meet them and not on their past performances. It would be absurd to suggest that the son who remained at home longer should pay 16.6 percent more, even though he is now earning 50 percent less than his sister. (If it really were a case of debt, notice, it would not be absurd: our business obligations are invariant with respect to our capacities to meet them, at least until we declare bankruptcy.) Second, it would be equally absurd to suggest that the debt children owe their parents might at some point be fully repaid and the children relieved of any further obligation to help parents, however ill they may be. Once contractual debts have been met, any special relationship between creditor and debtor dissolves. The two parties then stand in exactly the same relationship as before the debt was incurred. That is simply not how families or friendships work. A favor and a return favor do not cancel each other out and dissolve the relationship; instead, they strengthen it.[16]

What most fundamentally underlies the reciprocal duties of family life—of spouses to one another, of parents to their children, of children to their aged parents—is the vulnerability of those parties to one another. The protracted dependency of the human infant is, biologists tell us, one of the most striking features of the species. Much vulnerability is material in nature. Wageless members of the family depend on the wage earner(s) to bring home the bacon; children depend upon their parents to feed, clothe, and shelter them; in the absence of adequate collective provision, ill or infirm parents are often dependent upon their children for care of a very material sort.[17] But we must not focus exclusively upon these material forms of vulnerability. Much of the vulnerability, in family life and friendships more generally, is of an emotional sort. That fact provides a crucial link in the argument explaining why the material support in question has to come from the particular person it does (for example, the parent, child), instead of some unrelated other who might be in an objectively better position to provide it.[18]

One way to demonstrate the superiority of the vulnerability model would be to survey systematically those "special relationships" that we so readily acknowledge. Among the cases that might be discussed, in addition to the family responsibilities just mentioned, are the special responsibilities of businessmen for the safety of their employees and customers, of professionals (especially doctors and lawyers) for their clients, of friends to one another, and of beneficiaries to their benefactors. The aim would be to show that the vulnerability model can offer a plausible account of all features of all these special responsibilities, whereas the model of self-assumed obligations can at best account for only a few features of a few of them. Such a case-by-case demonstration is, however, beyond the bounds of the present chapter and is conducted elsewhere instead.[19]

The best quick demonstration of the superiority of the vulnerability model is this. Imagine someone who is utterly helpless. The model of self-assumed obligations says you have only such responsibilities with respect to that person as you voluntarily assume. You might agree to do all sorts of nice things for that person. It would be terribly kind of you to do so, and of course once you have assumed responsibilities, it would be obligatory at that point for you to discharge them. But, within this model, you are initially under absolutely no obligations to agree to do all (or any) of those favors. You are morally at liberty to press your bargaining advantage to the hilt and to exploit mercilessly the other's weakness. You can, and morally you *may,* force that person to agree to arrangements that are highly inequitable, to say the least. For examples, if any are needed, reflect upon the classic cases of "unconscionable contracts": peddling useless drugs to desperately ill patients at inflated prices, or charging a thousand dollars for a hamburger when you find yourself enjoying a monopoly on food at some disaster site.

Now, according to the model of self-assumed obligations, parties in strong bargaining positions like these would be violating none of their moral responsibilities by pressing their advantage to the hilt. The vulnerability model, in contrast, regards it as the height of immorality for them to exploit the other's weakness in this way. The same thing that would enable the stronger to drive a hard bargain with (and, within the model of self-assumed obligations, to evade altogether any responsibility for) the weaker would, within the vulnerability model, impose a heavy responsibility upon the stronger to look after the weaker. In such cases, the implications of the two models clearly diverge. And surely our considered moral judgments, backed up by all our "background theories," side with the vulnerability model on this score. As Green remarked, "There is no clearer ordinance of that supreme reason, often dark to us, which governs the course of man's affairs, than that no body of men should . . . be able to strengthen itself at the cost of the other's weakness."[20]

Protecting the Vulnerable

In spelling out the details of this vulnerability model of special responsibilities, I shall confine myself to three general remarks. The first concerns definitions of key terms: vulnerability, dependency, and responsibility. I use "vulnerability" and "dependency" interchangeably to refer to the following situation: A is vulnerable to B if and only if B's actions and choices have a great impact on A's interests. Here I equate "interests" with "welfare," following in reading "x is in A's interests" to mean "x increases A's opportunities to get what A wants."[21] Protecting the vulnerable is thus morally desirable because, *ceteris paribus,* it is morally desirable that people's interests and welfare should be furthered.[22]

Central to the concepts of vulnerability and dependency is the fact that they are relational. You are always vulnerable to, or dependent upon, some individual or group of individuals who have it within their power to help or to harm you in some respect(s). This relational character of the concepts is an enormous help in deciding where to settle responsibility for rendering assistance. If vulnerability gives rise to moral claims, then those moral claims must be principally against those agents to whose actions and choices one is vulnerable. Thus, this might be characterized as a "directed needs" model. Saying merely that "A is in need" leaves unspecified who should be responsible for meeting those needs. Saying that "A is vulnerable to B" provides a ready answer to that question.

Vulnerabilities are also relative. A is more vulnerable to B than to C if B's actions and choices make a greater impact on A's interests than do C's actions and choices. Those to whom one is relatively more vulnerable have relatively greater responsibilities. Anyone to whom A is uniquely vulnerable (no one else will help if that person does not) has the greatest responsibilities of all.

The fact that primary responsibility falls to whomever is in the best (or, in the limiting case, the unique) position to protect the vulnerable does not relieve others of responsibility altogether. Those who could help, albeit not as well as those with primary responsibility, retain a residual responsibility to do so should the others default, and they also have a continuing responsibility to monitor the situation to see whether or not their assistance is in fact required.[23]

Let us consider next the definition of responsibility. There are various forms, among them: causal responsibility (you produced this result); moral responsibility (you are to blame for it); and task responsibility (it's your job). Often we slide carelessly from one sense to another. To employ a pun that has frequently been mistaken for an argument, it is commonly said that those who are responsible should be made responsible. That is to say, (task) responsibility should be settled on those who are (causally) responsible. If A's actions have caused some unfortunate situation, then according to this rule it should be A's job to correct it. Most especially, if A got himself into a jam, it should be A's responsibility to get himself out of it.

My argument is that task responsibility and causal responsibility are logically separable and should often be separated in practice. On my analysis, how A got into his present state is irrelevant. All that matters now is who is best able to get him out.[24] Sometimes—maybe even typically, for all I know—the person causally responsible for producing a state of affairs will be able to reverse it. If so, then the pun will point us in the right direction. But in a great many cases, the agent best able to get a person out of a jam might well be someone other than the agent who got that person into it. Then, I would argue, task responsibility should be settled upon the former, even though that agent is in no way causally responsible. When the wake from a passing speedboat capsizes my sailboat, it must be the responsibility of other nearby sailors rather than the long-gone speeder to pull me out of the water.

That rule might, admittedly, tend to encourage improvident behavior. People could always rely on others to clean up their messes or get them out of jams they got themselves into. But providing appropriate counters to those perverse incentives is a practical rather than a moral matter. Incentives, as Rawls and Feinberg rightly emphasize, are nothing more than socially necessary bribes; they do not necessarily have anything at all to do with moral deserts.[25] On this nonmoralized view of incentives, encouraging people to get others out of bad situations is, in principle, just as important as discouraging those people from getting themselves into those situations in the first place. Where the emphasis should fall, in any particular instance, is simply a technical optimization exercise: we should just choose the most cost-effective method, or combination of methods, for avoiding suffering all around. This typically leads us to assign responsibility largely (and, on some analyses, almost exclusively) to people who were in no way causally responsible for the situations they are now being asked to remedy.[26] Furthermore, there are in any case clear limits on the use of incentives. Incentives must be effective in accomplishing their desired goal; they must be no larger than strictly necessary to do so; and they must be no more costly than the goal itself is worth. All this combines to suggest that incentive considerations will not lead us to deviate often or largely from the course of action recommended by my principle of protecting the vulnerable.

The separate question of moral deserts remains.[27] It presents itself as a counterargument to my vulnerability model in two respects. One argument concerns those who find themselves in difficulty through their own improvidence: some would say that they had it coming, that is, they deserve whatever they got, and it would actually be *wrong* for anyone to help them out of their difficulty. The other argument concerns those who have done nothing to cause another's distress but are (perhaps uniquely) in a position to help relieve it: some would insist that they have done nothing to deserve this burden and that it would be wrong to impose it on them, although of course it would be terribly nice of them if they chose to assume it.[28]

Both claims, however, extend the notion of deserts beyond its proper bounds. Take the second counterargument first. Incurring a duty or a responsibility is not necessarily, nor even characteristically, something that you deserve. More often than not, it is something that just happens to you. When walking along a deserted beach, you see a child floundering in shallow water. Nothing in your background or character suggests that you deserve to bear the burden of effecting the rescue. It would, however, be absurd to say that you are therefore morally at liberty to leave the child to drown.

The notion of deserts is ordinarily equally out of place in the first counterargument as well. By and large, the improvident should be regarded as foolhardy people whose recklessness is to be discouraged through appropriate disincentives, not as evil people whose wickedness deserves to be punished. In dealing with people in precarious situations, questions of fault, blame, and desert are simply out of place. When two victims of a traffic accident are brought into the hospital emergency room with similar injuries, surely they should be treated with equal care and attention, even though one caused the accident while the other was its innocent victim. The need, dependency, or vulnerability of the victims, not their deserts, is what dictates physicians' responsibilities.[29]

The third and final general point about my vulnerability model is that the agents to whom these responsibilities fall might be either individuals or collectivities. Consider the problem of famine relief. Millions of people are starving daily. But realistically what could I do to help? There are millions of them and only one of me. In such cases it may make little sense to hold anyone individually responsible; maybe, in my terms, those in need are just not very vulnerable to any single other individual.

Such invulnerability would, on my argument, relieve us individually of any responsibility for helping with famine relief efforts. Excuses of that sort, however, typically serve merely to get us out of the fire and into the frying pan.[30] The price of letting individuals off the hook in that way is to put collectivities there in their place. The starving people of the world certainly *are* vulnerable to the actions and choices of those of us in rich nations, taken collectively. Hence we collectively have heavy responsibilities in respect of them.

Collective responsibilities are laid, in the first instance, upon the group as a whole to organize and to implement a scheme of coordinated action to protect the vulnerable agent or agents' interests. But these group responsibilities ultimately devolve onto the individuals who constitute the group. Each member of the group is responsible, so far as that person is able, consistently with that person's other moral responsibilities, (1) to see to it that the group organizes a scheme of coordinated action that protects the interests of the vulnerable agent or agents as well as it can; and (2) to discharge fully and effectively the responsibilities allocated to him or her under any such scheme that might be organized, just so long as it protects the interests of the vulnerable agent or agents better than no scheme at all would protect them.[31]

In many ways, making something a collective responsibility only complicates matters. In one important respect, however, it simplifies them. Making something a collective rather than an individual responsibility removes any objection to the social enforcement of that responsibility. Individuals have many moral duties that, for one reason or another, we think society ought not compel them to discharge. Where the duty is a collective one from the outset, however, collective action is clearly appropriate. Then the collectivity is fully justified in compelling each of its constituent parts to play its full appointed role in discharging those obligations, duties, and responsibilities.

Broader Implications

The aim of this chapter is to demonstrate that we have a broader range of social responsibilities than we traditionally acknowledge. What I hope to establish here is essentially a point of principle. The practicalities—how best to discharge these broader responsibilities—remain as open questions, although at the end of this chapter I shall offer reasons for believing that the welfare state is a good way of discharging at least some of them.

The argument for broader responsibilities goes like this. We all acknowledge strong responsibilities toward our own families, friends, and certain others. Once we start examining the sources of those responsibilities, we discover there is nothing "special" about them. It is the vulnerability of the others, rather than any voluntary act of will on our part, that generates those responsibilities. There are many more people vulnerable to us, individually or especially collectively, than stand in any of the standard "special relationships" to us. If my analysis of the true basis of those standard responsibilities is correct, then we have strictly analogous (and, potentially, equally strong) responsibilities toward all those others as well. Aid to vulnerable strangers is thereby justified on the same basis as aid rendered to our own parents or children.

To see what all is at stake in this argument, its ramifications must be sketched, however briefly and unsatisfactorily. First and foremost, notice that state welfare services are essentially mechanisms whereby we attempt collectively to protect vulnerable members of our own society. They may or may not be the best mechanisms available for so doing, and I shall return to that issue presently. But for now, just note that the welfare state, as a device for protecting the vulnerable, can claim at least prima facie moral justifiability on my principle.

The vulnerability model, in its collective form, might also underwrite far stronger international obligations than are ordinarily acknowledged.[32] People in very poor countries are enormously vulnerable to the actions and choices of people in very rich ones. Again, how we might best go about discharging these responsibilities is an open question and turns heavily upon various matters of empirical fact. It seems very likely, however, that the responsibility imposed on the rich will turn out to be a collective rather than an individual one.[33]

Yet another potential application concerns our obligations to future generations. Intergenerational transfers, especially spanning several generations, are singularly one-way affairs. We can do whatever we like to our distant successors without fear of retaliation. Future generations are enormously vulnerable to the actions and choices of present people, individually and especially collectively. The things we destroy or use up will be unavailable for them to enjoy. Their extraordinary vulnerability to our actions and choices seems to be the best basis for assigning strong responsibilities to present generations to provide for the further future.

Finally, this model might entail responsibilities to protect animals and natural environments. "Dumb animals," delicate coral reefs, and ecosystems more generally have proven enormously vulnerable to the actions and choices of human agents, individually and especially collectively. Whether or not that gives rise to any responsibilities on our part to protect them depends on whether this constitutes vulnerability in the relevant sense. Earlier, vulnerability was defined in terms of the impact of our actions and choices on the *interests* of those who are affected. The question thus becomes whether animals and other nonhuman entities can have genuine interests. This is not the place to enter into that debate.[34] It is enough to say that if (and insofar as) we see sentient creatures, ecosystems, or the natural environments upon which they depend as having "interests" at all, then their vulnerability will once again generate prima facie responsibilities on our part to protect them.

Of course, we will have to balance one set of responsibilities against others. How much should we allocate to our collective responsibilities for social welfare, as against our private responsibilities for the well-being of our families and friends? How much to foreign assistance, as against domestic social services? How much to future generations, as against present people? How much to the protection of animals and environments, as against humans?

Some might regard these responsibilities as utterly incommensurable and therefore deny that any such balancing can ever be done. Recall Sartre's example of "the young man who is torn between remaining with his ailing mother and going off to join the Resistance. Sartre's point is that there is no way of adjudicating between these two strong claims on his moral allegiance through reason." But, as Taylor goes on to say, if there really were no bases for comparing the claims of kin and country, then the moral dilemma itself would disappear: the son should just "throw himself" one way or the other, as Buridan's ass should have done in choosing between two equally good haystacks; since neither choice would be right or wrong, there would be no point agonizing over the choice.[35] But that cannot be a correct analysis. We may find it hard to say which is the right choice, but we are quite confident that, whatever else, it is rightly to be regarded as a hard choice. That fact is conclusive evidence that the responsibilities cannot really be incommensurable, after all.

Here I suggest that the notion of vulnerability, cashed out in terms of the notion of interests, not only can account for the force of these dilemmas but also can help us resolve them. The dilemmas arise because discharging our responsibilities with respect to some of those who are vulnerable to us entails defaulting on our responsibilities with respect to some others who are also similarly vulnerable to us. Which we should favor depends, I suggest, upon the relative vulnerability of each agent. We must determine how strongly that agent's interests would be affected by our alternative actions and choices and whether or not that agent would be able to find other sources of assistance or protection should we fail to provide it.[36]

On balance, it seems likely that those relatively near to us in space and time probably will be rather more vulnerable to us in these ways. Hence my argument is saved from the traditional reductio of requiring us to give everything we have to starving Asians, or always to be saving everything for the ever-receding infinity of future generations, or to have our own lives and projects constantly interrupted to serve others. My argument would seem to allow—indeed, to require—us to show *some* bias toward our own kind, however defined. But that bias must not be absolute. The vulnerability of others—be they needy fellow citizens, foreigners, heirs, or hares—to our actions and choices may well be sufficiently large, and how we (and perhaps we alone) can help sufficiently clear, to require us to give their interests some substantial weight in reckoning our own responsibilities. Charity may indeed begin at home, but morally it must not stop there.

Reducing Immoral Vulnerabilities

Up to this point, my argument has taken vulnerabilities and dependencies as given. I have argued that, if people are vulnerable to us, then it is our responsibility to protect them. Sometimes, however, it might be even better to try to eliminate the conditions that make them vulnerable and dependent. A few of these conditions may be naturally fixed, inevitable, and immutable. But most vulnerabilities will turn out to have been created, shaped, or sustained at least in part through certain social arrangements.[37] In some respects, this is true even of those dependencies that would seem at first blush to be the most natural, such as those connected with childhood or old age.[38]

It is obviously immoral to hold people in an unnecessarily dependent status against their will. Moral theories built around notions of free choice, self-respect, or autonomy all yield that same conclusion. But in some cases people willingly do—and it seems morally and prudentially desirable that they should—render themselves vulnerable to a variety of other people for a variety of purposes. In personal relationships, love can plausibly be analyzed as putting yourself in one another's power. "A world in which no one had power over another, and in which no one was vulnerable, a world in which people could be moved to action by force or reason alone, would be a world without love, an inhuman world."[39] In commercial relations, interdependence is the essence of trade and hence of all mutually profitable business ventures. Similarly in politics, interdependence forms the basis of all kinds of alliances and coalitions.[40] Objectionable though we might find the particulars of any specific arrangement, there is surely nothing wrong with exchanges or alliances as such merely because they engender vulnerabilities of this sort.

Our moral theories must, then, allow for vulnerabilities, some of which are inevitable and some of which are self-selected. Yet at the same time we must recognize that such relationships are subject to abuse, and we must insist upon certain conditions to guard against that kind of abuse. The standard proposal is that, insofar as vulnerabilities or dependencies are within our power to create or alter or eliminate, they should be reciprocal or mutual. The real objection, various commentators observe, is not to dependency as such. It is instead to *unilateral* dependency, to *asymmetrical* power relations. That asymmetry is what creates opportunities for the strong to exploit the weak. Were each party equally dependent upon the other, there need be no fear of such behavior.[41]

It is, however, wildly unrealistic to demand that dependencies and vulnerabilities be completely symmetrical, that is, that each depend on the other in exactly the same measure. That condition is satisfied in virtually no trading relation, in virtually no alliance, and probably in very few personal relationships. Neither is complete symmetry strictly necessary for a morally acceptable dependency relationship. There are, in fact, two acceptable alternatives.

The first is described by a pair of conditions. One is interdependency: each party must get something out of the relationship; or, alternatively, each must stand to lose something if it were terminated. The other condition is that neither party be so heavily dependent upon the other that the dependent party would cease to meet basic needs were the relationship terminated.[42] The latter condition could be waived in cases of perfectly symmetrical vulnerabilities but becomes increasingly important the greater the asymmetry.[43]

The second alternative would permit monopoly suppliers of needed resources to exist. What it would crucially demand is merely that they have no discretionary control over the disposition of those resources. B, who needs the resource, would still be dependent upon A, the monopoly supplier of that resource. But A cannot *exploit* B's dependency unless A can withhold the resource at will. And it is exploitable dependencies that we find morally most offensive.

An Application: The Welfare State

The raison d'être of the welfare state clearly is to discharge in part the responsibility I have here been discussing, namely, to protect vulnerable members of society. The early British initiatives—old-age pensions, health and unemployment insurance, minimum-wage policies, and the like—were all aimed explicitly at "protecting the weakest and most vulnerable elements in society, such as the aged poor, the unemployed workman, the sweated worker."[44] The subsequent history of the welfare state has similarly consisted in the increasing recognition of, and response to, "states of dependency."[45] Contemporary arguments for the expansion of the welfare state are all likewise couched in terms of dependency and vulnerability.[46]

Assuming my earlier arguments have proven persuasive, it is clear that we have a strong moral responsibility to protect those who are vulnerable to our actions and choices. The only remaining question is whether the welfare state is the best way of doing so. Of course, any particular welfare state may fail for reasons peculiar unto itself. It is important, therefore, to separate out and concentrate on what is generic to the welfare state as such.

For purposes of this discussion, I shall assume that the defining features of the welfare state—and the features that must therefore be justified in any defense of it—are as follows. The welfare state necessarily entails *compulsory, collective provision for certain basic needs as a matter of right*. Welfare state provision is said to be compulsory and collective to distinguish it from private, voluntary charity; as distinct from more thoroughgoing egalitarian regimes, it provides only for people's basic needs; and as distinct from the old poor law, the welfare state allows beneficiaries to claim their entitlements as a matter of right.

The principal challenge facing any defense of the welfare state must surely be to show why protecting these vulnerable people should be a collective rather than an individual responsibility. There are basically two individualistic options available here. The first focuses upon the responsibilities of needy individuals themselves, while the second focuses upon the responsibilities of their families and friends.

Certainly it is true that people are even more vulnerable in even more ways to their own actions and choices than they are to those of the collectivity. For that reason, they should indeed bear primary responsibility for attending to their own needs. The state's responsibility is in the nature of a secondary, backup responsibility, activated only when those with primary responsibility have failed to discharge it. Why they have failed, I have argued, is morally irrelevant; my analysis of responsibilities is, recall, forward looking (asking only "Who is best able to help now?") rather than backward looking (asking "Who is to blame for this situation?").[47] All that matters is that these individuals are now at risk of failing to have their most basic needs satisfied. That in itself is quite enough to activate secondary responsibility on the part of others to protect them.

The second individualistic option is to admit any need for someone to bear second responsibilities in such a case but to lodge those responsibilities with some other private individuals rather than with the state. Specifically, this approach suggests that if people are unable to provide for themselves, it should be left to their families and friends to do so. That, curiously, is what "self-reliance" has come to mean in contemporary social policy debates.[48] No doubt families and friends do, on my account, have strong moral responsibilities to provide assistance in such situations, and at its best this system is no doubt preferable to state provision: material assistance from families and friends might betoken a deeper affection, in a way that state assistance necessarily cannot. The question is not whether families and friends should help out those in need. It is instead whether those in need should be forced to rely upon their families and friends for such support.

At this point, there is a strong case to be made for welfare-state provision as a kind of backup to the backup. An important part of this case is brutally empirical. One of the primary obstacles to an effective system of family responsibility for needy members is that needy people are ordinarily found in needy families, who are in no position to make any great sacrifices.[49] There is also a principled objection to such policies, however, that would prove decisive even if these empirical facts were otherwise.

This principled objection harks back to the standards of an acceptable dependency relationship laid down above. Dependency might be acceptable if: (1) it were symmetrical; or (2) basic needs were not at stake; or (3) no one were to enjoy discretionary control over needed resources. *Ex hypothesi* we are here discussing an asymmetrical relationship where the subordinate's basic needs are indeed at stake.

The only thing that could make such a relationship morally acceptable would be for the agent upon whom the subordinate depends not to have discretionary control over those needed resources. Where that agent is a person's family or friends, that condition cannot possibly be met: family and friends must inevitably enjoy discretionary control over resources that are, in the final analysis, still their own. Where the subordinate is dependent instead upon the state, however, it is possible to vest that person with a legal entitlement to assistance. Once such laws have been enacted, state officials (unlike families, friends, or private charities) lack any discretion in deciding whether or not to honor claims of needy.[50] The welfare state, defined as an institution that meets people's basic needs as a matter of right, is therefore a morally necessary adjunct to other more individualistic responses to the problems of vulnerability and dependency in our larger community.

Notes

This essay draws on work done while I was attached to the Social Justice Project at the Australian National University (Robert E. Goodin, *Protecting the Vulnerable: A Reanalysis of Our Social Responsibilities* [Chicago: Chicago University Press, 1985]). Earlier versions were read there and at the Universities of Auckland, Otago, Canterbury, Melbourne, and Essex. I am grateful for comments, then and later, from Annette Baier, Brian Barry, Stanley Benn, Ted Benton, Derek Browne, Tom Campbell, Jim Fishkin, Jim Flynn, Diane Gibson, John Kleinig, David Miller, David Novitz, Onora O'Neill, Carole Pateman, Philip Pettit, Val (Routley) Plumwood, Wojciech Sadurski,

Marian Sawer, Christine Swanton, Richard (Routley) Sylvan, David Tucker, Patricia Tulloch, Jeremy Waldron, Hugh Ward, and anonymous referees for *American Political Science Review.*

1. N. Daniels, "Wide Reflective Equilibrium and Theory Acceptance in Ethics," *Journal of Philosophy* 76 (1979): 256–82; John Rawls, *A Theory of Justice* (Cambridge: Harvard University Press, 1971), secs. 4, 9.

2. This is just updating and inverting Godwin's infamous example of being forced to choose between saving your mother or some greater public benefactor (Archbishop Fénelon) from a house fire (W. Godwin, *Enquiry Concerning Political Justice* [London: G. G. J. & J. Robinson, 1793], bk. 2, chap. 2). Williams's air crash example is related by R. M. Hare (*Moral Thinking* [Oxford: Clarendon Press, 1981], 138), who is highly critical of the conclusions reached by Williams there and elsewhere (B. Williams, *Moral Luck* [Cambridge: Cambridge University Press, 1981], 17–18). See similarly S. Gorovitz, "Bigotry, Loyalty, and Malnutrition," in *Food Policy,* ed. P. Brown and Henry Shue (New York: Free Press, 1977); L. A. Blum, *Friendship, Altruism, and Morality* (London: Routledge & Kegan Paul, 1980); A. Oldenquist, "Loyalties," *Journal of Philosophy* 79 (1982): 173–93; and E. R. Winkler, "Utilitarian Idealism and Personal Relations," *Canadian Journal of Philosophy* 12 (1982): 265–86.

3. W. D. Ross, *The Right and the Good* (Oxford: Clarendon Press, 1930), 21.

4. B. Williams, "A Critique of Utilitarianism," in *Utilitarianism: For and Against,* by J. J. C. Smart and B. Williams (Cambridge: Cambridge University Press, 1973), 110. See also Williams, *Moral Luck.*

5. D. Parfit, *Reasons and Persons* (Oxford: Clarendon Press, 1984), 95.

6. Michael Walzer, *Spheres of Justice* (New York: Basic Books, 1983), 31.

7. Parfit, *Reasons and Persons,* 95.

8. H. L. A. Hart, "Are There Any Natural Rights?" *Philosophical Review* 64 (1955): 175–91.

9. J. J. Thomson, "A Defense of Abortion," *Philosophy and Public Affairs* 1 (1971): 65. See also John Rawls, "Justice as Fairness," *Philosophical Review* 67 (1958): 158.

10. Hart, "Are There Any Natural Rights?" 183–84.

11. On businessmen, see P. S. Atiyah, *The Rise and Fall of Freedom of Contract* (Oxford: Clarendon Press, 1979); on professionals, see C. Fried, *Medical Experimentation* (New York: American Elsevier, 1974), 78; on families, see H. L. A. Hart, "Legal and Moral Obligation," in *Essays in Moral Philosophy,* ed. A. I. Melden (Seattle: University of Washington Press, 1958), 104; on friends, see M. Montaigne, "Of Friendship," in *The Complete Essays of Montaigne,* trans. D. M. Frame (Stanford, Calif.: Stanford University Press, 1958) (originally published in 1580).

12. Hence, I basically have no obligation to keep a promise when the promisee is not depending on me in any way to do so. The only reason I then would have is that everyone in society depends on the maintenance of the institution of promising, which is vulnerable to being undermined (however slightly) by my breach. That fact explains why the courts award damages, but only nominal ones, in cases where one party suffers no

loss from the other's breach of contract. See R. Braucher and E. A. Farnsworth, *Second Restatement of the Law of Contracts* (St. Paul, Minn.: American Law Institute, 1981), sec. 346; and, more generally, Atiyah, *Freedom of Contract*; G. Gilmore, *The Death of Contract* (Columbus: Ohio State University Press, 1974); and A. T. Kronman, "A New Champion for the Will Theory," *Yale Law Journal* 91 (1981): 404–23.

13. Hart, "Are There Any Natural Rights?" 187.

14. Braucher and Farnsworth, *Second Restatement,* sec. 90. See also Carole Pateman, "The Shame of the Marriage Contract" (University of Sydney, 1981, mimeo).

15. Champions of the voluntaristic model might reply that the parties have at least voluntarily assumed their roles and the concomitant (albeit unalterable) duties. Although that may explain why marriage partners have special responsibilities, no such voluntaristic analysis can explain what they are; for that, a separate account must be given. The vulnerability model, in contrast, provides a unified account of both the fact and the content of those duties.

16. See J. English, "What Do Grown Children Owe Their Parents?" in *Having Children,* ed. Onora O'Neill and W. Ruddick (New York: Oxford University Press, 1979), 345; A. Heath, *Rational Choice and Social Exchange* (Cambridge: Cambridge University Press, 1976), 59–60. Where families and friendships are concerned, reciprocal favors create bonds transcending the simple sort of trust that underlies longstanding commercial relationships, which amounts to little more than "trust to honor your debts and to keep your word" (R. Hardin, "Exchange Theory on Different Bases," *Social Science Information* 21 [1982]: 251–72). See also L. R. Macneil, *The New Social Contract* (New Haven: Yale University Press, 180).

17. I treat these as "social facts" that should, at least provisionally, be taken as given. In these and many other cases, people end up being vulnerable to certain particular individuals merely because society happens to assign those particular people responsibility for caring for them (e.g., parents for children). The only reason that this social allocation of responsibility matters morally is, I would argue, because of the vulnerability and dependency that it engenders. If it is regarded as your job and no one else will do it if you do not (and if furthermore it is a job that really ought to be done by someone), then there is a strong argument for you to do it. That is not to say that it should be your job, or that you (or we) should not try to get someone else to accept responsibility for doing it. It is merely to say that until and unless someone else does, you should keep on performing it. This is a topic to which I return in discussing collective responsibilities.

18. Thus, although the courts are committed to doing whatever is in "the best interests of the child," children are not removed from marginally less suitable natural parents whenever marginally more suitable foster parents can be found, and the reason given (the risk of "separation trauma") points, just as my argument here suggests it should, to the emotional vulnerabilities of the child. See R. H. Mnookin, "Foster Care: In Whose Best Interests?" *Harvard Educational Review* 43 (1973): 599–638; and, more generally, Parfit, *Reasons and Persons,* 96; and Blum, *Friendship, Altruism, and Morality,* 56.

19. Goodin, *Protecting the Vulnerable,* chap. 4.

20. T. H. Green, "Liberal Legislation and the Freedom of Contract," in *Works*, ed. R. L. Nettleship (London: Routledge, 1888), 322.

21. Brian Barry, *Political Argument* (London: Routledge & Kegan Paul, 1965), 176. See also A. Reeve and A. Ware, "Interests in Political Theory," *British Journal of Political Science* 13 (1983): 379–400.

22. My principle is more catholic than it might appear. Although the definition of "interests" is recognizably liberal, the slippage between what people want and what is objectively best suited to satisfying their desires allows substantial scope for Marxian notions of false consciousness to operate. Similarly, although my principle is welfare-consequentialistic in form, deontologists can embrace it just so long as the *ceteris paribus* clause is understood to include their cherished rights-based constraints on action. Notice also that my principle treats acts and omissions symmetrically. J. Glover (*Causing Death and Saving Lives* [Harmondsworth, England: Penguin, 1977], 94), Robert E. Goodin (*Political Theory and Public Policy* [Chicago: University of Chicago Press, 1982], 1–15), and J. Bennett ("Positive and Negative Relevance," *American Philosophical Quarterly* 20 [1983]: 185–94) show that, once other morally relevant correlates are factored out, not helping when you could have done so is morally indistinguishable from causing harm when you could have avoided doing so. That argument applies with particular force to bearers of standard special responsibilities (e.g., bodyguards and firemen) and would by extension apply equally forcefully to all vulnerability-based responsibilities that I have here argued are analogous.

23. Joel Feinberg, *Doing and Deserving* (Princeton, N.J.: Princeton University Press, 1970), 244. Notice an important asymmetry. When those with primary responsibility have acted, those with subsidiary responsibilities are relieved of any obligation to do so. But when those with subsidiary responsibility have, owing to the inability or especially the unwillingness of those with primary responsibility, been forced to act in their stead, that in no way relieves the latter of their obligations or excuses their defaulting.

24. This saves my principle from the counterintuitive consequence that we have stronger responsibilities for protecting the rich than the poor, because, *ceteris paribus*, people are more vulnerable the more they have to lose. But of course the more you have to lose, the better able you are to protect yourself from loss: the rich can protect themselves; it is the poor who need our help.

25. Rawls, *A Theory of Justice*, 1971, sec. 48; Feinberg, *Doing and Deserving*, 94.

26. The incentive problem posed here is discussed more fully by economists concerned with allocating the costs of accidents between those whose negligence created a dangerous situation, on the one hand, and those with the "last clear chance" to avoid the accident, on the other. D. Wittman ("Optimal Pricing of Sequential Inputs: Last Clear Chance, Mitigation of Damages, and Related Doctrines in the Law," *Journal of Legal Studies* 10 [1981]: 65–91) has shown that the optimal incentives there require us to impose the bulk of the charges on the latter party rather than the former one. This is consistent with my suggestion that task responsibility should be predominantly forward looking (who can remedy the situation?) rather than backward looking (who caused the situation?).

27. As a kind of hybrid between the incentive and desert arguments, there is a third proposition, which holds that it is our moral responsibility to protect the long-term interests of the profligate poor (or their or our successors who would otherwise have to pay their bills) by creating appropriate incentives in the present to encourage them to do what they (or their or our successors) will at some future time wish they had done. But the same limits apply to this argument as to the earlier incentive argument: it justifies incentives only insofar as they are necessary, effective, and entail less overall harm than benefit to the interests they are designed to protect. Thus, if the arguments of note 47 below are correct, the issue will simply not arise. Even if it does, this duty to be "cruel to be kind in the long term" might be counterbalanced by our duty not to be cruel in the short term.

28. The most famous counterexample of this sort is Thomson's of a dying violinist who can survive only if plugged into your circulatory system (Thomson, "A Defense of Abortion," 48). My principle does indeed require you to give the violinist's interests serious consideration; but they may of course be outweighed by the other responsibilities, including responsibilities to yourself, on which you would have to default to save the violinist's life. In this way my principle can wriggle out of Thomson's counterexample. Here it is to the credit of my theory that it requires some squirming: the simple answer, "It's my body, and that's that," surely makes far too short work of what truly is a terrible moral dilemma.

29. Robert E. Goodin, "Negating Positive Desert Claims," *Political Theory* 13 (1985): 575–98.

30. J. L. Austin, "A Plea for Excuses," *Proceedings of the Aristotelian Society* 57 (1956): 1–30.

31. Philosophers (M. McKinsey, "Obligations to the Starving," *Nous* 15 [1981]: 309–23) tend to recognize the latter duty but not the former; for more details, see Goodin (*Protecting the Vulnerable,* chap. 5). There is obviously some scope for trading off these two duties for one another, with political action designed to alter the scheme being preferred to cooperation under the scheme whenever it is likely to be sufficiently effective in instituting a scheme that is sufficiently better at promoting the interests of the vulnerable agent or agents sufficiently quickly to justify the short-term damage to those interests.

32. Peter Singer, "Famine, Affluence, and Morality," *Philosophy and Public Affairs* 1 (1972): 229–43.

33. L. Glover ("It Makes No Difference Whether or Not I Do It," *Proceedings of the Aristotelian Society [Supplement]* 49 [1975]: 171–90) points out that, although none of us acting alone could eliminate world poverty, virtually any of us acting entirely alone could lift at least several starving Asians out of poverty. The essential flaw with individualistic programs such as "adopt-a-child," though, is that they work on a child-by-child basis; consequently they can end up doing as much harm as good, both for the putative beneficiaries and for those around them. To be sure our well-intentioned gifts have the desired effects, they must be set in the context of some reasonably comprehensive and well-integrated scheme for restructuring the recipient community as a whole. That requires a kind of coordination well beyond anything isolated donors—or

even relatively large-scale voluntary charities—could reasonably hope to accomplish. R. Nozick (*Anarchy, State, and Utopia* [Oxford: Blackwell, 1974], 266–67) makes just such a case for organized collective action.

34. Joel Feinberg (*Rights, Justice, and the Bounds of Liberty* [Princeton, N.J.: Princeton University Press, 1980], 159–206) persuasively argues that animals, at least, do have interests and hence interest-based claims; and since Richard Routley and Val Routley ("Against the Inevitability of Human Chauvinism," in *Ethics and Problems of the Twenty-first Century*, ed. K. Goodpaster and K. Sayre [Notre Dame, Ind.: Notre Dame University Press, 1979]) are right to insist that the burden of proof must fall upon anyone who proposes to treat different agents' interests differently, animals' interests must at least presumptively enjoy the same status as our own.

35. Charles Taylor, "Responsibility for Self," in *The Identities of Persons*, ed. A. O. Rorty (Berkeley and Los Angeles: University of California Press, 1976), 290–91.

36. We also need to decide how to weight one agent's interests relative to another's. Where human beings are concerned, I am firmly inclined to weight everyone's interests equally (Robert E. Goodin, "How to Determine Who Should Get What," *Ethics* 85 [1975]: 310–21). I am just as firmly inclined to weight future generations' interests the same as our own (Robert E. Goodin, "Discounting Discounting," *Journal of Public Policy* 2 [1982]: 53–72). But where animals or inanimate objects are concerned, I am far less certain what the appropriate weighting should be.

37. R. M. Titmuss, "The Social Division of Welfare," in *Essays on "the Welfare State"* (London: Allen & Unwin, 1958).

38. See F. R. Marks, "Detours on the Road to Maturity," *Law and Contemporary Problems* 39 (Summer) 1975: 78–92; A. Skolnick, "The Limits of Childhood," *Law and Contemporary Problems* 39 (Summer 1975): 38–77; A. Walker, "The Social Creation of Poverty and Dependence in Old Age," *Journal of Social Policy* 9 (1980): 49–75; and A. Walker, "Dependence in Old Age," *Social Policy and Administration* 16 (1982): 115–35.

39. J. R. S. Wilson, "In One Another's Power," *Ethics* 88 (1978): 315.

40. D. A. Baldwin, "Interdependence and Power: A Conceptual Analysis," *International Organisation* 34 (1980): 471–506.

41. Wilson, "In One Another's Power," 315. See also Virginia Held, "Marx, Sex, and the Transformation of Society," *Philosophical Forum* 5 (1974): 168–83; Pateman, "Marriage Contract"; W. Thompson, *Appeal of One Half of the Human Race* (London: Longman, 1825); and M. Wollstonecraft, *A Vindication of the Rights of Women,* 2d ed. (London: J. Johnson, 1792). Symmetry must be subjectively defined: what one party gains from the relationship (or would lose were it terminated) must occupy as important a role in that party's overall life plan as what the other party gains or would lose plays in that other's.

42. Baldwin, "Interdependence and Power"; Henry Shue, *Basic Rights: Subsistence, Affluence, and U.S. Foreign Policy* (Princeton, N.J.: Princeton University Press, 1980).

43. Symmetrical dependencies, even very great ones, admit of no abuse. If each party depends equally upon the other for the satisfaction of basic needs, then neither could exploit the other through a credible threat to terminate the relationship.

44. W. A. Robson, *Welfare State and Welfare Society* (London: Allen & Unwin, 1976), 21.

45. Titmuss, "Social Division of Welfare," 42–43.

46. See E. van Lennep, "Opening Address," in *The Welfare State in Crisis* (Paris: Organisation for Economic Cooperation and Development, 1981), 9; and Australia, Royal Commission on Human Relationships, *Final Report* (Canberra: Australian Government Publishing Service, 1977), 1:63.

47. Backward-looking considerations are relevant only insofar as, through incentive effects, they might have future consequences. But there is a substantial body of evidence suggesting that the poor tend to be poor planners and hence are largely impervious to incentives whether these are positive (e.g., incentives to slack off work when guaranteed a minimal income) or negative (e.g., incentives to avoid hazardous jobs); see S. Danziger, R. Haveman, and R. Plotnick, "How Income Transfer Programs Affect Work, Savings, and Income Distribution," *Journal of Economic Literature* 19 (1981): 975–1028; W. K. Viscusi, *Employment Hazards* (Cambridge: Harvard University Press, 1979); and Robert E. Goodin, "Self-Reliance versus the Welfare State," *Journal of Social Policy* 14 (1985): 25–47. It is perfectly reasonable that the poor should be unresponsive to incentives; marginalist calculations are a costly business, and the poor have more pressing demands on their time and attention. Given that, however, restricting welfare benefits would probably amount to no more than bringing a gratuitous disincentive to bear on a group that is largely impervious to incentives of any kind.

48. Goodin, "Self-Reliance."

49. Goodin, "Self-Reliance"; G. Y. Steiner, *The Futility of Family Policy* (Washington, D.C.: Brookings Institution, 1981), 114.

50. Goodin, "Self-Reliance"; A. D. Smith, "Public Assistance as a Social Obligation," *Harvard Law Review* 63 (1949): 266–88; A. D. Smith, *The Right to Life* (Chapel Hill: University of North Carolina Press, 1955); and R. M. Titmuss, "Welfare 'Rights,' Law, and Discretion," *Political Quarterly* 42 (1971): 113–32. Discretion disappears only after such laws have been enacted; state officials are left with discretionary control over what laws they enact. But it is the exploitation of dependencies that worries us, and it is in the administration rather than in the enactment of welfare policies that the greatest danger (although certainly not the exclusive one) of such exploitation arises.

5

Rights, Obligations, and Needs

Onora O'Neill

Most of the ethical theories we commonly discuss pay little attention to needs. In utilitarian thinking, needs may be considered as they are reflected in desires or preferences; but we know that this is an imperfect reflection. Discussions of human rights often do not consider needs at all. And where they do, I shall argue, intolerable strains are placed on the basic structure of rights theory. Part of my plan here is to explore why this is the case. But the more positive part is to suggest that if we start from a theory of human obligations rather than of human rights, we can readily take account of human needs.

A complete approach to these tasks would no doubt require a complete theory of human needs, which I do not intend to provide. My failure to do so is not only a matter of prudence and ignorance but also is (to a reasonable extent) justified by the thought that our immediate concern is world hunger and poverty. It isn't controversial that human beings need an adequate diet, shelter and clothing appropriate to their climate, clean water and sanitation, and some parental and health care. Without these they become ill and often die prematurely. It is controversial whether human beings need companionship, education, politics, and culture, or food for the spirit—for at least some people have led long lives that were not evidently stunted without them. But these are issues that we don't need to settle for present purposes.

Since I shall claim that needs have a different relation to theories of rights and to theories of obligation, the first task is to show that such theories are not equivalent. In showing this, however, I shall not be arguing that *institutionalized* rights and obligations aren't equivalent (although I believe that they are not) but that fundamental—"natural" or moral—rights and fundamental obligations are not equivalent.

Obligation, Right, and Rights in the Abstract

If we consider the matters of obligation and of right sufficiently abstractly, there seems to be no distinction between a principle of obligation and a principle of right. Whenever it is right either for some assignable individual, A, or for unspecified parties to have some action, *x*, done or omitted by B, then it is obligatory for B to do or to omit *x* either for A or for unspecified parties. One and the same principle defines what it is right for A (or for unspecified parties) to receive from B and what it is obligatory (indeed right) for B to do for A (or for unspecified parties). Indeed, in many European languages the same word is used to convey the abstract notions of right and of obligation. The terms *droit* and *Recht*, for example, can serve as translation for either. At this level of abstraction, the only difference between the notions appears to be that the vocabulary of obligation looks at an ethical relationship from the perspective of agency and the vocabulary of right looks at the same relationship from the perspective of recipience. This correlativity is the most fundamental feature of action-centered ethical reasoning. Without it, discourse about what is owed to some cannot show that any action ought to be taken, and discourse about what is owed by some cannot show that anyone, specified or unspecified, has been wronged if nothing is done.

But at a less abstract level, it matters a lot whether discussion is conducted in the idiom of right or of obligation. This is initially puzzling. If correlativity holds, the choice between perspectives is surely a trivial one between equivalent vocabularies. But its significance emerges when we consider a shift that can take place *only* within a less abstract approach, which provides a basis for, and insists on the priority of, the vocabulary of right. This is the shift from discussion of *right action* to discussion of *rights*.

So long as we talk about what it is right for some agent or agency to do, we need not distinguish between what is owed to specified others and what is owed indeed, but not to specified others. But once we start talking about *rights*, we assume a framework in which performance of obligations can be *claimed*. Rights have to be allocated to specified bearers of obligations: otherwise, claimants of rights cannot know to which obligation bearer their claims should be addressed. In rights-based reasoning, rights can either be allocated to (and so claimed of) *all* obligation bearers (here the obligation is *universal*, such as perhaps an obligation not to injure others) or can be allocated to (and so claimed of) some *specified* obligation bearer(s) (here the obligation is *special*, such as perhaps a worker's right to receive agreed-upon wages from an employer). But action that neither can be performed for all nor is based on any special relationship remains unallocated, so cannot be claimed, for it is not specified against whom any particular claim should be lodged. Reasoning that begins with the notion of rights cannot take account of obligations that are neither universal nor special, where no connection is made between (universal or specified) bearers of obligations and holders of rights. Since the discourse of rights requires that obligations are owed to *all* others or to *specified others*, *unallocated* right action, which is owed to unspecified others, tends to drop out of sight. Beyond the most abstract level of action-centered reasoning, a gap opens between rights and obligations. It is a gap that makes a very great difference to action-centered reasoning about human needs.

Advantages and Disadvantages of the Shift to Rights Discourse

The shift from discussion of right to discussion of rights adopts not merely the passive perspective of the recipient of others' action but also the narrower perspective of the claimant of others' action. Within the recipient perspective, the attitude of claimants is indeed *less* passive than other possible attitudes. For claimants are not humble petitioners or loyal subjects begging for a boon or favor: they speak as ones who have been wronged and who demand others' action. Hence the eighteenth-century innovation of the perspective of rights had both heady power and political import. It spoke to the downtrodden over the heads of existing institutions and their categories and urged them to assert their rights. This could be liberating in a world of rulers and subjects. But those who claim rights still see themselves within an overall framework of recipience. They still demand that others act rather than that they do so themselves. To this extent, the rhetoric of rights is not the idiom of autonomous citizens but a more rancorous discourse appropriate to those who see others as agents and themselves as passive. For those who are themselves in need and powerless, it may be the most active form of ethical and political discourse available. For those who are powerful enough to take action to alter situations of need, the rhetoric of rights seems well designed not to recognize such power or the full range of obligations that might go with it. The passivity of this perspective produces a narrowing of moral vision and discourse.

Part of this narrowing of vision is reflected in what happens to unallocated obligations within a rights framework. When obligations are unallocated, it is indeed right that they should be met, but nobody can have a right—an enforceable and claimable right—to their being met. As a result, in discussion of rights it is *standardly* claimed that requirements to help others (or to be generous or sympathetic) are not owed to all others or to specified bearers of rights and that there thus can be no rights to receive help (or generous or sympathetic treatment).

Even when help, beneficence, and their like are seen as obligations, they then seem less important than obligations whose performance can be claimed by holders of rights. This has various results. First there is a standing temptation to "promote" certain obligations by insisting that they do indeed have corresponding rights, even if the supposed claimants of the "rights" can find nowhere to lodge their claim. But when "rights" are promulgated without allocation to bearers of obligation, they amount to empty "manifesto" rights, whose fulfillment cannot be claimed of any others. For example, if a "right to food" is promulgated without the obligation to provide food for particular right holders being allocated to specified agents and agencies, this so-called right will provide meager pickings. And this is not merely because obligation holders may not take their obligation seriously, but for the deeper reason that no obligation holders have been specified. The prospects of the hungry would be transformed if specified others were obliged to provide each of them with adequate food; but unless obligations to feed the hungry are a matter of allocated justice rather than unallocated beneficence, a so-called right to food, and many other "rights" that would be important for the needy, will be only manifesto rights.

The more extreme result of shifting from the discourse of right action to that of rights is that unallocated obligations to give help may be not only demoted in this way but entirely denied. When obligations are allocated, it is clear where those who claim their rights should lodge their claims. They can lodge them against the agents or agencies that fail to fulfill a universal obligation and against any specified agent or agency that fails to meet its special obligations. *Perfect* obligations can be handled within a rights approach. But those obligations traditionally termed *imperfect* obligations may be not merely downgraded but rejected. These obligations—for example, obligations to helpfulness, kindness, sympathy, and other forms of beneficence—are not owed to specified others and hence cannot be claimed. From a rights perspective, they are invisible and are often classified not as *any* sort of obligation but as unrequired supererogation. This classification assimilates mundane acts of kindness, generosity, or helpfulness to heroic or saintly action, which indeed goes beyond all duty. The strongest and most far-reaching result of shifting discussion from matters of right to matters of rights is that there is then nothing between justice and supererogation.

The choice of rights discourse as the idiom for ethical deliberation drives a powerful wedge between questions of justice and matters of help and benefit. Justice is seen as a matter of assignable, hence claimable and potentially enforceable, rights, which only the claimant can waive. Beneficence is seen as unassignable, hence unclaimable and unenforceable. This theoretical wedge is reflected in many contemporary institutional structures and ways of thought.

Legal and economic structures often define the limits of justice; voluntary and private activities, including charity work and personal relationships, are seen as the domain of beneficence. Others' need, even their hunger and destitution, will be thought injustice only if we can show either that there is a universal right to be fed, to which a perfect obligation corresponds, or that each hungry person has a special right to have his or her material needs met. Present institutional arrangements patently leave many persons without special claims for food against particular others, and the enterprise of showing that feeding the hungry is a matter of justice is (as we shall see) uphill work within a rights perspective. If that enterprise fails, ethical reasoning within a rights framework can do no more than suggest that beneficence is an imperfect set of duties that we may fulfill as we will; we may even deny that beneficence of any type is a duty. If we lavish our attention and help on those who already have enough, or on our own families, that will fulfill any imperfect duty of beneficence we may have. In discussions of rights, it seems that matters of need carry no independent weight. Unless the questions of need can somehow be brought under the heading of justice, the discourse of rights may have to relegate global famine and destitution to the withering inadequacy of private, optional charity.

Do the Needy Have Special Rights?

Yet rights discourse has major attractions, even if it appears least adequate in dealing with questions of need. It isn't surprising that there have been numerous attempts to show that, with plausible additions, the needs of the poor can be handled within a rights perspective. Such attempts fall into two major groups. The first group tries to show that current relationships between the needy and others, and specifically between richer and poorer parts of the world, are often unjust in terms of quite standard conceptions of justice. These approaches claim that, as things actually are in the world today, the poor have certain *special* rights against the rich, which for the most part are *rights to compensation for past or present injustice.*

The historical arguments point out that the plight of the underdeveloped world today has in some part been caused by the activities of the nations, corporations, and individuals of the developed world. Many Third World countries suffer from the legacy of a colonial past in which their economies were developed to the advantage of the imperial power. Profits made in the South were often "repatriated" rather than reinvested locally. (This intriguing metaphor suggests an image of economic growth analogous to an Aristotelian account of human reproduction: capital is the father of profit, while labor and raw materials are only its mother, and the offspring belongs wholly to the father.) Colonial industry and trade were often deliberately restricted. There is no doubt that development in the North was partly based on exploitation of the South. However, since the individuals whose rights were violated in the colonial past, and those who violated them, are long dead and the relevant institutions defunct, past exploitation often provides an indeterminate basis for claiming that any present individuals or groups or countries or regions have special rights to compensation from richer nations or corporations or individuals. The actual patterns of colonial violation of economic rights are complex and obscure. In the heart of darkness, everything is murky. Many former colonies were economically backward when colonized; some colonial powers did a good deal to modernize and develop the infrastructure of their colonies; in some cases, Third World economies are *less* prosperous now than they were under colonial administrations. And it is always uncertain what the present would have been had the past not been colonial. *If* the present plight of the poor could be traced to colonial or imperial activities in the past and harms could be allocated to surviving agents or agencies, we might perhaps be able to show that some of the poor have rights to compensation against specifiable agents and agencies. But precisely because justice has to be allocated within a rights approach, the rights of the poor to compensation will be no stronger than the proof of allocation. We cannot tell how far the predicaments of the present were produced by ancient wrongs, nor which of our contemporaries have been harmed by such wrongs, nor which have benefited, nor which have special obligations to bear the costs of just compensation.

A parallel set of considerations attributes much of the plight of the Third World not to ancient but to present wrong. The present world economic order, it is claimed, harms the most vulnerable. Laissez-faire is a mockery in a world where the rich and powerful control the ground rules of the international economic order and, in particular, the framework of monetary and trading arrangements. While the details of such charges are enormously intricate, their basic pattern is simple. Others' rights are not respected if there is massive interference in the basic circumstances of their lives. But there is such interference in the lives of the poor by the nations and institutions of the rich North. The activities of transnational corporations, the operation of trade barriers and of banking and credit institutions, and above all the regulation of the international monetary system by the International Monetary Fund show that the developed world still sets the ground rules of economic life for the poorer world and so limits liberty in many ways. In these circumstances, any claim that justice is a matter of laissez-faire is rank hypocrisy. While this argument is impressive in outline, its detailed implications are hard to follow. Does it point to rejection of policies of "dependent development" in favor of indigenous and autonomous, but perhaps slower, paths of development? Does it point to a massive scheme of restitution payments from the developed world to the former colonial world? If it does, is the present package of "aid" measures adequate restitution, despite its misleading label? Or are present policies, which are very unevenly spread and deeply affected by "donor" political interests, inadequate? Can policies that have produced developed enclaves in the Third World and left vast areas of rural hinterland yet more impoverished count as compensation for present—or for past—harm? Or are present arrangements in fact just to the poor of the world because they have been consented to by those whom they affect, or at least by their governments?

Poverty in the Third World cannot easily be grasped under the heading of compensatory justice. To claim special rights, we must show a specific relationship; but the causal patterns between the undoubted harms produced and the specific individuals who are harmed are not clear enough to allocate rights of compensation: and without allocation, rights are no more than the rhetoric of manifestos. In addition, some of the poorest peoples in the world have been relatively little touched by the colonial period; hence their needs would be least met by an emphasis on special rights to compensation. It therefore seems that a focus on special rights cannot deal adequately with the needs of the poor.

Rights and Needs

A second and more ambitious approach to needs within a rights framework functions not by showing that (some of) the poor have special rights but by arguing that (all of) the poor have rights to have their basic needs met. While an emphasis on special rights assumes only those rights that all rights theories take to be important for justice, an emphasis on "welfare" rights aims more ambitiously to show that justice comprises not only rights to liberty but also rights to certain goods and services that would meet human needs. To evaluate such proposals, it is necessary to consider the basis of all claims about human rights.

Appeals to the self-evidence of human rights, though still popular, are evidently irrelevant in this context, for we are considering a disagreement about what rights there are. Consequentialist arguments for rights clearly don't get hung up on an inability to take account of beneficence; their problem, rather, is that they cannot ground justice in a sufficiently clear way to make more than a derivative use of the notion of rights. The most plausible way of construing human rights takes them as the mutually consistent and collectively exhaustive components of human liberty, which provide each an equal and maximal liberty.[1] This formulation leaves open the question of how liberty should be understood (e.g., negatively or positively), so is acceptable to varieties of liberals. Those who hope to show that there are welfare as well as liberty rights emphasize that the relevant conception of liberty is a "positive" one and that rights should be seen as the mutually consistent and collectively exhaustive components of human autonomy.

Attempts to show that maximal liberty, when understood in this positive sense, includes welfare rights, which would enable people to claim their basic needs of others, have produced many difficulties. Yet the assertion seems initially plausible. For without minimal standards of subsistence—which meet human needs—agency itself fails, and so the point of liberty of action and hence even of liberty rights is gone. Must not the set of universal human rights, then, include rights to the basic material conditions of human agency? This conclusion contradicts the position traditionally held by many rights theories, which see all universal rights as *liberty* rights to others' noninterference. If correct, it is surely the most significant development of the theory of human rights since its origin. Arguments of this sort have been put forward in some detail in recent years, for example, by Shue and by Gewirth. I propose not to analyze the detail of their arguments here but to suggest why the enterprise, in spite of its admirable aims, will not succeed. To do this demands some consideration of the *individuation* as well as the *grounding* of rights.

Rights are often individuated in substantival or reifying ways (rights to life, liberty, and the pursuit of happiness). However, when we want to consider what a supposed right amounts to, we always have to spell out which actions it permits and requires of whom. The reifying vocabulary is only a convenient shorthand—and not an entirely innocent one. It suggests, for example, a misleading proprietorial image of what a right is, as though it were some good that we could grasp and possess—an interpretation that does not hold up even for property rights, which are always rights to act in specified ways with specified items to the exclusion of specified sorts of interference by others. But, more significantly, a reifying way of individuating rights makes it hard to tell whether various alleged rights are mutually consistent or how the obligations that are their counterparts are allocated.

But a universal right is only a manifesto right if there is no corresponding allocated obligation. Standardly, rights theorists take it that the counterpart to a universal right is a universal obligation. The question of the allocation of obligation is then immediately solved. It is this that accounts for the "negative" character of traditional rights, that is, for the fact that they are all liberty rights. For it seems quite clear that it is possible for all to refrain from intervention or interference in a situation.[2] But it isn't clear what it would be for all to get involved in, or to take positive action with respect to, some situation. A universal right to be fed or to receive basic shelter or health care is unlike a universal right not to be killed or to speak freely in that it is plausible to think that the rights not to be killed or to speak freely are matched by and require universal obligations not to kill or not to obstruct free speech, but a universal right to food cannot simply be translated into a universal obligation to provide an aliquot amount of food. The asymmetry of liberty and welfare rights, on which libertarians rest so much of their refusal to broaden their conception of justice, is, I think, well grounded. (I doubt, however, that this result should give much comfort to libertarians, since the basic construction on which they rely is [unless a physicalist framework is assumed] indeterminate between alternative sets of possible liberty rights, and there are no convincing arguments to show that any set of liberty rights is maximal, nor indeed that any specified right must be a component of maximal liberty. However, this is not the occasion for pursuing these wider claims; I have done so elsewhere.)[3]

Our present concern is whether we can broaden our conception of rights and so of justice to include some rights to claim basic needs. It appears that we can do so only if we talk about rights so abstractly that we can avoid talking about their allocation to bearers of obligation, that is, at the level of abstraction at which we do not determine against whom claims may be lodged. We can talk quite fluently in a reifying way about rights to food or to a minimal standard of life or to basic health care. The reifying idiom serves well at this abstract level. But it obscures the point that there is a real asymmetry between rights to such goods and services and rights not to be killed or injured or coerced in various ways. The latter rights clearly can correspond to universal obligations, but it does not seem that welfare claim rights can have as their counterpart universal obligations to make available an aliquot amount of some good or to provide an aliquot service.

Shue has pointed out, quite correctly, that once we start talking about the *enforcement* of rights, the distinction between liberty rights that demand only noninterference and welfare rights that require positive action fades: "the very most 'negative'-seeming right to liberty, for example, requires positive action by society to protect it and positive action by society to restore it when avoidance and protection both fail."[4] But once we start talking about enforcement, we *assume* that the allocation of obligations, and so the individuation of rights, is settled. Otherwise we would not know what rights there are to enforce. Hence arguments from the requirements of enforceability cannot settle questions about what rights there can consistently be. Although it is true that the enforcement of a right not to be tortured demands positive action, just as enforcement of a right to food does, the difference between the two rights remains, whether or not there is enforcement. If, in the absence of enforcement, A tortures B, we are quite clear who has violated B's right; but if A does not provide B with food, or even with an aliquot morsel of food, we are not sure whether A has violated B's rights. There is nothing to show that it is against A that B's claim to food should be lodged, rather than against others, or to show that it is a legitimate claim.

Professor Gewirth's route to establishing rights to have needs met has related problems. He argues that "freedom and well-being" (understood in a limited sense that encompasses human needs rather than a comprehensive conception of well-being) are "necessary goods," in the sense that they are needed for human agency—as indeed they are. But then he suggests that this amounts to claiming that an agent must have "freedom and well-being" and hence has "rights to freedom and well-being." But this is no mere paraphrase. Granted that I must have freedom and well-being in order to act, what shows that I must, that is, ought, to be accorded freedom and well-being? In the first case, the term "must" is used in an instrumental sense: freedom and well-being are required for agency; in the second case, "must" is used in a moral sense: freedom and well-being ought to be accorded. Gewirth does not vindicate the transition from the instrumental sense in which agents must indeed have what they need in order to be agents to his claim about the rights human beings ought to have. Any claim about rights carries with it a claim about obligations and their allocation. Gewirth acknowledges this point and renders it as the claim that "others ought at least to refrain from removing or interfering with my freedom and well-being." But this formulation does not make it clear that securing rights to *well-being* cannot be just "a matter of refraining from removing and interfering," so cannot be a universal right. Yet unless an argument to ground rights to have needs met allocates to obligation bearers obligations to fulfill those rights, the alleged rights are no more than manifesto rights. While liberty rights correspond to universal obligations not to interfere with liberty, there is no parallel correspondence in the case of rights whose counterpart obligations demand positive action *whether or not there is enforcement*. The asymmetry between liberty rights and supposed welfare rights has not been shown to be illusory, and the assimilation of meeting needs to the requirements of justice, as these can be conceived within the rights framework, remains dubious.

There are, no doubt, other strategies that might be used to argue that human rights include rights to have needs met. Since there is no way to discuss these exhaustively, I intend to turn now to the perspective of obligations. This may seem a dismal project, given the contemporary intellectual and political scene. Human rights are discussed everywhere, and there is a diversely institutionalized human rights movement. There is, so far as I know, no human obligations movement, and obligations enter academic debate largely as the counterparts of human rights. Yet the perspective of obligation is not only the older perspective but also the one more widely current in daily, professional, and public life. It is also, I shall argue, a perspective that affords a better prospect for incorporating discussion of needs into our ethical thinking.

Starting with Obligations

The argument so far has established two significant points about obligations. The first is that a theory of obligations can be broader than a theory of rights, in that it can allow for unallocated, hence "imperfect" (literally incomplete), obligations and so is not bound to classify whatever good action is not a matter of perfect obligation as supererogation. The second is that it is the discourse of obligations rather than that of rights that is the primary vocabulary of action-centered ethics. When we discuss obligations, our direct concern is with what should be done; but when we discuss rights, our direct concern is with what should be received, yet we can only make this definite by considering what should be done.

If the discourse of obligations is fundamental for action-centered reasoning, it may be a more suitable context for considering a construction, analogous to those proposed by Shue and Gewirth and many others, of those obligations that can be held by all agents. And this, as is well known, is the core of the Kantian ethical enterprise. Kant derives the principles of obligation by considering on what principles all agents *could act* (not either *would* or *should* act, as in so many misreadings). Universalizable principles are those that *can* serve all agents as principles of action. Nonuniversalizable principles, which rational agents are obliged to eschew, are principles that cannot, in principle, be universally acted on.

The Kantian enterprise is in one very important way *unlike* the construction of human rights by considering which rights all agents could enjoy. The construction of rights works by determining what the greatest possible liberty (understood negatively or positively as the case may be) amounts to. In determining whether a right is one that could be universally enjoyed, we ask not just whether the right is *internally* consistent but also whether it is consistent with all other members of a proposed set of rights. Because this is the method of construction, rights to have needs met are standardly rejected by those who ask what the greatest possible set of liberties is: for they discover that the obligations that would have to be allocated for needs to be met are obligations that would be incompatible with central liberty rights, which they take to be the more important rights. We cannot, for example, combine a level of economic welfare for all with unrestricted liberty of economic action for all. But in constructing principles of obligation on the Kantian scheme, the aim is initially to discern some principles of action that are *internally* inconsistent and so cannot, even considered individually, be universally shared, and so must be rejected if all agents are to have the same fundamental obligations.[5] There is, therefore, an important respect in which the Kantian construction of obligations is *weaker* than counterpart constructions of human rights. It allows us to determine *some* principles of obligation—principles that cannot serve as universal principles—without having to establish *all* such principles. By contrast, to establish that any rights are components of human liberty, it is necessary to determine all rights. Because the construction of rights has to determine what rights there are collectively, liberty rights are often taken to be the least controversial of rights: their mutual coherence is thought uncontroversial. (I have argued elsewhere that this is an illusion.)[6]

Since the Kantian enterprise depends on determining what principles are nonuniversalizable, it is essential to work out at what level of act description the enterprise is to take place. Clearly superficial and detailed act descriptions must be ruled out, for these can never be universally shared. We cannot all of us eat the same grain nor share the same roof. The level of description that is important—that of the Kantian maxim of action—is the level of description that is *fundamental* to a given action. Roughly speaking, we have to distinguish between ancillary act descriptions, which must vary with circumstances, and those on which the doing of an act was contingent. The maxim is the guiding or controlling principle of an action, the principle that makes sense of, and orchestrates ancillary aspects of, action. On Kant's account, neither agents nor others have privileged knowledge of the maxim of a given act; this is always a matter of judgment and, given the opacity of self and of other knowledge, no more beyond dispute than any other empirical matter. Hence we cannot definitively judge others' actions or our own. But this does not preclude guiding deliberation by reference to the criterion of avoiding reliance on those principles that are clearly not ones on which all agents could act. Agents can strive to avoid acting on nonuniversalizable principles even if they cannot guarantee that they have succeeded.

The Kantian method of construction allows us to isolate at least two major principles of justice, namely, those of noncoercion and nondeception. The background arguments here show that it is impossible for a principle of coercion to be universally shared—for those who are coerced are denied agency and so cannot share that principle of action, and those who are deceived are denied knowledge of the agents' maxim, so cannot, in principle, share it.

The same construction yields some principles of imperfect obligation. These are not nonuniversalizable in the strict sense that holds for all possible rational beings but are only nonuniversalizable among beings who, like human beings, have desires that they are not naturally able to fulfill. However, the construction does not depend upon *what* is desired.[7] Kant's thought is simply that rational beings whose desires, unlike those of creatures of instinct, standardly outrun both their own resources and those of their species must, regardless of the specific content of their desires, reject certain further principles as nonuniversalizable.[8] Such beings cannot rationally will that they should be part of a world in which a principle of neglect of others' ends is universally adopted. Nor can they rationally will to be part of a world in which a principle of neglect of talents is universally adopted. Either of these principles of action would on occasion be incompatible with whatever particular ends they may seek, given that they are committed (by the principle of hypothetical imperatives) to some means for any end to which they are committed and by their natural character to desires that exceed naturally available capacities. The claim is not that maxims such as those of principled nonbeneficence or of principled neglect of talents are nonuniversalizable for any rational beings but specifically that rational beings whose desires exceed their individual resources (and to whom instinct provides inadequate species support) cannot rationally adopt these maxims. For such beings must will to be given help when their own resources are inadequate or to rely on skills developed by someone or other in seeking whatever ends they pursue. However, the nonuniversalizability of neglect of beneficence and of talents does not entail that there are obligations to help all others in all their projects or to develop all possible talents, for this is impossible. The Kantian construction respects the asymmetry of duties to refrain and duties to intervene.

This construction has already revealed one of the advantages of starting with obligations rather than with rights. It allows the development of principles of imperfect obligations and so is not torn between showing, on one hand, that what have traditionally been thought imperfect duties (such as beneficence) are really matters of justice or conceding, on the other hand, that they are only supererogatory and in no way obligatory. However, the construction still allows us to talk about rights, considered as the reciprocal of perfect obligations. When it is either relevant or politic to adopt the perspective of recipience, the idiom of rights will be available for discussing matters of justice where obligations are allocated. And it will not be muddied by any attempt to show that imperfect obligations are matters of right. All of this might, however, be thought to show precisely that the central part of a theory of obligation cannot incorporate consideration of needs. If perfect duties, and specifically matters of justice, are a matter of noninterference, and if the allocation of beneficence is undetermined by fundamental ethical considerations, may we not allocate it without regard to human need? So the Kantian enterprise is often read.

Obligations and Needs

The Kantian construction can, however, take full account of basic human needs. I shall sketch how that can be done and then will point briefly to some textual grounds for thinking that this is the reading that makes best sense of the Kantian enterprise as a whole.

Kant stresses repeatedly that his principles of obligations are principles for *finite* rational beings and in particular that human beings are finite not only in rationality but also in many other ways. Consequently, casuistry and deliberation are essential if we are to work out what the principles of noncoercion, nondeception, and nonneglect of beneficence and talents imply about specifically human duties.

The principle of noncoercion clearly cannot be interpreted for the human condition unless we have an account of what constitutes coercion in that condition. It is generally agreed that physical force is coercive: when A pushes B, B's movement is no reflection of B's agency, which indeed is preempted. However, it is also generally thought that threat and duress constitute coercion. However, the notion of a threat cannot be explicated without reference to context. What constitutes a threat depends on what powers the threatener has to harm—hence also on the reciprocal of power, namely, the vulnerability of those threatened. There is no feasible way of describing what constitutes a threat that can abstract from the questions of the relative power and vulnerability of the parties concerned. Only when the context of power and vulnerability is fixed can we raise questions about the credibility of the threat. If we consider simplified situations, such as guns being pointed at unarmed others, we get an immediate and clear view of the relation of vulnerability and power. But in complex social relations, things are not so patently visible.

One very basic form of social vulnerability is the vulnerability of the needy to those who have the power to grant or refuse them the means of life, whether directly by help or hindrance or indirectly by the mediation of social institutions. Material need is standardly reflected in powerlessness, and so in vulnerability to others' action. Only the powerless remain long in absolute need. When we are in great need, others do not have to threaten much for compliance to be as ready as it would be, under other circumstances, to a pointed gun. Nor does a threat to those in need have to be made with the standard rhetoric and gestures of armed conflict. It may well be couched in the language of standard commercial bargaining or political negotiation. But these modes of discourse respect others' agency only when used among those who are (approximately) equal in power (cf. Aristotle's insistence that justice is a relation among equals). Where there are vast differences of power and vulnerability, it is all too easy for the powerful to make the vulnerable "an offer they cannot refuse." Like the Mafia, they can use the civil language of commerce or politics or labor relations, while exerting a pressure that coerces. Unlike the Mafia, they may well even believe that the outward form in which the "offer" is couched guarantees its justice.

Once we take account of the actual, partial, and vulnerable nature of human autonomy, Kantian deliberations about human justice will have to take account of whatever is required if the needy are not to be coerced. The offers that are made to them must be offers that they can choose—or refuse. But this demands more than outward forms of bargaining; it demands either that circumstances of justice will make such offers refusable or that the offers made are adapted so that even the vulnerable can turn them down. To deal justly with the neediest, we must ensure that vulnerability to the demands of the powerful is not total, and so we must reduce their need. It is unjust to pretend a relationship of laissez-faire and to assume that those who are in basic need can genuinely accept or reject the offers of powerful individuals or institutions. Interaction with those whose autonomy is greatly reduced by need can be just only if it ensures that offers are refusable. This standard of justice would demand great changes in the present international economic order, which determines the circumstances of life of the powerless yet takes no steps to guarantee them any way of refusing their part in that order. Their vulnerable circumstances of life preclude refusal even of arrangements that often bring them meager advantage or institutionalized disadvantage. If, indeed, parts of our world were still America, in the sense that Locke thought much of it was in his day, then Kantian justice would not demand that those whose whole lives were led beyond the pale of modernity be considered in the construction of modern institutions. But the world is no longer America, and global economic and political structures affect the lives of all but a few isolated human beings. Justice to those in need demands that they not be the victims of institutional arrangements that they cannot refuse. When the option of refusal is genuine, the needy can insist that needs be met as a condition of their involvement. In his essay *Perpetual Peace*, Kant remarked that the problem of justice can be solved even for a "nation of devils"; it can be solved for the human nation too—but only if we do not impute idealized and inaccurate conceptions of human autonomy to actual, vulnerable human beings and so fail to consider what it actually takes to avoid coercing vulnerable others. Avoiding coercion in human life demands far more than avoiding the fist and the gun. While the abstract principle of noncoercion makes no mention of human need, its implementation in human conditions cannot avoid taking account of need.[9]

Analogous considerations can be introduced in considering the implications of principled nonneglect of beneficence in human conditions. Kant defines beneficence as a matter of not failing to help at least some others achieve their ends. Since these ends include ends sought because desired, it may seem that Kantian beneficence could have only the contingent relation to human need that utilitarian thinking can have. Desires are only an imperfect reflection of need, and intensity of desire often diverges from seriousness of need. Will not Kantian beneficence then, too, be readily diverted to satisfying desires even when basic needs remain unmet? Two comments seem in order. First, there is a major difference between the context of beneficence in Kantian and in utilitarian thinking. Beneficence is the whole of right action in the latter, and justice a matter of basic beneficence rather than of prior obligation. Second, since Kantian beneficence is directed toward helping agents achieve their ends and not simply toward providing whatever they may desire, it must pay central attention to agents' ability to pursue ends, hence to the conditions of agency, for which meeting material needs is fundamental. Kantian beneficence is not a matter of producing desired results for others but of helping them achieve their ends. It is therefore fundamentally unpaternalistic and, when faced with circumstances of injustice in which basic needs are unmet and abilities to determine and seek ends are impaired, must give priority to the development, repair, and support of capacities for action, for these are the basis of the Kantian construction of principles of obligation.

All of this is said in some haste and without detailed reference to the Kantian texts. Some implications for aid, trade, and development policies are, however, fairly clear. Kantian justice requires changes in the fundamental principles of institutions that make or leave others so vulnerable that their agency is impaired. The single most important change for many will be the abolition of material need. Those whose need is absolute, or who can be plunged into absolute need by others' action, are so vulnerable that they cannot refuse offers that do not suit. If they are not to be coerced, the structure of some of the basic institutions in which their lives are led must be changed. However, since the restitution and maintenance of capacities for agency are at the heart of Kantian concerns, the methods used in seeking change and development cannot themselves, without injustice, undermine or destroy the agency of those whose material needs are now unmet. Only development policies that take seriously the participation of those whose lives are to be transformed, even when their priorities are not those that others might share, can be seen as just development strategies. Analogously, Kantian beneficence—while unavoidably selective—cannot but take seriously the claims of unmet need and impaired agency. Even where desires for unneeded objects are overwhelmingly strong, they do not have the same claims on beneficence as do unmet needs that damage agency.

There are evident respects in which the argument of this last section is un-Kantian. It is certainly not the Kant of the *Groundwork*, who was engaged in the more abstract task of setting out the principles of obligation for rational beings as such (who might have no material needs and might not be mutually vulnerable), yet who unfortunately illustrated these principles with examples drawn from determinate duties as known in eighteenth-century Königsberg. Nor is it the Kant constructed by commentators who have chosen to take those examples as their guide to what he might have meant and have drawn a variety of pictures of rigoristic and formalistic ethics. It is closer to the Kant of the *Doctrine of Virtue*, where the abstract principles of obligation of the *Groundwork* are related more closely to the human condition. However, the main reasons for taking this reading seriously lie deeper than a preference for one rather than another Kantian text. There are deep reasons why any Kantian determination of more specific principles of duty must take need seriously. When we consider what it is for a community of finite rational beings to be agents, we cannot but note that their agency is partial and mutually vulnerable. Any community of finite rational beings faces the problem that differences of power and vulnerability may leave some without even the basic needs of life, and so without effective agency. Hence the Kantian construction can be filled in for the case of finite and mutually vulnerable beings only by obligations to construct institutions that control variations of power enough to prevent absolute need. Only such institutions can ensure that no persons are so vulnerable to others' denying their basic needs that they cannot refuse what others propose.

Notes

1. When rights are constructed on this principle, there is evidently no possibility of justifying any but perfect obligations, because there is, so to speak, no space remaining after the allocation of maximal sets of liberties to each agent. Any unallocated "space" will be absorbed into a right to do as one chooses in "self-regarding" matters. Maximal liberty demands that no requirements be placed on agents other than those essential to avoid leaving some with submaximal liberty: beyond those perfect obligations lies the space of liberty.

2. This takes Shue's point that it is strictly duties rather than rights to which the positive/negative distinction applies.

3. See Onora O'Neill, "The Most Extensive Liberty," *Proceedings of the Aristotelian Society* 80 (1979–80): 45–59; and Onora O'Neill, *Faces of Hunger: An Essay on Poverty, Development, and Justice* (London: George Allen & Unwin, 1986), chap. 6, esp. sec. 7.

4. Henry Shue, *Basic Rights: Subsistence, Affluence, and U.S. Foreign Policy* (Princeton, N.J.: Princeton University Press, 1980), 53.

5. The idea of the Kingdom of Ends points to, but I think does not provide a principle for constructing, a complete set of universalizable principles.

6. See the references in note 3, and for a wider treatment of the issues, see Onora O'Neill, *Towards Justice and Virtue: A Constructive Account of Practical Reasoning* (Cambridge: Cambridge University Press, 1996), esp. chaps. 2, 5.

7. Kant denies not only that desires can be the basis of morality but even that we can form a determinate conception of human happiness or of the desires whose satisfaction would constitute that happiness.

8. Kant's assumptions are therefore much weaker—so more plausible—than those Rousseau makes when he contrasts natural and artificial desires. See Jean-Jacques Rousseau, *A Discourse on Inequality* (1755), trans. Maurice Cranston (Harmondsworth, England: Penguin, 1984).

9. It is a corollary of this account of coercion that offering the needy bribes that they cannot refuse also coerces their action, and so is unjust. Although a bribe may meet some needs, it doesn't provide the security to accept or refuse others' "offers." Unconditional gifts to the needy do not coerce, since the recipients are left to choose their own action. However, a policy of *relying* on such gifts to meet others' needs is one that neglects justice and relegates its tasks to beneficence. Since beneficence is an imperfect duty, it cannot provide the poor the security that just policies can give. Too great reliance on beneficence is likely to give scope for paternalistic and manipulative action, which is incompatible with the unpaternalistic beneficence to which a Kantian account of imperfect obligations points. The capricious action of a Lady Bountiful cannot secure either beneficence or justice of the sort Kantian reasoning justifies. See Onora O'Neill, "Consistency in Action," in *Constructions of Reason: An Exploration of Kant's Practical Philosophy* (Cambridge: Cambridge University Press, 1989), 81–104.

6

Equality, Justice, and the Basic Needs

David Copp

The thesis that there is a right to be enabled to meet one's basic needs is a minority view in contemporary political philosophy. Such a right would license redistributive schemes under which a state would transfer resources from better-off to worse-off members of society to enable the latter to meet their basic needs. Libertarians reject such schemes,[1] and many philosophers reject the idea that there are "positive rights," of which the right to be enabled to meet one's needs would be an example. Egalitarians and liberals would presumably agree that redistributive schemes can sometimes be justified, but familiar liberal and egalitarian principles target people's welfare, or their control over resources or Rawlsian primary social goods, rather than their ability to meet their basic needs.[2]

In this chapter, I try to establish the plausibility of the view that there is a right to be enabled to meet one's basic needs. I call this The Right. I argue that The Right is best understood to be a right against the state, a right to be enabled to meet one's basic needs, provided that one's society is in favorable circumstances. I explain the basic human needs as, roughly, requirements of rational autonomy. I conclude by arguing that The Right does exist.

I do not discuss the problem of implementation. I take it that if The Right exists, then a state in favorable circumstances ought to provide economic and social institutions that enable each person to meet her needs. We would have to resolve some difficult empirical issues in order to support more specific claims about implementation. To ensure that those with special needs are cared for, a market economy would have to be regulated and supplemented by a variety of programs, including such things as a universal health care insurance scheme. Yet regulations and supplementary programs would have to be designed carefully to minimize negative effects on incentives and self-respect. Given the need for self-respect, and given that dependency tends to undermine self-respect, it would certainly be advisable to create an institutional environment in which as many as possible are enabled to meet their needs through gainful and worth-while work.[3]

Rights against the State

I propose that The Right is best understood as a right against the state. Many other putative rights, including the civil liberties and the right to an education, are similar in this respect. For example, a person who believes in the right to an education will typically believe that the state has a duty to provide education for its citizens, provided it is in a position to do so. I believe that The Right is similar in this respect to the right to an education.

If The Right exists, it is a right held by each of us against some other agent (or agents) that we be enabled to meet our needs. That other agent has (or those agents have) an obligation to enable us to meet our needs. The following argument, a version of which was discussed by Rodney Peffer, helps to explain why it would be implausible to think that The Right is held against individual persons:[4] there is no one in particular against whom The Right would be held, to the exclusion of other people. Because of this, if The Right is held against other people, it appears that it would have to be held against every other person. Every other person would have an obligation to ensure that a person with The Right is enabled to meet her needs. Hence, if everyone has The Right, then everyone would have an obligation to enable every other person to meet her needs. This seems quite implausible.

There is an additional problem with the idea that The Right is held against individual persons. Few if any individual persons are in a position to address the large-scale economic and social issues that would typically have to be dealt with in order to satisfy The Right in situations where some people have not been enabled to meet their needs. The state, or its agent, the government, does have at least some ability to address these large-scale issues.

I propose, then, that if The Right exists, it is held against the state. The state has the duty to ensure that its members are enabled to meet their basic needs; at least, it has this duty if it is in favorable circumstances. It may seem that it would be better to describe The Right as a right of the citizen against the society as a whole, since the state is the agent of the society. But since a society could not act effectively to satisfy The Right unless it were organized into a state (or some similar governing entity), I prefer saying that The Right is held against the state. Government action would be necessary in order to secure effective recognition of The Right, but governments come and go, while the responsibility to satisfy the right remains with the state.

Enabling People to Meet Their Basic Needs

It will be useful to consider the impact that implementing John Rawls's principles of justice would have on our ability to meet our basic needs. Imagine, then, a society in which there is equality of opportunity and the basic liberties are securely guaranteed. Rawls's "difference principle" implies that any remaining social and economic inequalities are justified in this society if and only if they work to the advantage of the worst-off. That is, inequalities in the "primary goods" of income and wealth, power and authority, and the "social bases of self-respect," are justified if and only if they improve the position (in respect of these primary goods) of a representative member of the group in society that is worst-off (in respect of these same primary goods).[5] Notice, however, that if you must spend a significant portion of your income to buy the drugs you need to stay alive, while I am in perfect health, I may be better able to meet my needs even if you have a greater command over Rawlsian primary goods. People may require different kinds and quantities of primary goods in order to meet their basic needs.[6] Because of this, and because the difference principle does not take account of our basic needs, the principle does not guarantee that the result of the process of transferring primary goods to those who are disadvantaged in terms of their command over primary goods will be that they are enabled to meet their basic needs.[7] Moreover, the principle could mandate reducing the expectations of the better-off to the point that some of them are no longer able to meet their needs. It is quite possible that a situation in which people with especially costly needs had the resources they require would be in violation of the difference principle. They might have sufficiently large incomes that they would count as among the best-off people in society on the basis of their command over primary goods even if they were barely able to meet their needs. If their greater command over primary goods did not work to the advantage of the less well-off, the situation would be unjust on Rawlsian grounds even if their living standards were lower than the living standards of people who had less in the way of primary goods.

It seems to me that if the people in Rawls's "original position" realized that the difference principle has these implications, they would choose on Rawlsian grounds, behind the "veil of ignorance," to recognize a right to be enabled to meet one's basic needs, and they would give it priority over the difference principle. They would not accept redistribution that might undermine people's ability to meet their basic needs.[8]

In short, Rawls's theory might count a society as just even though many people in it are unable to meet some of their basic needs and even though economic resources could be redistributed in a way that would result in everyone's being able to meet her needs. I think such a society would in fact be unjust. It would be unjust because it *could enable* people to meet their needs, but it has not done so.

Justice does not require the state to ensure that people do meet their basic needs, but I think it does require a society to provide people with the resources they must have in order to meet their basic needs, provided it is able to do so. We require a nutritious diet for our health, but justice does not mandate that the state ensure that everyone has a nutritious diet. What it requires, I think, is that the state ensure the availability of a food supply sufficient to enable everyone to have a nutritious diet. Again, justice does not require the state invariably to make good to people losses that they incur as a result of their own voluntary choices, assuming that they can properly be held responsible for their own choices. The foolish and the improvident must be given the opportunity to meet their needs, but if they squander the opportunity, and if they can properly be held responsible for their own choices, they cannot complain that they have been treated unjustly. Accordingly, I shall say, The Right requires a state that is in favorable circumstances to *enable* everyone to bring it about that she meets her basic needs. That is, it must both provide each person with the ability to meet her basic needs and also make it possible that all people meet their needs.[9]

Consider the following simplified example. Suppose that a given stock of resources is provided to a person by the state, a stock that is sufficient to enable her to meet her basic needs. But suppose that, as an adult, and fully aware of what she is risking, she gambles away these resources. And suppose that she is not able to recoup her loss, so that she finds herself living in poverty. She clearly can ask for charity, and morality may give her additional grounds for argument. Perhaps, for example, she can stand on egalitarian considerations and argue that there is injustice in a situation in which she is in poverty while others are living well. Perhaps, if she is a parent, she could invoke the right of her children to an adequate standard of living and their need for parenting, in an argument that she ought to be given further help by the state. But she could hardly justifiably complain of being treated unjustly simply on the ground that the situation resulting from her gambling is one in which she cannot satisfy some of her basic needs.

There is a need to qualify my formulation of The Right in a way that I will explain here but not mention again. The Right requires that each person be enabled to achieve a standard of living *as nearly* adequate to her basic needs as is possible, given the existing technology and the facts of the case. A person with a terminal illness cannot be enabled to regain her health and well-being, but this obviously does not show that she has been wronged by the state. A paraplegic will never walk, but she can be given a wheelchair that will enable her to move about. This may be sufficient to satisfy her claim under The Right.

Favorable Circumstances

If The Right exists, it demands nontrivial resources for its fulfillment, and sufficient resources are not always available. Because of this, a state that fails to give some of its citizens the ability to meet their needs has not by that very fact failed to meet a requirement of justice. This may seem to argue against the existence of The Right, but I think instead that it explains why The Right must be understood to be conditional on favorable circumstances.

The Right is not unique in this respect. The civil liberties, such as the right to a fair trial, presuppose the existence of a legal system, and they could not be implemented without the creation of effective judicial and policing agencies. The right not to be subject to arbitrary arrest or detention, for example, which may seem a paradigm civil liberty, cannot be implemented in a modern society unless there is a set of legal restrictions on arrest and a set of institutions capable of enforcing the restrictions. In unfavorable circumstances, a state may be unable to sustain such institutions. In a prestate society, such as an aboriginal hunting and gathering society, the civil liberties would have few, if any, implications. A person who was detained arbitrarily in such circumstances would not have had her civil liberties violated. More obviously, if the right to education is understood to include a right to a formal education, it could not be fully implemented in a primitive or a poverty-stricken society. It should be understood to be conditional on favorable circumstances.

To be in relevantly favorable circumstances, a society would have to be wealthy enough to enable every member to meet her basic needs. But we need to consider the *means* by which a society could bring it about that everyone can meet her needs. I will say that a society is in "favorable circumstances" if it is wealthy enough or otherwise well enough placed that there is a "feasible" and "morally realizable" future state of affairs in which every citizen is able to meet her needs. It should be clear enough what is meant here, although there are nontrivial complications.

The idea is that in favorable circumstances, a state has at its disposal policy options that would actually bring about a situation in which each person would have the ability to meet her basic needs if she used the available opportunities. And the state could implement these options without violating any moral constraint of equal or higher priority than The Right. I have not yet discussed the relative moral priority of The Right, and I shall have little enough to say about it. But a society would not be in favorable circumstances, for these purposes, if, for example, it would have to invade and conquer a weaker neighboring state and deprive its citizens of their rights in order to enable its own people to meet their needs. Nor would a society be in favorable circumstances if it would have to resort to murderous means of population control to reduce the demands on it sufficiently to be in a position to provide its citizens with the ability to meet their needs.

In summary, if a society is wealthy enough or otherwise well enough placed that there is a feasible and morally realizable future state of affairs in which every citizen is able to meet her basic needs, then The Right requires the state to bring about or maintain a state of affairs in which every individual is well enough placed to make it the case, if she so chooses, that she meets her basic needs. If a citizen has dependents within her family, she must be well enough placed to bring it about that they too enjoy an adequate standard of living.

Now consider a poor society, a society that is *not* in favorable circumstances. A person who belongs to such a society and who is not able to meet her needs could not properly complain of unjust treatment on that basis alone. Yet if there is The Right, then she has the property, whatever it is, that grounds possession of The Right, the property in virtue of which the society would have the duty to enable her to meet her needs if it were in favorable circumstances. Everyone has this property. Because of this, The Right presumably should be taken to imply that a poor society has both of the following duties: First, it ought to strive for the capability of enabling all of its members to meet their needs, and to strive to achieve this result as soon as it can. And second, subject to this longer-term goal, it ought to do as well as it can to enable as many as it can to come as close as possible to meeting their needs, while treating each of its members fairly. Call this second duty "the fallback duty."

It is not entirely clear how best to interpret the fallback duty.[10] On one interpretation, it is a duty to ensure substantive equality. It implies that a poor state ought to enable each person to come as close as possible to meeting her needs, given the constraint that each person is to be enabled to enjoy approximately the same standard of living as everyone else. In circumstances of very extreme poverty, however, a requirement of substantive equality could lead to everyone's living a life that no one would view as worth living. On a second interpretation, the fallback duty requires only what could be called "procedural equality." It requires a poor state to give each person an equal chance of being enabled to meet her needs and to enable as many as possible to meet their needs, while doing as well as possible for the remaining people, given the remaining resources. On this interpretation, The Right would at least give every person a chance of being enabled to live a life worth living. Hence, in very bad circumstances, the procedural interpretation will seem more plausible than the substantive. But in circumstances where substantive equality would give everyone a life she would view as worth living, the substantive interpretation may seem more plausible than the procedural, since the latter might leave some people with a life no one would regard as worth living. I will have to set these difficulties to one side, for there are additional possible interpretations of the fallback duty, and the existence of people with extraordinarily costly needs leads to further complications.

Costly Needs

Some people have needs that could only be met with a very large investment of resources. Some are dying, but even so, their lives can be prolonged and made more comfortable, if only at tremendous cost. Some of the severely ill and disabled can have their needs met, but only given a large expenditure of resources. If there are great numbers of people in these categories, the costs of meeting their needs can be significant. And with advances in medical technology, the numbers of people in these categories and the costs of treatment will presumably increase.

Would a state be required by The Right to enable the very needy to meet their basic needs even if, in order to do so, it would have to reduce to bare adequacy the standard of living of everyone else? If it would *not* be required to do so, then the duties of a state under The Right must be limited by what I shall call a "stop-loss provision." A stop-loss provision would specify that a state is not obligated to go past a specified point in order to enable any given person to meet her basic needs. Hence, a state, even a state in favorable circumstances, might fail to enable some people to meet their needs without thereby abridging any requirement of justice.

The problem, however, is to explain what can justify treating extraordinarily costly needs differently from more ordinary needs. Why should we suppose, for example, that The Right implies that the state has a duty to ensure that routine medical needs are met but not that all medical needs are met that can be met? And where is the line between the routine and the costly? A principled solution to this problem would derive a stop-loss provision directly from the underlying rationale of The Right. But the interest in autonomy and rational agency, which I think grounds The Right, does not lose its urgency when a person comes to have extraordinary needs.

If the interest underlying The Right is in living one's life as a rational and autonomous agent, then it may be that the state's obligation to enable a person to meet her needs comes to be less pressing after she has enjoyed a "normal lifetime." A normal lifetime might be specified in terms of the median life expectancy. It is arguable that, once a person has enjoyed a normal life span, she cannot complain of injustice if the state limits the amount of resources it is prepared to expend to enable her to meet her needs and thereby to extend her lifetime. This is a very difficult issue, and it clearly needs more attention than I am able to give it here.[11]

In any event, it seems to me that the rationale underlying The Right would permit a state to limit benefits to the very needy in order to protect the ability of the better-off to meet their own basic needs. If institutions could be created and funded that would enable the very needy to meet their needs without compromising the ability of the better-off to meet their needs, then The Right would require the state to create the institutions. But in circumstances where the state could not enable the very needy to meet their needs without putting at risk the ability of other people to meet their needs, the interest of the very needy in being able to meet their needs would be balanced by the interest of the remaining citizens in continuing to be able to meet their needs. In these conditions, it seems to me that the underlying rationale of The Right would permit limiting the expenditure of resources to help the very needy. If so, then the fallback duty must be understood not to permit the state to reduce anyone's standard of living to the point that she is not able to meet her basic needs.

Of course, there are other moral considerations that are relevant to the evaluation of social institutions, and, in some cases, they will come into conflict with The Right and may override it. Accordingly, there may be moral considerations that justify abridging The Right of people with extraordinarily costly needs when doing so is necessary to prevent the reduction of everyone else's standard of living to bare adequacy. This means that recognizing The Right does not necessarily commit one to holding that expenditures by the state to enable people to meet their costly needs cannot be limited until everyone else has had his living standard reduced to mere adequacy. But, considered by itself, The Right would mean this.

The problem of extraordinarily costly needs afflicts many theories of social justice. In order to bring about equality, for example, whether it be equality of welfare, equality in the opportunity for welfare, equality of resources, or equality in the ability to meet basic needs, it may be necessary to worsen the situation of the better-off to the point that they do not enjoy even an adequate standard of living.[12] As I conceive of it, The Right does at least impose two cutoff points on the process of transferring resources from the better-off to the worse-off. First, it does not require worsening the situation of the better-off to the point that they are unable to meet their basic needs. And second, it does not require any further redistribution once the extraordinarily needy have been provided with the opportunity to meet their basic needs.

A more detailed story would have to say much more about the relative weight of The Right by comparison with other moral considerations. But a theory of rights and of justice would be required before anything very deep could be said. The Right is not a complete account of distributive justice. At the very least, other rights against the state would have to be recognized in a complete theory. And there are of course other moral considerations besides justice, such as consequentialist ones, including the consideration that redistribution might undermine economic productivity. Rights have an urgency and a special status, including a priority over the ordinary goals of the state, such as economic efficiency. But this does not mean that competing rights or a sufficiently important combination of goals cannot override or limit a right.

Needs, Tastes, Capabilities, and Resources

There is a difference between the merit of a claim to additional resources made by a person with an expensive and unfilled taste and the merit of a claim made by a person with an expensive and unfilled need. The idea that there is a right to be enabled to meet one's basic needs can explain this difference. For example, a lover of fine champagne who cannot afford to satisfy her desire has no ground for complaint on that score, even if she is not in any way responsible for the fact that she has the desire. Assuming that she does not require the champagne in order to meet her basic needs, she cannot expect resources to be transferred to her to enable her to indulge her desire. But a person with a breathing disability who cannot afford a supply of bottled oxygen may have a valid complaint against her society, assuming that she requires a supply of bottled oxygen in order to meet her need for oxygen. If she has The Right, and if her society is in favorable circumstances, then her right has been abridged.[13] People with expensive addictions may need the substance to which they are addicted. Given their addiction and the cost of the substance they require, they may be unable to meet their basic needs, and they may therefore have a basis for complaint under The Right. If so, they ought to be given access to the substance they require, or to be helped to overcome the addiction. Yet those who became addicted owing to simple foolishness and who are responsible for their own foolishness, if there are any in this category, may be viewed as having squandered their entitlements under The Right if they otherwise would have been able to meet their needs. People in this category may have to depend on charity for additional help.

Fulfilling the basic needs is important instrumentally, as a means to living a decent life. If its importance is merely instrumental, one might think, a theory of justice should not give pride of place to enabling people to meet their basic needs but should instead focus on enabling people to live good or worthwhile lives. However, the ability to meet one's basic needs is central to a decent life in a way that may be missed if it is viewed merely as a means to such a life. Amartya Sen has pointed out that a person who is "poor, exploited, overworked and ill, but who has been made satisfied with his lot by social conditioning," is hardly doing well "just because he is happy and satisfied." Nor would we view his situation differently if we were informed that he has fulfilled his desires.[14] We would think his desires must also be due to social conditioning. Nor would we think better of his life if we were told that he would not have any different desires even if he considered his life calmly, clearly, and with full information, without making any errors of reasoning. We would think that the conditioning must have been especially effective.[15] When we think of a person's quality of life, we think of an objective measure in which her ability to meet basic needs is of central importance.

An objective measure could be defined in terms of possession of commodities or resources. Sen quotes A. C. Pigou's characterization of a minimum standard of living: "The minimum includes some defined quantity and quality of house accommodation, of medical care, of education, of food, of leisure, of the apparatus of sanitary convenience and safety where work is carried on, and so on."[16] However, to follow Sen's reasoning, one person may have more income than another and succeed in buying and consuming more food, but if he "has a higher metabolic rate and some parasitic disease," he may be more "undernourished and debilitated." If so, then on any reasonable account, he would have a lower standard of living. In general, variations in psychological, social, medical, climatic, and other factors mean that a given commodity bundle can be associated with quite different standards of living.[17] Sen concludes that "the focus has to be on what life we lead and on what we can or cannot do, can or cannot be." He calls the various living conditions we can or cannot achieve, our "functionings," and our ability to achieve them, our "capabilities."[18]

In order to give content to the idea of an adequate standard of living in these terms, however, we obviously need to decide which functionings a person would have to have the capability of achieving in order to enjoy an adequate standard of living. There is the capability of nourishing oneself adequately, but there is also the capability of getting the champagne one desires. Unfortunately, Sen's account does not provide or suggest a natural and principled way of deciding on the relative importance of different capabilities. Still, in Sen's terminology, one functioning is a living condition in which our basic needs are satisfied, and one capability is the ability to achieve such a condition or the ability to satisfy our basic needs. What I propose is that the ability to satisfy basic needs is a nonarbitrary and theoretically defensible criterion of the minimal adequacy of a standard of living. The basic thing about food intake is that it be sufficient for one's nourishment, for that is what one needs. And the basic thing about housing is that it be usable in a way that satisfies one's needs for shelter, for a sanitary means of waste disposal, and so on. Hence, while Sen's proposal is plausible, the required minimum quantity and quality of the various commodities and resources Pigou mentions is surely at least a quantity and quality sufficient to satisfy basic needs.

Basic Human Needs

There are things that a person needs in order to achieve a goal or to satisfy a desire and that she would not otherwise need. Needs of this sort I shall call "occasional needs," since they are occasioned by goals or desires. Hence, if I want to speak with a friend, I may need to make a telephone call. The matters of basic need, however, are things a person requires regardless of her goals or desires. Thus, each person needs a nutritious diet. There is, then, a distinction between basic needs and occasional needs.[19]

David Braybrooke distinguishes between one's basic needs and the things required to meet them, which are needed in their own right as "forms of provision" for the basic needs.[20] Hence, medical care may be required by someone in order to meet her basic need to preserve her body intact, and the need for a nutritious diet gives rise to needs for certain specific foods. It will be helpful to bear in mind this distinction between the basic needs and the forms of provision. Every human needs a nutritious diet, but differences in metabolism, gender, climate, health, and so on contribute to differences in what kinds and amounts of food a person must have in order to meet this need. Everyone needs a sense of self-respect, but different things are required in different cultures and circumstances in order to sustain this sense. And there are relevant differences between people due to differences in their psychologies. Every human has basic needs that are the same at some level of description as those of every other human, even though the forms of provision may vary from person to person and circumstance to circumstance, depending on a variety of factors, including culture.[21]

There is obviously a distinction between a preference and a basic need. I need a nutritious diet regardless of what kind of diet I prefer. And although I prefer chocolate to vanilla ice cream, I personally do not need ice cream at all.[22]

There is also a distinction between basic needs and all-purpose resources, such as Rawls's primary goods.[23] Primary goods would be instrumental to virtually any goal, and they are also usually required by us if we are to meet our basic needs. But they are not themselves matters of basic need. I do not have a basic need for income and wealth, for example. Matters of basic need are, of course, required in order to achieve many of our goals, and so they are also usually needed instrumentally, but they are needed independently of our goals and regardless of our circumstances. We do not need to know anything about our goals or desires or circumstances in order to know that we need a nutritious diet.

Any credible analysis of the concept of a basic need would imply that all or most of the following are either basic needs or forms of provision for a basic need: the need for nutritious food and for water; the need to excrete; the need otherwise to preserve the body intact; the need for periodic rest and relaxation, which I presume to include periodic sleep and some form of recreation; the need for companionship; the need for education; the need for social acceptance and recognition; the need for self-respect and self-esteem; the need to be free from harassment.[24] This list is perhaps not complete, and it may contain some redundancy, but it can help to orient our thinking.

I should perhaps remind the reader that I am proposing a right to be *enabled* to meet one's basic needs, I am not proposing a right to be *provided* with what one needs. Hence, for example, although the state can hardly *provide* people with self-respect, companionship, and social acceptance and recognition, it may be able to design institutions that enhance the ability of people to meet these psychological and social needs. Since a state clearly could not ensure that people are able to meet needs of these kinds, The Right must be qualified. It entitles people to call on the state to enable them to meet their basic needs, but only insofar as it is possible in the nature of the case for the society to enable them to do so.

There seems to be a conceptual connection between the basic needs and the avoidance of harm; if a thing is a matter of basic need for a person, then the idea is that the person requires it in some quantity and in some form in order to avoid harm. David Wiggins suggests that deprivation of a matter of basic need would constitute a harm or create a probability of harm, given the "laws of nature, unalterable and invariable environmental facts, or facts about human constitution."[25] Garrett Thomson suggests that a person needs something only if the thing is "practically necessary" for the person, in the sense that his "life will be blighted or seriously harmed without it."[26] There may be something that one person needs in this sense as a form of provision for a matter of basic need that is not itself a matter of basic need. For example, a person may have a breathing disability in virtue of which she requires a supply of bottled oxygen. But a supply of bottled oxygen is not itself a matter of basic need even though some people require a supply of bottled oxygen in order to meet their basic needs. Matters of basic need are things anyone would require in some quantity and in some form in order to avoid a blighted or harmed life.

This account is vague, but it is perhaps as much as we can expect from the concept of a basic human need. We require, however, an account of what is meant by a blighted or harmed life in order to unify, and provide a theoretical justification for, the list of matters of basic need. Braybrooke has suggested that, in brief, basic needs are things that are "essential to living or to functioning normally." More fully, basic needs are things that, at some time in the course of the life of every member of the population, are "[presumptively] indispensable to mind or body in performing [without derangement] the tasks assigned [them] under a combination of basic social roles, namely, the roles or parent, householder, worker and citizen."[27] The idea here presumably is not that a person is inevitably leading a blighted life if she is not performing in a combination of these basic social roles. It is rather that a person's life is blighted if she does not have the things needed to perform in this combination of roles. We do not want to be committed to the claim that a person who has freely chosen the life of an ascetic, and who is living alone on a mountain in the desert, must be living a harmed and blighted life. But if she had the choice of what kind of life to live, and if she made it freely, then she must have had available to her the necessities of a more standard life. A person may not *choose* to live such a life, but if she is *unable* to choose it and take it up because she is deprived of one of the necessities, then her life is blighted. Perhaps then Braybrooke's account would be more plausible if he were to say that the basic needs are things that are required in order to have the opportunity to choose and to live a standard life.

If a person's life would be blighted if she were unable to choose and live a standard life, it would also be blighted if she were unable to choose and live anything *but* a standard life. Hence, there is the more general point that a person's life is blighted if she is not able to choose how to live her life and to implement her choice, if she is not able to form her own values and evaluate her life in relation to them and to choose a life and to live a life that suits them. Now, the inability to form values, or to evaluate one's life in terms of one's values, or to choose how to live one's life, or to implement such a choice seems to mark a degradation of one's autonomy or rationality. Hence, I shall say, a person with inabilities of these kinds is falling short of full "autonomy" or "rationality." Using this terminology, then, I suggest that the kind of harm relevant to understanding the basic needs would consist in being deprived of the things that are indispensable to one's acquiring and preserving over one's life the status of autonomous rational agent. I propose therefore that the basic needs are the things that, at some time in the course of life, are indispensable in some form and quantity to a rational and autonomous life for a human, given the "laws of nature, unalterable and invariable environmental facts, or facts about human constitution."

I cannot here fill in all the details of this account of the basic needs.[28] The idea of a rational and autonomous agent needs more attention. Such an agent has a set of values that are her own, but the sense in which they are her own needs to be explained. The idea that the matters of basic need are essential to one's status as a rational and autonomous agent also needs more attention. The idea that certain things are essential to rational autonomy needs to be explained. And it is important to preserve the distinction between the matters of basic need and the forms of provision.

The most important test of my account is whether it can account for the items on the above list of matters of need. It is a commonplace that people who lack the basic necessities of life have limited options. They are at risk of exploitation and have no choice but to devote their attention to these basic needs.[29] I hope it is clear, therefore, that my account supports the claim that people need food, water, shelter, sanitation, health care, and the like. Both physical and psychological integrity are obvious requirements of rationality and autonomy. Without self-respect and self-esteem, one would be incapable of genuine choice. Without companionship and social acceptance and recognition, one would lack the assurance needed for genuine choice. And without education in one form or another, one would lack the needed information and skills to make genuine choices. To be sure, the notion of a genuine choice is vague and needs further explanation. And these remarks need to be qualified to take into account the fact that the details of what any given individual requires to provide for the basic needs depend on one's specific biological, psychological, and social circumstances.

There are many remaining questions that I cannot address in this chapter, but I will discuss some problematic examples.[30] A person's rationality and autonomy are not inevitably undermined by an inadequate diet, yet we think that there is a need for a nutritious diet. Moreover, some people may be able to meet the conditions of autonomous rationality without any formal education and with only the most minimal companionship, but we still view education and companionship as matters of basic need. There are at least three ways to deal with such examples within the account of basic needs that I have proposed. First, we can focus on what is needed over a lifetime. People need a generally nutritious diet over a lifetime. Different people in different stages of life and in different states of health will be affected in different ways by their diet. Second, we can explain differences between people as differences in what they require in order to achieve what they basically need rather than as differences in what they basically need. Third, we can seek a more abstract description of the underlying matters of basic need and describe companionship and education, and perhaps a nutritious diet, as things typically required in order to meet the basic needs. We could even claim that rationality and autonomy are the most fundamental matters of basic need and that the items on the list are typically required in order to satisfy these basic needs. For present purposes, I do not need to decide among these strategies. We can live with the remaining looseness in my account provided that it seems at least plausible in outline.

Arguments for the Existence of The Right

To this point in the chapter, I have mainly attempted to explain what I mean by claiming that there is a right to be enabled to meet one's basic needs. In this concluding section, I shall argue that this right does exist.

Elsewhere, I have argued that morality calls for society to ensure that its members are able to meet their basic needs with rough equality.[31] The argument is too complex for me to attempt to summarize it here. In any event, it shows at best that a society has a *duty* or *obligation* to ensure that its members are enabled to meet their basic needs with rough equality. To show that its members have a *right against the state* to be enabled to meet their needs, I would have to show that this duty properly belongs to the state and that it is a duty with the kind of status that it must have in order to correspond to a right.

The special status of rights has been thought to have three aspects. First, rights have priority over the ordinary goals and duties of the state and over the goal of promoting the general welfare. Rights can be overridden only in the interest of a goal or duty of special urgency.[32] Second, rights can be claimed as their due by the people who possess them. Right holders are wronged if their rights are abridged.[33] Third, a person who claims something to which she has a right does not thereby demean herself or undermine her grounds for self-respect or self-esteem. On the contrary, a person with proper self-respect and self-esteem would claim the things to which she had a right, unless she had a good reason not to do so.[34]

I believe the idea that rights have this threefold special status makes it more plausible to claim that there is The Right than to claim merely that states (in favorable circumstances) have the duty to ensure that people are enabled to meet their needs. People have to meet their basic needs in order to be successful in most of their endeavors. I have argued that people must have the ability to meet their basic needs in order to be fully autonomous. These are reasons to think that a state ought to give high priority to enabling people to meet their basic needs. Many people, including people with special needs, require help at certain times in their lives. Because of this, it is important to view the grounds of self-respect and self-esteem as secure against the need to seek help. Now, if citizens have The Right, then (in favorable circumstances) a citizen has been wronged if she has not been enabled to meet her basic needs, and she is entitled to demand assistance in meeting her needs without this in any way undermining the grounds of her self-respect. Of course, people may in some circumstances actually feel that their self-respect is undermined if they need to ask the state for help. Nevertheless, the idea that there is The Right implies that people are entitled to ask for help and that asking for help is no reason to feel less worthy. Because of this, it seems more plausible to hold that there is The Right than to hold that a state (in favorable circumstances) merely has the duty to enable people to meet their basic needs.

Many moral views, including Kantian and Aristotelian views, suggest that a good society would foster the rational agency of its members. On my account, fostering this would involve promoting a situation in which each member is able to meet her basic needs. Kantians and Aristotelians can see enabling people to meet their basic needs as a way for society to promote the rational agency of each person, and utilitarians can see it as a way for a society to promote the welfare of its members. Hence, each of these theories supports the claim that a good society would bring it about that its members are able to meet their basic needs.

There is reason, moreover, to think that society has a *duty* to bring this about. For if meeting one's basic needs is necessary to avoid harm, then any theory that implies a duty to help people avoid harm would imply a duty to help people meet their basic needs. And since one particularly important kind of harm threatened by failure to meet one's basic needs is damage to one's rational autonomy, any theory that implies a duty to promote the rational autonomy of others as well as of oneself would imply a duty to help people meet their basic needs. Certain forms of consequentialism and certain interpretations of Kantianism would presumably imply such duties, although I cannot here explore the details.

In order effectively to promote people's ability to meet their basic needs, it seems that a society would have to be efficiently organized, and in the modern world the state is the typical form of organization. Given this, and given that the state is the agent of the society as a whole, then if the society has the duty to bring it about that its members are enabled to meet their basic needs, the state has this duty.

This is not yet an argument for the claim that individuals have a *right*. If there is a right to an adequate standard of living, then the duty of the state to enable people to meet their basic needs has the special status I discussed before. I have already argued that it is plausible to suppose that it has this special status. It is reasonable to claim that the goal of respecting the autonomy of the citizen ought to have priority over the goal of promoting the general welfare or economic efficiency. The ground of other rights against the state, such as the rights of free speech and freedom of association, is surely at least in part that they protect our autonomy from the encroachment of government. If so, then recognizing rights of this kind, and recognizing them for this reason, commits one to regarding the goal of not abridging the autonomy of the citizen as having a higher priority than the goal of promoting the general welfare, except perhaps in extraordinary circumstances. The reason for giving priority to this goal is presumably the value accorded to autonomy. It is a small additional step to claim that, except in extraordinary circumstances, the state ought to give priority to enabling the citizen to preserve and promote her rational autonomy. On my account, this means that the state ought to give priority to enabling each citizen to meet her basic needs. I conclude, then, that a good case can be made in favor of a right against the state to be enabled to meet one's basic needs.

I agree, of course, that if there are rights not to have one's autonomy abridged, these rights may have priority over the right to be enabled to meet one's basic needs, for the latter boils down to a right to be enabled to meet the conditions required to achieve and maintain one's rational autonomy. It may be that, in cases of conflict, the duty of government not to encroach on people's autonomy would override its duty to promote the conditions of their autonomy.

This concession does not amount to accepting the libertarian view, however, that taxation of the better-off to enforce transfers from the better-off to the less well-off must inevitably violate the rights of the better-off,[35] for I also claim that ordinary citizens have a duty to assist the state in discharging its duty by contributing to programs intended to enable every citizen to meet her basic needs. I argued before that people do not have a right against every other ordinary citizen to be enabled to meet their basic needs. The state has a special responsibility for the condition of the society as a whole. And the state is typically the only agent capable of promoting the economic and social conditions required to enable the citizens to meet their basic needs. Ordinary citizens are ordinarily poorly placed to do anything except of a piecemeal nature. For these reasons, the state has a special responsibility, at least with respect to most of its citizens. Hence, an ordinary citizen does not have a right against every other citizen to be enabled to meet her needs. Yet this explanation of why The Right is a right against the state is compatible with my claim that ordinary citizens have a duty to assist the state in discharging its duty to enable people to meet their needs.

The state cannot discharge its duties without the support of individual members of society, and the state is the agent of the society, which is an aggregate of its members. I would argue on this basis that, at least in ordinary cases, if a state has a moral duty, its citizens have a duty to support it in discharging that duty. This means that the state would not have to rely on voluntary contributions. It would need only to ask people to do their duty, and it would not inevitably be violating their rights if it required them to do their duty. If I am correct, then, there is a duty to pay one's share of the cost of programs designed to fulfill the government's responsibility to enable people to meet their basic needs. Perhaps it is true that the government is not entitled to enforce transfers from the rich to the poor once the point has been achieved that the worst-off are enabled to meet their basic needs. My claim is simply that in favorable circumstances, the better-off have a duty to pay their share *until* the worst-off are enabled to meet their basic needs.

To summarize, I have claimed that the right to an adequate standard of living amounts to a right against the state to be enabled to meet one's basic needs, insofar as it is possible for the state to be of assistance, and provided that one's society is in favorable circumstances. I attempted to defend this thesis on the basis of a theory that takes the basic needs to be things that are needed in order to achieve and maintain one's status as an autonomous and rational agent.

People ought to be able to develop their talents to the full and to enjoy happy and thriving lives; it may therefore seem quite modest to demand merely that they be enabled to meet their basic needs. Moreover, given the inequalities between poor and wealthy societies, it is arguable that citizens of the poorer societies have claims against the wealthier societies. Because of this, it may not seem adequate to consider only the claims they have against their own societies. Yet the richest societies do not even assure the ability of their own citizens to meet their basic needs, so there is surely some value in arguing that justice requires that they do this.

Notes

This chapter is an abridged, reorganized, and partially rewritten descendant of "The Right to an Adequate Standard of Living: Justice, Autonomy, and the Basic Needs," *Social Philosophy and Policy* 9 (1992): 231–61. The paper was originally presented to the Social Philosophy and Policy Centre conference "Economic Rights," San Diego, 11–14 October 1990. I would like to thank all the participants for their helpful comments. I also received very useful comments and suggestions from Harry Brighouse, Carl Cranor, David Dolinko, John Fischer, Marc Fleurbaey, Jean Hampton, Craig Ihara, Steve Munzer, Mark Ravizza, and the editor of *Social Philosophy and Policy*, and I want to express my appreciation to all of them.

1. Robert Nozick expresses a libertarian view in his *Anarchy, State, and Utopia* (New York: Basic Books, 1974).

2. John Rawls, *A Theory of Justice* (Cambridge: Harvard University Press, 1971), 7, 64–65. See Richard J. Arneson, "Liberalism, Distributive Subjectivism, and Equal Opportunity for Welfare," *Philosophy and Public Affairs* 19 (1990): 158–94; Ronald Dworkin, "What Is Equality? Part 1: Equality of Welfare" and "What Is Equality? Part

2: Equality of Resources," *Philosophy and Public Affairs* 10 (1981): 185–246, 283–345. David Braybrooke is an exception. See Braybrooke, *Meeting Needs* (Princeton, N.J.: Princeton University Press, 1987), 143–50, 293–301. Virginia Held proposes a similar right in her *Rights and Goods: Justifying Social Action* (New York: Free Press, 1984), 184–85.

3. See Gregory Kavka, "Disability and the Right to Work," *Social Philosophy and Policy* 9 (1992): 262–90.

4. Rodney Peffer discusses a version of this argument in "A Defense of Rights to Well-Being," *Philosophy and Public Affairs* 8 (1978): 65–87, at 71.

5. Rawls, *A Theory of Justice*.

6. Amartya Sen, "Justice: Means versus Freedoms," *Philosophy and Public Affairs* 19 (1990): 118. Sen speaks of "variable conversion rates of primary goods into achievements." See also Amartya Sen, *The Standard of Living*, The Tanner Lectures, Cambridge, 1985, ed. Geoffrey Hawthorn (Cambridge: Cambridge University Press, 1987), 18. It is worth mentioning that Rawls sets aside the problem of costly needs as a "difficult complication." He claims only to deal with "the fundamental case" of a society in which "no one suffers from unusual needs" and "all citizens are fully cooperating members . . . over the course of a complete life." See John Rawls, "Kantian Constructivism in Moral Theory: The Dewey Lectures, 1980," *Journal of Philosophy* 77 (1980): 546. But the problem of variable conversion rates is different from the problem of costly needs.

7. Held makes related points in *Rights and Goods*, 187.

8. Rawls's argument from the original position depends crucially on the claim that those in the original position would choose on the basis of the "maximin" choice rule, which of course is controversial. Rawls explains and gives the rationale for maximin in *A Theory of Justice*, 152 ff. Here, for the sake of argument, I do not question Rawls's basic assumptions except, mainly, the assumption that the parties to the original position would be concerned with their command over the primary goods. I claim that they would be concerned to be able to meet their basic needs.

9. Suppose a society introduces a lottery in which the prize is a fund of resources sufficient to guarantee the ability to meet one's basic needs. Only one person can win the prize, but everyone is given a ticket. There is a sense in which everyone is enabled by this system to meet her basic needs, but not a relevant sense, for it is not possible in this system for every person to meet her needs. To have the opportunity in the relevant sense implies being in a position to bring it about that one meets one's needs, and no one under the lottery system is in such a position.

10. Jean Hampton and the editor of *Social Philosophy and Policy* helped me to see different interpretations of the duty.

11. I am grateful to Harry Brighouse and Marc Fleurbaey for helpful discussion of the idea of a normal lifetime.

12. Arneson, "Liberalism, Subjectivism, and Equal Opportunity"; Dworkin, "What Is Equality?" parts 1 and 2; and Braybrooke, *Meeting Needs*.

13. Arneson denies that it is possible to justify "discriminating in the treatment of physical handicaps and other expensive preferences." See "Liberalism, Subjectivism,

and Equal Opportunity," 194. I claim that the fact that handicaps are deprivations of what we need is what justifies treating them differently from unfulfilled preferences.

14. See Sen, *Standard of Living*, 8, 11.

15. Arneson proposes to answer Sen's objection by invoking hypothetical desires. He also proposes to invoke considerations about the conditions under which desires are formed, to avoid the worry about conditioning. But I submit that we already know enough about a person who is "poor, exploited, overworked and ill" to know that she does not have a decent life. We do not have to inquire into the conditions under which her desires were formed. See Arneson, "Liberalism, Subjectivism, and Equal Opportunity," 167–70, 163.

16. Sen, *Standard of Living*, 14, quoting A. C. Pigou, *The Economics of Welfare* (London: Macmillan, 1952), 759.

17. Sen, *Standard of Living*, 15–16.

18. Sen, *Standard of Living*, 16.

19. There are discussions of the distinction in many places. For a particularly good discussion, see Garrett Thomson, *Needs* (London: Routledge & Kegan Paul, 1987), 1–10.

20. Braybrooke, *Meeting Needs*.

21. There are complications that would need to be addressed in a full treatment of the issue. Suppose, for example, that the culture of one's society views a kind of housing as contemptible, although housing of this kind would be adequate to satisfy anyone's need for shelter. If so, housing of this kind might be inadequate to sustain a sense of self-respect, and so a case could be made for enabling everyone to have better or different housing than is strictly needed to provide adequate shelter. But differences in psychology can lead to unwelcome complications. Suppose, for example, that a person's self-esteem comes to depend on his having much fancier housing than most other people. He should not be viewed as having an entitlement to the fancier housing. For, assuming that there are other routes to self-esteem, he should be expected to look for another route, and his case should not be assimilated to a case of costly needs.

22. Arneson says, "The conviction that mere preferences are analytically distinguishable from true human needs may prove to be illusory." See Arneson, "Liberalism, Subjectivism, and Equal Opportunity," 191. The distinction is discussed by several authors, including Braybrooke, *Meeting Needs*; David Wiggins, "Claims of Need," in *Needs, Values, Truth* (Oxford: Blackwell, 1987), 1–57; and Thomson, *Needs*, 98–107.

23. Rawls, *A Theory of Justice*, 62, 90–95.

24. The list is adapted from Braybrooke, *Meeting Needs*, 36.

25. Wiggins, "Claims of Needs," 15, 10. See also Joel Feinberg, *Social Philosophy* (Englewood Cliffs, N.J.: Prentice-Hall, 1973), 111; D. W. Stampe, "Need," *Australasian Journal of Philosophy*, 66 (1988): 135.

26. Thomson, *Needs*, 8.

27. Braybrooke, *Meeting Needs*, 31, 48.

28. For additional discussion, see David Copp, *Morality, Normativity, and Society* (New York: Oxford University Press, 1995), chap. 9.

29. Held stresses this point in *Rights and Goods*, 184–87.

30. Mark Ravizza and Richard Arneson urged me to confront these examples.

31. See *Morality, Normativity, and Society*. The heart of the argument is given at 201–3, but it cannot be understood without taking into account the overall theory developed in the book.

32. See Ronald Dworkin, *Taking Rights Seriously* (Cambridge: Harvard University Press, 1977), xi, 91–92, 188–92. See also Richard Wasserstrom, "Rights, Human Rights, and Racial Discrimination," in *Rights,* ed. David Lyons (Belmont, Calif.: Wadsworth, 1977), 46–57.

33. See David Lyons, ed., introduction to *Rights,* 1–4. Joel Feinberg uses the idea of a claim in explaining the idea of a right in "The Nature and Value of Rights," *Rights,* ed. Lyons, 78–91, at 84–85. Wasserstrom speaks of rights as entitlements in his "Rights, Human Rights, and Racial Discrimination," in *Rights,* ed. Lyons, 48.

34. Feinberg relates respect for rights to respect for persons in "The Nature and Value of Rights," in *Rights,* ed. Lyons, 87. See also Thomas E. Hill Jr., "Servility and Self-Respect," in *Rights,* ed. Lyons, 111–24. Steve Munzer suggested the importance of self-esteem in a personal communication. See also David Sachs, "How to Distinguish Self-Respect from Self-Esteem," *Philosophy and Public Affairs* 10 (1981): 346–60.

35. See, e.g., Nozick, *Anarchy, State, and Utopia*, 167–74.

7

Aristotelian Social Democracy

Martha Nussbaum

Aristotle spoke about the human being and good human functioning. He also spoke about the design of political institutions in the many areas of life that should, as he saw it, fall within the province of the lawgiver's concern. He connected these two levels of reflection through a certain conception of the task of political planning. That task, as he saw it, is to make available to each and every citizen the material, institutional, and educational circumstances in which good human functioning may be chosen; to move each and every one of them across a threshold of capability into circumstances in which they may choose to live and function well. The aim of this chapter is to give a philosophical outline of a political conception based upon these elements in Aristotle, to describe the relationship of this conception to some forms of liberalism, and to explain why I find it a valuable and promising political conception. As my title indicates, I believe that this conception provides the philosophical basis for a certain sort of social democracy—one that shares a number of important features with some forms of liberalism that have been defended in the recent debate, but one that also breaks with liberalism at some crucial points. We can begin investigating this conception by reading three passages from Aristotle's *Politics (Pol.):*[1]

> The things that we use most of and most frequently where our bodies are concerned, these have the biggest impact on health. Water and air use things of that sort. So good political planning should make some decisions about these things. (*Pol.* 1330b11.)

> We must speak first about the distribution of land and about farming. . . . For we do not believe that ownership should all be common, as some people have urged. We think, instead, that it should be made common by way of a use that is agreed upon in mutuality. At the same time, we believe that no citizen should be lacking in sustenance and support. As for the common meals, everyone agrees that

they are a valuable institution in a well ordered city. . . . And all citizens should participate in them, but it is not easy for poor people both to bring in the required contribution and to manage the rest of their household affairs. . . . Then we must divide the land into two portions—the one to be held in common, the other to belong to private owners. And we must divide each of these two portions in half again. Of the commonly held portion, the one part will be used to support the cost of religious festivals, the other part to subsidize the common meals. Of the privately held portion, one part will be on the frontiers, the other part near the city. Each citizen will be given two hats, in such a way that all have a share in both sorts of land. That way is both equal and just. (*Pol.* 1329b39 ff.)

Political government is government of free and equal citizens. (*Pol.* 1255b20.)

Our first passage makes a quick transition. From the fact that water and air are of great importance for health, a central part of good human functioning, it is inferred directly that the adequate provision of these resources (by which is meant, we later see, a clean public water supply and healthy air) is the job of government.

Our second passage makes a similar move, with an even more striking result. The argument seems to go as follows. Participation in the common meals is a valuable part of social functioning. But a system of unqualified private ownership will produce a situation in which the poor are unable to join in, so that they will lose out on a valuable part of citizenship. (We shall examine this premise in a moment.) Nor, for reasons not given in this passage (and we shall discuss these reasons later), is a system with no private ownership altogether acceptable. Aristotle's conclusion: we want a system that includes some private ownership but that also guarantees that no citizen will be lacking in sustenance—both with respect to common meals and, presumably, with respect to other valued functionings. The solution chosen is an extraordinary one, even from the point of view of the contemporary welfare state. For it is clear, first of all, that fully half the city's land will be held in common. Half of the product of this part will subsidize civic festivals (including, for example, the festivals at which tragedies and other music will be performed—so this looks above all like a subsidy for education). The other half will directly subsidize the participation of all citizens in the common meals.

Aristotle here tells us his own solution to a problem he has discussed before. Common meals, he has argued, are a very important part of the provision of nourishment for all and also of civic participation and sociability (*Pol.* 1272a19–2). In Sparta, each citizen is required to pay a subscription to join, out of his private property. The citizen who is unable to pay is excluded not only from the common meal but also, as a penalty for failing to join, from all civic participation (*Pol.* 1271a26–37, 1272a12–21). Aristotle has criticized this system, praising instead the arrangement in Crete that he calls "more common to all"—for the common meals there are subsidized out of publicly held produce and cattle, as well as by a tariff paid by dependent noncitizen farmers in the surrounding area. Here, in his own ideal city, he follows the Cretan model but goes even further, for, since he omits the tariff from noncitizen dependents, he is required to devote an extremely large proportion of the city's land to the common project.

But matters do not end there. For Aristotle has told us, as well, that there will be a "common use" of the land that is still privately held. What does he mean by this? The passage refers to one in book 2, in which Aristotle tells us that the lawgiver must ensure that citizens make their property available to others, not only to personal friends but also for "the common use of all." He gives some examples: "In Sparta, for example, men use one another's slaves as if they were their own, and one another's horses and dogs. And when they are on a journey, if they need food, they take it from the farmers in the area" (*Pol.* 1263a30 ff.). Aristotle does not tell us there how the lawgiver will effect this result. What is clear is that things in Aristotle's city will be arranged, through and through, with a view to the full sustenance of every citizen at all times. Even where private property is permitted, it is to be held only provisionally, subject to claims of need. This complex result is defended on grounds of both justice and equality.[2]

Finally, our third passage defines government of a political sort—the sort Aristotle is describing in our first two passages—as a government "of free and equal citizens." It becomes clear elsewhere that this "of" has a double sense: for both ruler and ruled are, in fact, to be free and equal, and they are to be the same people, taking turns in exercise of office.[3]

What we see, then, are three elements. First, we have a conception of good human functioning. Second, we have a conception of political rule, which involves full support for these functionings and insists that this support is to be provided in such a way as to treat citizens as free and equal. Third, we have a sketch of institutional arrangements that both preserve some private ownership and circumscribe it, both by a scheme of common ownership and by a new understanding of private ownership as provisional, subject to claims of need. There are many difficulties in understanding the concrete details of what will go on. But this much appears evident.

My aim is to articulate the connections among these three elements, showing how a certain view of good human functioning gives rise to a political conception, through an understanding of political rule. We must ask, first of all, how the Aristotelian conception defends the need for a substantial theory of the human good prior to the selection of a political structure. A large part of our task will then be to examine this account of good human functioning and to ask how the Aristotelian conception arrives at it. I shall argue that the account of good human functioning is based upon a conception of the human being, and I shall call this conception the "thick vague conception of the human being." The associated conception of good functioning I shall call the "thick vague conception of the good," in order to distinguish it from conceptions of the good used in some liberal theories. By this name I mean to suggest that it provides a (nearly) comprehensive conception of good human functioning (in contrast to Rawls's "thin" theory), but at a high level of generality, admitting of multiple specifications. I shall argue that this conception of the human being is not metaphysical in the sense in which it is frequently taken to be by liberal theorists who contrast their own conceptions with Aristotle's. It is, instead, an ethical-political account[4] given at a very basic and general level, and one that can be expected to be broadly shared across cultures, providing focus for an intercultural ethical-political inquiry. We shall then see how choice figures in the Aristotelian conception and ask how political rule is understood to be a rule of free and equal citizens.

The Priority of the Good and the Task of Political Arrangement

The Aristotelian conception believes that the task of political arrangement cannot be understood or well performed without a rather full theory of the human good and of what it is to function humanly. The task of political arrangement is, in fact, defined in terms of such a theory. Aristotle writes, "It is evident that the best *politeia* is that arrangement according to which anyone whatsoever might do best and live a flourishing life." His criterion for excellence in a political arrangement is that the people involved should be enabled, by that arrangement, to choose to function well and to lead a flourishing life, insofar as the polity's material and natural circumstances permit.[5] But this means, he argues, that we cannot understand what good arrangement is, or which arrangements are good, without first having an account of good human functioning in terms of which we can assess the various competitors. He concludes, "A person who is going to make a fitting inquiry into the best political arrangement must first get clear about what the most choiceworthy life is—for if this is unclear, the best political arrangement must remain unclear also" (*Pol.* 1323alF17).

This priority of the good is the most conspicuous difference between the Aristotelian conception and all major liberal theories. But the difference is actually not easy to grasp; and it is a far more subtle difference than has sometimes been supposed. So we must do more work to understand exactly what the Aristotelian conception requires in this regard. We shall proceed in two stages. In this section we shall develop a general account of Aristotle's idea of the priority of the good by examining his arguments against two alternative views. We then try to situate these arguments in the contemporary debate, giving some examples to show just what is at stake. In the next section we examine the Aristotelian theory of good itself, asking just how far away it is from "thin" theories of the good that a liberal could accept and how it is used in assessing political arrangements.

The Aristotelian conception argues that the task of political arrangement is both *broad* and *deep*. It is *broad* in that it is concerned with the good living not of an elite few but of each and every member of the polity. It aims to bring every member across a threshold into conditions and circumstances in which a good human life may be chosen and lived. It is *deep* in that it is concerned not simply with money, land, opportunities, and offices, the traditional political distributables, but with the totality of the functionings that constitute the good human life.[6] It opposes itself to three other conceptions of the relationship between an idea of the good and a political arrangement—all of which have their analogues in contemporary liberal theory. It needs to be stressed that liberal theories, too, give priority to a certain sort of conception of good: for, as Rawls says, we need to know what we are distributing and to know that these things are good.[7] So the question is, how does each conception conceive of the account of good that is to be used in defining the task of political arrangement itself, prior to the selection of distributive patterns and principles?

Aristotle's first opponent defines the good of an arrangement in terms of the total (or average) opulence it produces. This view does not ask what this opulence does for and in people's lives; nor does it ask how the opulence is distributed. Aristotle mentions an example of this sort: the view that the good city is the wealthy city, no matter what this wealth is doing and who has it. And he frequently alludes to political views that have this tendency, finding them in regimes such as that of Sparta.[8] A contemporary example of this sort of view is the tendency to measure economic development in terms of GNP (total or average) and to rank countries accordingly, where development is concerned, without asking any further questions.

The Aristotelian objection to this view is that it treats as an end in itself something that is only a tool. And it imagines that there is no limit to the goodness of money and possessions, whereas in fact (according to the Aristotelian) they have no value beyond what they do for and in the lives of human beings.

The second group of theories still thinks of money and possessions as good. But it asks about their distribution, as well as their total or average amount. A simple example of this type of theory in the ancient world, and a direct ancestor of contemporary liberalisms, is the theory ascribed by Aristotle to Phaleas according to which a political arrangement is good just in case it distributes property and money equally among the citizens.[9]

More sophisticated versions of this type of view can be found in the liberal political theories of Dworkin and Rawls. Dworkin defends equality of resources as a criterion of good distribution, and thus of good arrangement.[10] Rawls's theory of the good has by now become extremely complex, but we can begin with the core of the theory, in its initial statement. In *A Theory of Justice*, Rawls argued that we need, prior to the selection of principles of justice, a "thin theory" of good, "restricted to the bare essentials." The list of "primary goods" is, as Rawls conceives it, a list of things that rational individuals, whatever else they want and plan, desire "as prerequisites for carrying out their plans of life." "Other things being equal, they prefer a wider to a narrower liberty and opportunity, and a greater rather than a smaller share of wealth and income."[11] An index of primary goods (above all, at that stage, of wealth and income)—and not, for example, an index of capability or activity—is used to judge which people in the society are the "worst off," what counts as an improvement in someone's condition, and so forth. Rawls's second principle of justice permits inequalities only if they improve the condition of the worst-off, so defined.

The basic intuitive idea used by the Aristotelian conception to argue against this is the idea that wealth, income, and possessions simply are not good in themselves. However much people may actually be obsessed with heaping them up, what they have really, when they have them, is just a heap of stuff—a useful heap, but a heap nonetheless, a heap that is nothing at all unless it is put to use in the doings and beings of human lives.[12] But this means that to answer any of the interesting questions about the distribution of resources—how much we should give, to whom, under what institutional structures—we need to see them at work in human functioning, seeing which of the important functions of human beings they promote or impede and how various schemes for their arrangement affect these functionings.[13] They all "have a boundary, like tools: all are useful for something" (*Pol.* 1323b7–8). The right amount and the right ordering can be seen only be taking a stand on the question, "What *for*?"

Several more concrete observations can be added to support this general argument. First, the Aristotelian insists that more is not, in fact, always better where wealth and income are concerned. At any rate, we have no right to assume that this is so, in advance of developing a theory of good living. If something has worth in itself, then more of that thing is probably always better. But once we grant that wealth and income are not like that but are means, albeit of a very versatile sort, it seems inconsistent to assert confidently that more is always better.[14] This is a heretical and a deeply peculiar thought to those brought up in liberal capitalism. It seems as if more cannot help being better. To Aristotelianism, by contrast, the thought is not peculiar, but obvious and central. The Aristotelian really does not see any point in heaping these things up more and more, either for herself or for others. Too much wealth may produce excessive competitiveness or excessive focus on technical and managerial tasks, distracting people from social interaction, from the arts, from learning and reflecting. If this is so, then Aristotle is quite prepared to say so much the worse for wealth. And he entertains perfectly seriously the possibility that wealth might have these bad results.[15]

Second, the Aristotelian recognizes wide individual variation in the functional role of the instrumental goods. In Aristotle's famous example, the right amount of food for Milo the wrestler, given his activity level, size, and occupation, is an amount that would be too much for most people. On the other hand, Milo would be very badly off, from the point of view of functioning, if he had an amount of food that is just right for a small sedentary philosopher. Again, as Aristotle prominently recognizes, the needs of pregnant women for food and other goods associated with health are very different from the needs of a nonpregnant woman. We might add that the protein needs of a child are altogether different from those of an adult. Again, a person with mobility problems or a missing limb will require a much larger subvention in order to be minimally mobile than will a person with no such deficiency.[16] If we look further into social context, still more variety appears. Children from disadvantaged minority groups need more money spent on them, if they are really to have access to education, than do middle-class children: we can see this by looking at what they are able to do and to be. Again, as things currently are, women need more support in terms of child care and so forth, if they are to work as they choose, than do others who do not face similar social obstacles.[17] All this is one more reason why the Aristotelian wishes to make the central question not "How much do they have?" but rather "What are they able to do and to be?" And she wishes to say that government has not done its job if it has not made each and every one of them capable of functioning well—even if it has given them many *things*.

Turning now from the subject of individual variation to our third objection, we must insist that in any actual and conceivable contemporary structure of allocation, decisions are in fact made one way or another about which resources are allocated, about how and through what channels they are allocated, and about the areas of human life in connection with which they will be allocated. Governments do not, in fact, stay completely out of the business of choosing to support certain human functions rather than others. No modern state simply puts income and wealth into the citizens' pockets; instead, programs are designed to support certain areas of life—health, education, defense, and so forth. Any other approach would produce confusion. Even to answer the question "Which things that we have to hand are the useful and usable resources?" requires *some* implicit conception of the good and of good human functioning. In short: to answer any of the interesting, actual political questions about resources and their allocation through programs and institutions, we need to take some stand, and do all the time take a stand, on the Aristotelian questions, "What human functions are important? What does a good human life require?"

Finally, a list of functionings can show us one very important thing that an account of good based on wealth and resources alone cannot. It can show us where tensions and conflicts might be present in the ends that human beings try to promote. I am thinking here not of conflicts between persons, as when A's pursuit of A's good conflicts with B's pursuit of B's good. I am thinking of conflicts among the demands of generally agreed components of the good life, as when certain sorts of industrial or scientific progress may come to be in tension with ecological or health-related values, or where the demands of work may compete with the function of child care. Here, first of all, we want to know about these conflicts and who faces them, since these people—for example, women or men who combine a full-time career with family responsibilities—will usually need extra resources and support systems if they are to live as well as people without such conflicts. Simply giving them an equal amount will not do enough; and we will not even find out about their problems if we concern ourselves with resources without having a view of the good. Beyond this, the promotion of the good of all citizens, in cases where pervasive conflicts exist among components of the good, will require deep reflection about the good and about how resources and institutional arrangements might mitigate conflict. In some cases, reflection on conflict may lead to large-scale institutional changes, changes that would not even have been imagined had the exercise been confined to the provision of equal amounts of resources all round.

These are some of the Aristotelian's arguments against the Rawlsian liberal. But Aristotle's third opponent must now be confronted. This is, of course, the utilitarian, whose approach dominates much of the contemporary scene in economics and public policy. The utilitarian agrees with Aristotle that resources are valuable because of what they do *for people*. But she is a liberal, or a quasi liberal, in wishing to leave the decision about goodness to each person. In particular, she wishes to make it a function of the satisfaction of desires or preferences that people happen, as things are, to have. She rejects the idea that any more objective account of good human functioning is either necessary or desirable.

The central difficulty with this proposal is one that is recognized both by the Aristotelian conception and by many liberal conceptions, including

Rawls's.[18] It is the fact, frequently emphasized by Aristotle,[19] that desire is a malleable and unreliable guide to the human good on almost any seriously defensible conception of good. Desires are formed in relation to habits and ways of life. At one extreme, people who have lived in opulence feel dissatisfied when they are deprived of the goods of opulence. At the other extreme, people who have lived in severe deprivation frequently do not feel desire for a different way or dissatisfaction with their way. Human beings adapt to what they have. In some cases, they come to believe that it is right that things should be so with them; in other cases, they are not even aware of alternatives. Circumstances have confined their imaginations. So if we aim at satisfaction of the desires and preferences that they happen, as things are, to have, our distributions will frequently succeed only in shoring up the status quo.[20]

The Aristotelian takes desire seriously as *one* thing we should ask about in asking how well an arrangement enables people to live. But she insists that we must also, and more insistently, ask what the people involved are actually able to do and to be—and, indeed, to desire. We consider not only whether they are asking for education but also how they are being educated; not only whether they perceive themselves as reasonably healthy but also how long they live, how many of their children die—how, in short, their health is.

In all of this, the Aristotelian approach understands the job of government to be, as we have said, both broad and deep. It takes cognizance of every important human function, with respect to each and every citizen. But now we must introduce an extremely important qualification. The conception does not aim directly at producing people who function in certain ways. It aims, instead, at producing people who are capable of functioning in these ways, who have both the training and the resources to function so, should they choose. The choice itself is left to them. And one of the capabilities Aristotelian government most centrally promotes is the capability of choosing: of doing all these functions in accordance with one's very own practical reasoning.[21] The person who is given a clean public water supply can always put pollutants into the water she drinks. The person who has received an education is free, later on, to waste it. The government aims at capabilities and leaves the rest to the citizens.

Many questions need to be raised here. For now, we should simply notice how much this qualification narrows the gap between the Aristotelian and the liberal. For it was the liberal's desire to create a context of choice for individuals that made her stop with the thin theory of good. The Aristotelian's claim is that stopping with such a thin theory neither shows the point of those instrumental goods nor gives sufficient guidance to promote their truly human use. And we can now add that such a thin theory may actually not show the legislator how to produce the capability of choosing, a human function that has institutional and material conditions like any other.

The Thick Vague Conception of the Good

But if we are to give priority to the good, we must have a conception of the good. And this is where the liberal becomes apprehensive. For it appears that any substantial notion of the good that might be used by political thought will be biased in favor of some projects that citizens might choose and hostile toward others. Such a conception will, it seems, therefore be objectionably paternalistic in its tendency to support some ways of life rather than others. Liberals suspect, furthermore, that the Aristotelian's decision to base her substantial conception of the good on an account of the human being will import metaphysical elements that are controversial among the citizens and thus will prove unable to ground a political consensus. So the Aristotelian must show what her concept of the good is, how much determinate content it has, how (using what background concepts) it is derived, and what political work it can do.

The Aristotelian uses a conception of the good that is not "thin," like Rawls's "thin theory"—that is, confined to the enumeration of all-purpose means to good living—but "thick"—dealing, that is, with human ends across all areas of human life. The conception is, however, vague, and this in a good sense. It admits, that is, of many concrete specifications; and yet it draws, as Aristotle puts it, an "outline sketch" of the good life.[22] It draws the general outlines of the target, so to speak. And yet, in the vague guidance it offers to thought, it does real work. The Aristotelian proceeds this way in the belief that it is better to be vaguely right than precisely wrong and that, without the guidance of the thick vague theory, what we often get in public policy is precise wrongness.

The thick vague theory is not, in the sense that worries liberals, a metaphysical theory. That is, it is not a theory that is arrived at in detachment from the actual self-understandings and evaluations of human beings in society; nor is it a theory peculiar to a single metaphysical or religious tradition. Indeed, it is both internal to human history and strongly evaluative;[23] and its aim is to be as universal as possible, to set down the basis for our recognition of members of very different traditions as human across religious and metaphysical gulfs. The theory begins, as we shall see, from an account of what it is to be a human being. But this account, far from being based on "metaphysical biology" (as some critics of Aristotle have held),[24] is actually based on the commonness of myths and stories from many times and places, stories explaining to both friends and strangers what it is to be human rather than something else. The account is the outcome of a process of self-interpretation and self-clarification that makes use of the storytelling imagination far more than the scientific intellect. In "Aristotle on Human Nature and the Foundations of Ethics" (HN) I describe this process as occurring within a single community whose members wish to clarify to themselves and to their children the meanings they have found in living as human beings. But an equally important part of such stories, as I try to show in "Non-Relative Virtues" (NRV), is that they are recognitions of humanness across distance. Aristotle wrote, "One can see in one's travels to distant countries the ties of recognition and affiliation that link every human being to every other" (*Nicomachean Ethics [EN]* 1155a21–2). The vague thick theory is a set of stories about such ties. In this way, it is a most general and preliminary evaluative theory: for it recognizes that certain aspects of human life have a special importance. Without them, we would not recognize ourselves or others as the sort of beings we are; and they provide the basis for our recognition of beings unlike ourselves in place, time, and concrete way of life as members of our very own kind.

The basic idea of the thick vague theory is that we tell ourselves stories of the general outline or structure of the life of a human being. We ask and answer the question, "What is it to live as a being situated, so to speak, between the beasts and the gods, with certain abilities that set us off from the rest of the world of nature, and yet with certain limits that come from our membership in the world of nature?" The idea is that we share a vague conception, having a number of distinct parts, of what it is to be situated in the world as human and of what transitions either "up" or "down," so to speak, would turn us into beings no longer human—and thus into creatures different from ourselves. Frequently this conception is elucidated (and perpetuated) by myths of nonhuman yet anthropomorphic creatures, either bestial or godlike,[25] which force our imaginations to ask, "Why, if these creatures resemble humans, don't we count them as human?" In this way, we learn something about ourselves.[26]

Take, for example, the Cyclopes, beings who have human shape and form but who live in isolation from community and who lack all sensitivity to the needs of others, all sense of commitment and affiliation. What do we learn about our own self-understanding when we notice that our stories treat such creatures as nonhuman monsters?

This is the way the exercise proceeds. (In HN, I develop in detail some concrete examples.) And the great convergence across cultures in such storytelling, and in its singling out of certain areas of experience as constitutive of humanness, gives us reason for optimism that if we proceed in this way, using our imaginations, we will have, in the end, a theory that is not only the parochial theory of our local traditions but also a basis for cross-cultural attunement. In fact, it would be surprising if this were not so, since the question we are asking is, What are the features of our common humanity, features that lead us to recognize certain others, however distant their location and their forms of life, as humans and, on the other hand, to decide that certain other beings who resemble us superficially could not possibly be human? The question we ask directs us to cross boundaries.[27]

The list we get if we reflect in this way is, and must be, open ended. For we want to allow the possibility that some as yet unimagined transformation in our natural options will alter the constitutive features, subtracting some and adding others. We also want to leave open the possibility that we will learn from our encounters with other human societies to revise certain elements in our own standing account of humanness, recognizing, perhaps, that some features we regarded as essential are actually more parochial than that. We must insist that, like most Aristotelian lists, our working list is meant not as systematic philosophical theory but as a summary of what we think so far and as an intuitive approximation, whose intent is not to legislate but to direct attention to certain areas of special importance. And the list is not only intuitive, but also heterogeneous; for it contains both limits against which we press and powers through which we aspire. This is not surprising, since we began from the general intuitive idea of a creature who is both capable and needy.[28]

Here, then, as a first approximation, is a kind of story about what seems to be part of any life that we count as a human life.

Level A: The Constitutive Circumstances of the Human Being (or: The Shape of the Human Form of Life)

Mortality. All human beings face death and, after a certain age, know that they face it. This fact shapes more or less every other element of human life. Moreover, all human beings have an aversion to death. Although there are many circumstances (varying among individuals and from culture to culture) in which death will be preferred to the available alternatives, it is still true that in general human beings wish to live, and leave with fear and grief "the sweet light of life."[29] If we did encounter an immortal anthropomorphic being, its way of life would be so different from our own that we could hardly regard it as a part of the same kind with us. The same would be true if we encountered a mortal being that showed no tendency to avoid death or to seek to continue its life.[30]

The Human Body. We live our entire lives in bodies of a certain sort, whose possibilities and vulnerabilities do not as such belong to one human society rather than another. These bodies, similar far more than dissimilar (considering the enormous range of possibilities) are our homes, so to speak, opening to us some options and denying others. We are so used to our bodies that we tend to forget how different from other bodies and conceivable bodies (and from the condition of bodilessness) they are, how far and how deeply they demarcate our possibilities. The fact that any given human being might have lived anywhere and belonged to any culture is a great part of what grounds our mutual recognitions; this fact has a great deal to do with the general humanness of the body, its great distinctness from other bodies. The experience of the body is culturally shaped; but the body itself, not culturally variant in its requirements, sets limits on what can be experienced, ensuring a lot of overlap.[31]

There is of course much disagreement about *how much* of human experience is rooted in the body. Here metaphysics enters into the picture in a nontrivial way. So in keeping with the general nonmetaphysical character of the list, I shall include at this point only those features that would be agreed to be bodily even by metaphysical dualists. I shall discuss the more controversial features (perceiving, thinking, etc.) as separate items, taking no stand on the question of dualism.

1.   *Hunger and thirst; the need for food and drink.* All human beings need food and drink in order to live; and all have comparable, though varying, nutritive requirements. Being in one culture rather than another does not make one metabolize food differently. Furthermore, all human beings have appetites that are indices of need. Appetitive experience is to some extent culturally shaped; and sometimes it is not parallel to the body's actual level of need. And yet, we discover enormous similarity and overlap. Moreover, human beings in general do not wish to be hungry and thirsty (though they might choose to fast for some reason).

2.   *Need for shelter.* A recurrent topic in myths of humanness is the nakedness of the human being, its relative fragility and susceptibility to heat, cold, the elements in general. Stories that explore the difference between our needs and those of furry or scaly or otherwise protected creatures remind us how far our life is constituted by the need to find refuge from the cold or from the excessive heat of the sun, from rain, wind, snow, and frost.

3.   *Sexual desire.* Though less necessary as a need than the needs for food, drink, and shelter, sexual desire is a feature of more or less every human life. Aristotle includes it among the desires whose complete absence would be the sign of a being far from human. It is, and has all along been, a very strong basis for the recognition of others different from ourselves as human beings.

4. *Mobility.* We are, as the old story goes, featherless bipeds—that is, creatures whose form of life is in part constituted by the ability to move from place to place in a certain way, not only through the aid of tools we have made, but also with our very own bodies. Human beings like moving about and dislike being deprived of mobility. An anthropomorphic being who, without disability, chose never to move from birth to death would be hard to view as human; and a life altogether cut off from mobility seems a life less than fully human.

Capacity for Pleasure and Pain. Experiences of pain and pleasure are common to all human life—though once again their cultural expression and perhaps, to some extent, the experience itself, will vary. Moreover, the aversion to pain as a fundamental evil is a primitive and, apparently, unlearned part of being a human animal. A society whose members altogether lacked that aversion would surely be considered to be outside the bounds of humanness.[32]

Cognitive Capability: Perceiving, Imagining, Thinking. All human beings have sense-perception, the ability to imagine, and the ability to think, making distinctions and, as Aristotle famously says, "reach(ing) out for understanding."[33] And these abilities are regarded as valuable. It is an open question what sorts of accidents or impediments to individuals in these areas will be sufficient to make us judge that the form of life is not human, or no longer human. But it is safe to say that if we imagine a tribe whose members totally lack sense-perception, *or* totally lack imagination, *or* totally lack reasoning and thinking, we are not in any of these cases imagining a tribe of human beings, no matter what they look like.

Early Infant Development. All human beings begin as hungry babies, aware of their own helplessness, experiencing their alternating closeness to, and distance from, that, and those, on which they depend. This common structure to early life—which clearly is shaped in many and varied ways in different social arrangements—still gives rise to a great deal of overlying experience that is of great importance for the formation of emotions and desires, and that is a major source of our ability to see ourselves in the emotional experiences of those whose lives are otherwise very different from our own. If we encountered a tribe of apparent humans and then discovered that they never had been babies and had never, in consequence, had those experiences of extreme dependency, need, and affection, we would, I think, have to conclude that their form of life was sufficiently different from our own that they could not be considered part of the same kind.

Practical Reason. All human beings participate (or try to) in the planning and managing of their own lives, asking and answering questions about what is good and how one should live. Moreover, they wish to enact their thought in their lives—to be able to choose and evaluate, and to function accordingly. This general capability has many concrete forms and is related in complex ways to the other capabilities, emotional, imaginative, and intellectual. But a being who altogether lacks this would not be likely to be regarded in any culture as fully human.[34]

Affiliation with Other Human Beings. As Aristotle claimed, all human beings recognize, and feel a sense of affiliation and concern for, other human beings. Moreover, we value the form of life that is constituted by these recognitions and affiliations—we live to and with others and regard a life not lived in affiliation with others to be a life not worth living.

Relatedness to Other Species and to Nature. Human beings recognize that they are not the only living things in their world, that they are animals living alongside other animals, and also alongside plants, in a universe that, as a complex interlocking order, both supports and limits them. A creature who treated animals exactly like stones and could not be brought to recognize some problem with that would probably be regarded as too strange to be human. So, too, would a creature who did not care in any way for the wonder and beauty of the natural world.

Humor and Play. Human life, wherever it is lived, makes room for recreation and laughter. The forms that play takes are enormously varied, and yet we recognize other humans, across many and varied barriers, as the animals who laugh. Laughter and play are frequently among the deepest and also the first modes of our mutual recognition. Inability to play or laugh is taken, correctly, as a sign of deep disturbance in an individual child; if it is permanent, the consequence may be that we will prove unable to consider the child capable of leading a fully human life. An entire society that lacked this ability would seem to us both terribly strange and terribly frightening.[35]

Separateness. However much we live for and to others, we are, each of us, "one in number," proceeding on a separate path through the world from birth to death. Each person feels only his or her own pain and not anyone else's. Each person dies alone. When one person walks across the room, no other follows automatically. These obvious facts need stating, since they might have been otherwise; we should bear them in mind when we hear talk of the absence of individualism in certain societies.

Strong Separateness. Because of separateness, each human life has, so to speak, its own peculiar context and surroundings—objects, places, a history, particular friendships, locations, sexual ties—that are not the same as those of anyone else and in terms of which the person to some extent identifies herself. On the whole, human beings recognize one another as beings who wish to have some separateness of context, a little space to move around in, some special items to use and hold and cherish.[36]

This is an open-ended list. One could subtract some items and/or add others. But it is a thick vague starting point for reflection about what the good life for such a being might be.

Level B: Basic Human Functional Capabilities

This brings us to the second stage of our thick vague conception, for now we are in a position to specify vaguely certain basic functionings that should, as constitutive of human life, concern us. We shall actually introduce the list as a list of the related capabilities, rather than of actual functionings, since we have argued that it is capabilities, not actual functionings, that should be the legislator's goal.

1. Being able to live to the end of a complete human life, as far as is possible; not dying prematurely or before one's life is so reduced as to be not worth living.

2. Being able to have good health; to be adequately nourished; to have adequate shelter; having opportunities for sexual satisfaction, to move about from place to place.

3. Being able to avoid unnecessary and nonuseful pain and to have pleasurable experiences.

4. Being able to use the five senses, to imagine, to think, and to reason.

5. Being able to have attachments to things and persons outside ourselves; to love those who love and care for us, to grieve at their absence; in general, to love, grieve, feel longing and gratitude.

6. Being able to form a conception of the good and to engage in critical reflection about the planning of one's own life.

7. Being able to live for and to others, to recognize and show concern for other human beings, to engage in various forms of familial and social interaction.

8. Being able to live with concern for, and in relation to, animals, plants, the world of nature.

9. Being able to laugh, to play, to enjoy recreational activities.

10. Being able to live one's own life and nobody else's.

10a. Being able to live one's own life in one's very own surroundings and context.

This is a list of functional capabilities that are very basic in human life. The claim is that a life that lacks any one of these, no matter what else it has, will be regarded as seriously lacking in humanness. So it would be reasonable to take these things as a focus for concern, if we want to think how government can actually promote the good of human beings. The list provides a minimal theory of good. The approach to the list through myths and stories promises that we will go on exploring the various items in many different imagined combinations, seeing how they support one another and where they conflict. And the whole approach being suggested here insists, throughout, on recognizing a plurality of good things, things distinct from one another in quality.

The Task of Politics, in Relation to the Thick Vague Conception

The task of Aristotelian politics is to make sure that no citizen is lacking in sustenance.[37] With respect to each of the functionings mentioned in the thick vague conception, citizens are to receive the institutional, material, and educational support that is required if they are to become capable of functioning in that sphere according to their own practical reason—and functioning not just minimally but well, insofar as natural circumstances permit. Politics examines the situations of the citizens, asking in each case what the individual's requirements for good functioning are in the various areas. Both the design of institutions and the distribution of resources by institutions are done with a view to citizens' capabilities.

The Aristotelian aim should be understood along the lines of what has been called *institutional*, rather than *residual*, welfarism. That is, politics does not just wait to see who is left out, who fails to do well without institutional support, and then step in to bail these people out. Its aim is, instead, to design a comprehensive support scheme for the functionings of all citizens over a complete life. Aristotle's common-meal plan, we recall, did not simply assist the poor. It subsidized the entire common meal program for all citizens, so that nobody could ever come to be in a situation of poverty with respect to that program. In a similar way, the Aristotelian conception (and Aristotle himself) promotes a comprehensive scheme of health care and a complete plan of public education for all citizens over a complete life, rather than simply giving aid to all those who cannot afford private health care and private education. This way is defended as more equal and more just.

The Aristotelian uses the available resources to bring all citizens across a threshold into a condition in which good human functioning, at least at a minimal level, can be chosen. In "Nature, Function, and Capability," I give a more extensive account of this aim, in terms of levels of capabilities. To summarize briefly, the Aristotelian program aims at producing two types of capabilities: internal and external. Internal capabilities are conditions of the person (of body, mind, character) that make that person in a state of readiness to choose the various valued functions. External capabilities are internal capabilities plus the external material and social conditions that make available to the individual the option of that valued function. Internal capabilities are promoted, above all, by schemes of education, by health care, by appropriate labor relations. But over and above this, the legislator must work to make sure that a capable individual has the chance to function in accordance with that capability: and this calls for another, slightly different, set of concerns with labor and with the circumstances of personal and social life.

In all of these areas, as I have said, treating citizens as free and equal means moving all of them across the threshold into capability to choose well, should the available resources at all permit this. The focus is always on getting more to cross the threshold rather than further enhancing the conditions of those who have already crossed it. This is so for two reasons: first, because that is what it is to treat citizens as free and equal; second, because, as we have noted, once a person has crossed that threshold, more is not necessarily better. The limit of money's usefulness in human life is set by its role in getting an individual across the threshold into good living; after that, more of it is not clearly better and may well be worse.

If we now examine our list of basic capabilities, remembering that what we aim at in each sphere is the capability to function, in that sphere, according to both practical reason and affiliation, we can begin to imagine what the conception requires. It requires comprehensive health care; healthy air and water; arrangements for the security of life and property; protection of the autonomous choices of citizens with respect to crucial aspects of their medical treatment. It requires sufficient nutrition and adequate housing; and these are to be arranged so as to promote the choices of citizens to regulate their nutrition and their shelter by their own practical reason. (This would, for example, lead one to place emphasis on health education, drug education, and so forth.)

It requires the protection of the capability of citizens to regulate their own sexual activity by their own practical reason and choice. (Here once again, support for educational programs would seem to play a crucial role.) It would require protection from assaults and other preventable pains. For the senses, for the imagination, and for thinking, it would require, beyond medical support, education and training of many kinds, aimed at the fostering of these capabilities; and the protection of the arts, as essential for the good functioning of imagination and emotion, as well as as sources of delight. For practical reason, it would require institutions promoting a humanistic form of education and the protection of citizen choices in all contexts, including the context of designing the political conception itself. For affiliation and the emotional life, it would require support for rich social relations with others, in whatever way it will emerge, through argument, that the institutional and political structures can best support and protect these relations. It would require reflective policies promoting due respect for other species and for the world of nature. It would require the provision both of recreational facilities and of forms of labor that permit the choice of recreation and enjoyment. And finally, for separateness and for strong separateness, it would require protection of a larger or smaller sphere of noninterference around the person so that, according to practical reason and in relationship with others, each person can choose, in his or her own context, to lead his or her very own life.

The idea is that the entire structure of the polity will be designed with a view to these functions. Not only programs of allocation but also the division of land, the arrangement for forms of ownership, the structure of labor relations, institutional support for forms of family and social affiliation, ecological policy and policy toward animals, institutions of political participation, recreational institutions—all these, as well as more concrete programs and policies within these areas, will be chosen with a view to good human functioning.

Notes

1. Citations in this chapter are from *Politics,* ed. W. D. Ross (Oxford: Oxford Classical Texts, 1957); and *Nicomachean Ethics,* ed. I. Bywater (Oxford: Oxford Classical Texts, 1894).

2. On the distinction between ownership and use, see *Pol.* 2.5 as a whole; for an excellent discussion of the history of this distinction in Greek political thought, see W. Newman, *Aristotle's Politics: Text and Commentary* (Oxford: Oxford University Press, 1887), commentary on 2.5.

3. *Pol.* 1332b25–7;. cf. 1325b7, 1334a27–9.

4. It is not possible to make a sharp distinction between the ethical and the political in discussing Aristotle's views.

5. *Pol.* 1323a17–19.

6. For textual references and discussion, see Martha Nussbaum, "Nature, Function, and Capability: Aristotle on Political Distribution," in *Oxford Studies in Ancient Philosophy*, supplementary vol., 1988: 145–83 (hereafter referred to as NFC); and "Reply to David Charles," in Oxford Studies in Ancient Philosophy, supplementary vol., 1988. Cf. esp. *Pol.* 1323a17–19, 1324a23–5, 1325a7, *EN* 1103b2–6.

7. John Rawls, *A Theory of Justice* (Cambridge: Harvard University Press, 1971), 396. For further development of the view of primary goods, see John Rawls, "Social Unity and Primary Goods," in *Utilitarianism and Beyond*, ed. A. Sen and B. Williams (Cambridge: Cambridge University Press, 1982), 159–86; and John Rawls, "The Priority of Right and Ideas of the Good," *Philosophy and Public Affairs* 17 (1988): 251–76.

8. See esp. *Pol.* 1.8, 7.1.

9. On Phaleas, see *Pol.* 1266a39 ff.; and for discussion, see NFC.

10. See Ronald Dworkin, "What Is Equality? Part 2: Equality of Resources," *Philosophy and Public Affairs* 10 (1981): 283–345; and Ronald Dworkin, "Liberalism," in *A Matter of Principle* (Cambridge: Harvard University Press, 1985), 181–204, originally published in S. Hampshire, ed., *Public and Private Morality* (Cambridge: Cambridge University Press, 1978).

11. Rawls, *A Theory of Justice,* 396. In "Social Unity and Primary Goods" and "Priority of Right," Rawls refines and expands the list, making it far more heterogeneous and focusing less attention on wealth. Thus the latest version of the list in Rawls, "Priority of Right," divides primary goods into five categories: (1) basic rights and liberties; (2) "freedom of movement and free choice of occupation against a background of diverse opportunities"; (3) "powers and prerogatives of offices and positions in the political and economic institutions of the basic structure"; (4) income and wealth; (5) the social bases of self-respect. Rawls suggests he is willing to add other goods, "for example, leisure time, and even certain mental states such as the absence of physical pain." On the one hand, this alteration of the list addresses some of the Aristotelian's criticisms, since it now includes a number of human capabilities that the Aristotelian, too, regards as basic human goods. But insofar as it does so, the new list seems to depart from the original notion of "primary goods," the notion of all-purpose means that are neutral among conceptions of the good. Rawls's unpublished "Reply to Sen" shows that he still wishes to maintain the original conception against Sen's more Aristotelian proposal; thus there now seems to be considerable tension and ambiguity in the position. Some elements of that reply are incorporated in John Rawls, Political Liberalism (New York: Columbia University Press, 1993), 183–86.

12. See *Pol.* 7.1.

13. See A. Sen, *Equality of What?* Tanner Lectures on Human Values 1, ed. S. McMurrin (Cambridge: Cambridge University Press, 1980); and A. Sen, *The Standard of Living,* Tanner Lectures on Human Values 1985, ed. C. Hawthorne (Cambridge: Cambridge University Press, 1987).

14. Cf. *Pol.* 7.1 and note 7 above.

15. See esp. *Rhetoric* 2.15–17, discussed in Martha Nussbaum, *The Fragility of*

Goodness: Luck and Ethics in Greek Tragedy and Philosophy (Cambridge: Cambridge University Press, 1986), 339–40. The bad effects of wealth include insolence, arrogance, and a mercenary attitude to other valuable things.

16. On Milo, see *EN* 1106b3; Aristotle discusses the nutritional and exercise needs of pregnant women at *Pol.* 1335b12 ff.

17. On women's capabilities and the support they require, see A. Sen, *Resources, Value, and Development* (Oxford: Blackwell, 1984); and A. Sen, *Commodities and Capabilities* (Amsterdam, N.Y.: North-Holland, 1985).

18. See Rawls, *A Theory of Justice,* 258–65. See also Rawls, "Priority of Right."

19. The point is most frequently expressed as a criticism of the thesis that pleasure is identical with the good: cf. *EN* 7.11–14, 10.1–4; cf. also the account of "bestial vice" and of desires malformed through bad experiences in *EN* 7.5, 1148b15 ff.

20. See Sen, *Resources, Value, and Development*; Sen, *Commodities and Capabilities*; Sen, *Standard of Living*; Onora O'Neill, "Justice, Gender, and International Boundaries," in *The Quality of Life,* ed. Martha Nussbaum and A. Sen (Oxford: Clarendon Press, 1990); and E. Allardt, "Having, Loving, Being: An Alternative to the Swedish Model of Welfare Research," in *The Quality of Life,* ed. Nussbaum and Sen.

21. For further discussion of Aristotle's views on this point, see NFC; and Martha Nussbaum, "Aristotle on Human Nature and the Foundations of Ethics," in *World, Mind, and Ethics: Essays on the Ethical Philosophy of Bernard Williams,* ed. J. Altham and R. Harrison (Cambridge: Cambridge University Press, 1990) (referred to hereafter as HN).

22. *EN* 1098a20–23; for full discussion of this passage, see HN.

23. For this terminology, see Charles Taylor, *Sources of the Self: The Making of Modern Identity* (Cambridge: Harvard University Press, 1989); and Charles Taylor, "Explanation and Practical Reason," in *The Quality of Life,* ed. Nussbaum and Sen.

24. See Alasdair MacIntyre, *After Virtue* (South Bend, Ind.: University of Notre Dame Press, 1981); and B. Williams, *Ethics and the Limits of Philosophy* (Cambridge: Harvard University Press, 1985). Both, in general sympathetic to Aristotle, find a serious difficulty for his account at this point.

25. On the role of reflection about beasts and gods in arriving at a conception of the human, see Nussbaum, *Fragility of Goodness;* Martha Nussbaum, "Transcending Humanity" in *Love's Knowledge: Essays on Philosophy and Literature* (New York: Oxford University Press; Oxford: Clarendon Press, 1990); and HN.

26. See HN for a further account of this procedure.

27. An obvious problem is that some agents who ask this question will arbitrarily exclude certain humans from humanity, and Aristotle himself is guilty of this in his reflections on women and natural slaves. On how the Aristotelian approach can confront this difficulty, see HN; and see also Martha Nussbaum, "Reply to Onora O'Neill," in *The Quality of Life,* ed. Nussbaum and Sen.

28. HN approaches the list by focusing on the two architectonic capabilities and briefly describes the limits; Martha Nussbaum, "Non-Relative Virtues: An Aristotelian Approach" (NRV) (in *The Quality of Life,* ed. Nussbaum and Sen) focuses on the

limits as they give rise to a unitary debate about the virtues. Here I try to put these pieces together.

29. Lucretius *De Rerum Natura* 5.989; cf. Martha Nussbaum, *The Therapy of Desire: Theory and Practice in Hellenistic Ethics* (Princeton, N.J.: Princeton University Press, 1994), chap. 6.

30. Aristotle discusses mortality in *De Anima* 2.4 and in the discussions of courage in the ethical works. See also Nussbaum, "Mortal Immortals"; and Nussbaum, "Transcending Humanity."

31. On the role of the body in the conception of the human being, see also NRV.

32. NRV discusses a Stoic argument that holds the belief that pain is bad to be a cultural artifact; this view seems highly implausible, although one should certainly grant that *conceptions* of the painful and the pleasant are shaped by cultural learning.

33. *Metaphysics* 1.1.

34. On practical reason and affiliation, see HN.

35. Aristotle's emphasis on this element is striking: see *EN* 4.6–8. Few moral philosophers place so much emphasis on this.

36. "Strong separateness" is defended by Aristotle in his criticisms of Plato in *Politics* 2: see Martha Nussbaum, "Shame, Separateness, and Political Unity: Aristotle's Criticism of Plato," in *Essays on Aristotle's Ethics,* ed. A. Rorty (Berkeley and Los Angeles: University of California Press, 1980), 395–435.

37. On this task, see the further discussion in NFC.

8

A Theory of Human Need

Len Doyal

The coherence of the concept of social progress depends upon the belief that some modes of social organization are better suited to satisfying human need than others. Unless increases in need satisfaction can be shown to follow from policies that purport to promote such progress, their moral purpose will be blurred. This can be seen as regards the varied attempts to defend and improve the welfare state. In light of national differences between welfare provision and differing levels of benefits within nations, some criterion is required to distinguish good and bad welfare systems, to enable the one to be defended and the other to be reformed.

Attempts to deny the objectivity of need have proved popular and superficially plausible. People do have strong feelings about what they need, and these feelings can vary enormously between cultures. Conflicting evidence of this kind suggests that subjective feeling is not a reliable determination of human need, a point reinforced by the fact that we can strongly desire things that are seriously harmful and, in our ignorance, not desire things that we require to avoid such harm. But the intelligibility of this fact seems to depend on the belief that there is something objective and universal about human need: "objective" in that its theoretical and empirical specification is independent of individual preference, and "universal" in that its conception of serious harm is the same for everyone. This chapter identifies these nonpreferential features of human need and outlines some of the moral consequences that follow from such an identification.

The Concept of Human Need

The word "need" is used explicitly or implicitly to refer to a particular category of *goals* that are believed to be *universalizable*. Needs in this sense are

157

commonly contrasted with "wants," which are also described as goals but which derive from an individual's particular preference and cultural environment.

Referring to needs as universalizable goals risks obscuring the reason why universality is imputed to some aims and not others. The imputation rests upon the belief that if needs are not satisfied by an appropriate "satisfier," then serious harm of some specified and objective kind will result.[1] Not to try to satisfy needs will thus be seen to be against the objective interests of the individuals involved and will be viewed as abnormal and unnatural. When goals are described as "wants" rather than needs, it is precisely because they are not believed to be linked to human interests in this sense.

But what counts as serious harm? Our approach equates serious harm with fundamental disablement in the pursuit of one's vision of the good—not contingent subjective feelings like anxiety or sadness. Another way of describing such harm concerns the impact of poor need satisfaction on the success of social participation.

Unless individuals are capable of participating in some form of life without arbitrary serious limitations being placed on what they attempt to accomplish, their potential for private and public success will remain unfulfilled, whatever the detail of their actual choices. Our private and public goals must always be achieved on the basis of past, present, or future successful interaction with others. We build a self-conception of our own personal capacities through learning from others—how they assess what we think we have learned and how they respond to changes in our actions on the basis of such assessment.

It follows that the search for objective basic needs becomes that for universalizable preconditions that enable nonimpaired participation both in the form of life in which individuals find themselves and in any other form of life that they might subsequently choose if they get the chance. Without the discovery of such conditions, we will be unable to account for the special moral significance that we wish to impute to basic need satisfaction.[2]

Physical Survival/Health and Autonomy as Basic Human Needs

For individuals to act and to be responsible, they must have both the physical and mental capacity to do so—at the very least a *body that is alive* and that is governed by all of the relevant causal processes and the *mental competence to deliberate and to choose*. Let us identify this latter competence and capacity for choice with the most basic level of personal "autonomy."[3]

Since physical survival and personal autonomy are the preconditions for any individual action in any culture, they constitute the most basic human needs—those that must be satisfied to some degree before people can effectively participate in their form of life to achieve any other valued goals.

Let us now look at each of these basic needs in further detail. Beginning with survival, it is clear that the need for physical survival on its own cannot do justice to what it means to be a person. The victim of a motor accident who survives in deep coma on a life-support system, incapable of independent action, demonstrates why. So it is *physical health* rather than just mere survival that is a basic need, one that it will be in the interest of individuals to try to satisfy before they address any others. To complete a range of practical tasks in daily life requires manual, mental, and emotional abilities with which poor physical health usually interferes.

On this view, the physical health needs of individuals have been met if they do not suffer in a sustained and serious way from one or more particular diseases.[4] For our purposes, the usefulness of such a perspective should be clear. Serious diseases ordinarily keep sufferers from participating as well as they might—and as might be expected from them—in the particular form of life in which they find themselves. In short, physical health can be thought of transculturally in a negative way. If you wish to lead an active and successful life in your own terms, it is in your objective interest to satisfy your basic need to optimize your life expectancy and to avoid serious physical disease and illness conceptualized in biomedical terms. The same applies to everyone, everywhere.[5]

Yet clear and potentially useful as the negative definition of physical health is, it is rightly regarded by many as problematic. For much more is involved in the preconditions for sustained successful human action than the absence of serious biological disease.[6] Individual autonomy must also be sustained and improved. One can easily imagine a situation where an actor has met her primary need for physical health but is still capable of initiating very little.

Three key variables affect levels of individual autonomy: the level of *understanding* a person has about herself, her culture, and what is expected of her as an individual within it; the *psychological capacity* she has to formulate options for herself; and the objective *opportunities* enabling her to act accordingly or impeding her from doing so.[7]

The degree of understanding of self and culture depends on the availability and quality of teachers. People do not teach themselves to act; they have to learn from others. Which skills are learned will differ from culture to culture, but they are not totally variable. There are some activities that are common to all cultures and for which all people must be prepared if they are to be able to participate successfully and to understand what goes on within those cultures. Braybrooke correctly classifies these social roles as those of parent, householder, worker, and citizen.[8]

This is why autonomy can be impaired in formal education, for example, by a curriculum that is irrelevant to the vocational needs of the community or the emotional needs of individual students.[9] It can equally be damaged by the way in which people are taught. If their curiosity is not sparked and their intellectual confidence is not reinforced, the scope of their potential choices will be artificially constrained, along with their ability to affect the world and others.[10] As a result, they will be objectively disabled.

The second key determinant of autonomy is the individual's *cognitive capacity and emotionality*—ultimately, his or her *mental health*. Rationality is an important component in all the definitions of autonomy that we have considered. But what does it mean in relation to mental health? Since all actions have to embody a modicum of reason to be classed as actions at all, it is difficult to give a precise definition of the minimum levels of rationality and responsibility present in the autonomous individual. Generally speaking, the existence of even minimal levels of autonomy will entail the following sustained characteristics:

- that actors have the intellectual capacity for the formulation of aims and beliefs common to their form of life

- that actors have enough confidence to want to act and thus to participate in some form of social life

- that actors sometimes actually do so through consistently formulating aims and beliefs and communicating with others about them

- that actors perceive their actions as having been done by them and not by someone else

- that actors are able to understand the empirical constraints on the success of their actions

- that actors are capable of taking moral responsibility for what they do

Therefore, again like physical health, autonomy at its most basic level should be understood negatively—with reference to the serious objective disablement to which the absence of one or more of these characteristics will lead.[11] Those who are seriously and permanently ill in this sense have either lost or never possessed a level of autonomy sufficient for more than minimally successful levels of intentional social interaction, if that.

The third variable that affects the degree to which autonomy can be increased is the range of *opportunities* for new and significant action open to the actor. By "significant," we mean activities that are deemed of social significance in any of Braybrooke's preceding categories or that the actors deem of significance for the rational improvement of their participation in their form of life. This means that when we link improvements in autonomy to increased choices, we do not mean any old choices.[12] Significant choices require social opportunities. Those who are denied them have their freedom and their autonomy artificially constrained and are unable to explore some of their capacities as people.[13] More than anything else, it is this that makes tyranny so abhorrent.

In further exploring the links between autonomy and freedom, many writers within the liberal tradition argue that both should be seen as the absence of constraints on actions that have not been chosen by actors themselves. Yet if "constraint" is taken to mean "self-sufficiency," then we must take great care. For the opportunity to express individual autonomy requires much more than simply being left alone—more than negative freedom. If we really were ignored by others, we would never learn the rules of our way of life and thereby acquire the capacity to make choices within it.

In other words, to be autonomous and to be healthy, we also require *positive freedom*—material, educational, and emotional need satisfaction of the kind already described.[14] Against the background of the general socialization on which their cognitive and emotional capacity for action depends, autonomous individuals must understand *why* they should not physically constrain the actions of others and must possess the emotional competence to act accordingly. But again, they only learn with positive assistance to follow the rules embodied in such constraint. This is why the concept of serious harm is so intimately linked with that of impaired social participation.

Critical Autonomy

Even the oppressed can make choices. Their lives are full of mundane choices in interpreting the rules that shape the social roles over which they have no say. Were freedom of the oppressed illusory—were there no opportunities—it would make little sense to encourage and to assist them to throw off the chains of their oppression. Slavery is the most dramatic example and underlines the political importance of the *freedom of agency* of individuals in such groups—their ability in principle to choose—even though at any given time members may do little to challenge their oppression. What is equally clear, however, is that freedom of agency should not be confused with higher levels of autonomy and opportunities associated with *political freedom*.[15] Our analysis of autonomy as a basic need has thus far focused on the necessary conditions for participation in any form of life, no matter how totalitarian. Individual autonomy can obviously reach greater levels than this. Where the opportunity exists to question and to participate in *agreeing to or changing* the rules of a culture, it will be possible for actors significantly to increase their autonomy through a spectrum of choices unavailable to the politically oppressed. In such circumstances, actions that hitherto actors could only be said to choose through interpreting the already existing rules of their particular social environment become chosen and their own in a much more profound sense. What was autonomy becomes "critical autonomy."

It is for this reason that we prefer the distinction between autonomy as freedom of agency, which is compatible with relatively high levels of critical reflection, and the higher degrees of critical autonomy that are entailed by democratic participation in the political process at whatever level. For critical autonomy to be a real possibility, individuals must have the opportunity to express both freedom of agency and political freedom.[16] Without both types of opportunity, they will again be objectively disabled, even though their levels of understanding and cognitive and emotional competence may be quite high.

Satisfiers and "Intermediate Needs"

While the basic individual needs for physical health and autonomy are universal, many goods and services required to satisfy these needs are culturally variable. For example, the needs for food and shelter apply to all peoples, but there is a potentially infinite variety of cuisines and forms of dwelling that can meet any given specification of nutrition and protection from the elements. We have called all objects, activities, and relationships that satisfy our basic needs "satisfiers."[17] Basic needs, then, are always universal, but their satisfiers are often relative.

"Satisfier characteristics" are a subset of all characteristics having the property of contributing to the satisfaction of our basic needs in one or more cultural settings. Let us now subdivide this set further to identify *universal satisfier characteristics*: those characteristics of satisfiers that apply to all cultures. Universal satisfier characteristics are thus *those properties of goods, services, activities, and relationships that enhance physical health and human autonomy in all cultures*. For example, "calories a day" for a specified group of people constitutes a characteristic of (most) foodstuffs that has transcultural relevance. Similarly "shelter from the elements" and "protection from disease-carrying vectors" are characteristics that all dwellings have in common (although to greatly varying degrees). The category of universal satisfier characteristics thus provides the crucial bridge between universal basic needs and socially relative satisfiers.

Universal satisfier characteristics can be regarded as goals for which specific satisfiers can act as the means. For this reason, and because the phrase is less clumsy, let us refer to universal satisfier characteristics as intermediate needs. If this reasoning is correct, such needs can provide a secure foundation on which to erect a list of derived or second-order goals that must be achieved if the first-order goals of health and autonomy are to be attained. Our theory dictates that intermediate needs are most important for basic need satisfaction, why this is so, and why they are the same for all cultures. These intermediate needs can be grouped as follows:

- nutritional food and clean water

- protective housing

- a nonhazardous work environment

- a nonhazardous physical environment

- appropriate health care

- security in childhood

- significant primary relationships

- physical security

- economic security

- appropriate education

- safe birth control and childbearing

The only criterion for inclusion in this list is whether any set of satisfier characteristics universally and positively contributes to physical health and autonomy. There is one partial exception. Significant biological differences within the human species may occasion specific requirements for distinct satisfier characteristics. The most significant of such differences by far is the sex difference between men and women. This entails one further universal satisfier characteristic the satisfaction of which is essential to the health and autonomy of one half of the human race. Women require access to safe birth control and childbearing if they are to enjoy the same opportunities as men to participate in their respective societies.

The evidence about what is universally necessary is derived from two principal scientific sources: (1) the best available technical knowledge articulating causal relationships between physical health or autonomy and other factors; (2) comparative anthropological knowledge about practices in the numerous cultures and subcultures, states, and political systems in the contemporary world.[18] Thus both the natural and social sciences play their part in rationally determining the composition of intermediate needs.

Needs, Rights, and Moral Responsibilities

So far we have argued that health and autonomy are basic needs common to all humans irrespective of culture. But we have not been concerned with the moral issue of whether people's needs should be met. Not everyone accepts that they have an obligation to aid those in serious need. Without such a moral theory we can only preach to the converted. This is by no means a pointless task, given the assaults of relativism and the withering attacks from upholders of rather crass forms of individualism—the "me-now" ethic—in recent years. Those who uphold the morality of meeting basic needs require as much rational support for their beliefs as possible. But their arguments need situating within a broader moral context if others are to be convinced. Otherwise why should they be expected to move from the "is" of need to the "ought" of the responsibility to do something about it?

It is not only social life that requires moral responsibility; so, too, does the success of our own individual participation within it. Unless we just happen fortuitously to have the power to inflict our will on others, social success will depend on our capacity to understand what our moral responsibilities are and our willingness to act accordingly. The duties that moral responsibilities entail are just as *real* for us in our social lives as is our physical environment. The reality of duties apparently entails the reality of *rights*—the entitlement of one group of individuals to what is required for them to carry out obligations that they and others believe they possess. However, the logical relationship between rights and duties is highly complex. For this reason we shall argue that duties only entail rights against the background of an already existing network of moral beliefs that clearly specify the conditions of entailment.[19]

The Right to Minimal Levels of Need Satisfaction

Let us begin with an individual A who believes that she has a duty of some kind toward others in group B who expect her to act accordingly. Also assume that she is aware of, and accepts the legitimacy of, their expectation. The group in question could be a small face-to-face community or a large anonymous collectivity. But whatever its size and however well its members know one another, for her and them to believe that she should do her duty presupposes that they also believe that she is in fact able so to do. In other words, "'ought'" implies "can."

Therefore, the ascription of a duty—for it to be intelligible as a duty to those who accept it and to those who ascribe it—must carry with it the belief that the bearer of the duty is entitled to the level of need satisfaction necessary for her to act accordingly. Thus A must believe that she has the right to such satisfaction if, say, she suddenly becomes impoverished but is still expected by the members of B to execute the duties she did before this occurred. For *without at least minimal levels of need satisfaction, A will be able to do nothing at all, including those acts that are specifically expected of her*. And the same applies to those who believe that they have a right to A's actions. They also must accept that, unless her basic needs are minimally satisfied, she will be unable to do what they think she should. Therefore, she has a right to such satisfaction in proportion to the seriousness with which they take her duty and expect her to fulfill it. And the converse also holds.

Of course, the acceptance of such a right does not specify exactly how it should be respected in particular circumstances. The members of B, for example, may accept that A has a right to a minimal level of need satisfaction without accepting that they have a corresponding duty *directly* to provide it. This will be likely if, say, welfare agencies exist that have the institutional responsibility for meeting needs. But remember, someone or some group must accept the duty to act for A if her right is to have substance. Therefore, the members of B cannot escape from the responsibility at least to *contribute toward* A's minimal need satisfaction—provided that an *agency* exists for this purpose.[20]

The Right to Optimal Need Satisfaction

The argument so far has justified the rights of all peoples to the minimal satisfaction of their basic needs. It has not, however, provided a justification for anything more than the avoidance of gross suffering or enabling people just to "get by." Let us now extend the argument to higher levels of need satisfaction, up to and including "optimal" levels.

Fulfilling one's perceived obligations in public and private life usually involves much more than the minimal amount of action made possible by a minimal level of need satisfaction. There will always be some goals that individuals take very seriously and that they believe that they have a duty to achieve *to the best of their ability*. These will usually be aims that they perceive as central to the conduct of their lives, the achievement of which will determine whether or not they will regard themselves and be regarded by others as of high moral character. Personal goals of this kind are informed by cultural values—the types and levels of performance expected by those toward whom one experiences moral obligations.

Thus, attempts at excellence are symbolic of the commitment to a specific way of life and thereby to a particular vision of the good. The degree of this commitment will ultimately be judged by others who share the same values. In these situations, for us to expect less of ourselves than our best or to believe that less would be acceptable to those to whom we are obligated calls into question our and their commitment to the shared good that informs our action. It would mean that the good was not really believed to be *that* good after all.

If, however, we agree that those who are committed to the same morality have the duty to do their best—to be good in its terms—then this commits us to a further belief: that those concerned have a *right* to the goods and services necessary for their best effort to be a realistic possibility. It is inconsistent for us to expect that others should do their best and also to think that they should not have the wherewithal to do so—the *optimal* as opposed to the minimal satisfaction of their basic needs. And, of course, the same applies to ourselves. The only way in which this conclusion does not follow is for us to believe that, all things being equal, less than the best effort is compatible with the pursuit of the good.

But again, what would "the good" mean in this context? If we really take our moral beliefs seriously, then we have no option but to take equally seriously the entitlement of other members of our community to those things that will optimize their capacity for moral action. As was the case with minimal need satisfaction, this entails two things: negatively, not inhibiting persons from trying to do their best; and positively, doing what we can to provide access to the same levels of need satisfaction that we claim in our own pursuit of moral virtue. All other members of our own culture who take their morality seriously incur the same duties toward us, and for the same reasons.[21]

Of course, what is regarded as "best" and "optimal" in the above terms will vary between cultures, depending on their particular moral codes and the resources that are available for need satisfaction. Therefore, when we use the term "optimal," we are obviously not maintaining that those who share moral values have a right to *everything* that might conceivably reinforce their pursuit of moral excellence. Since the scope of such satisfiers is potentially infinite, no individual or group within the culture could assume the corresponding duty of providing them, and without such a duty there can be no identifiable right.

Our point is rather that the members of specific cultures will already have reasonably clear ideas of what doing one's best amounts to *in practice*. These will be linked to exemplars of what ordinary individuals can hope to achieve if they apply themselves to the best of their ability, along with theories about the levels of health, learning, and emotional confidence that are usually associated with such application. To be consistent, therefore, a commitment to a vision of the good must be linked to that culture's best available understanding of what is required for optimal individual effort. Consistency also dictates that everyone who is expected to do her best to be good in our terms—and is encouraged to try to do so—is given a fair share of the resources available for this to be a real possibility.

The Right of Aliens to Need Satisfaction

So far we have seen how a collective commitment to optimal need satisfaction should follow from a collective commitment to a vision of the good and to a system of rights and duties associated therewith. But what of social justice among those who do not share the same system of moral values and, therefore, the same moral vision? Does our sense of moral imperative apply only to members of our own culture?

The measure of our moral commitment is our willingness to take seriously its categorical character—its applicability to everyone and not just to those with whom we already profess agreement. If our good is *the* good, then we must believe that all individuals should do their best to act accordingly, irrespective of their own moral values. If one believes, for example, that female circumcision is an affront to all women, or that the isolation of old people is an outrage, then the practice must be morally condemned, whatever the justification used by participants. However, if we believe that others should do their best to be good in our terms, then we must also accept that they have the right to try to do so. Yet for this prescription to be any more than a hollow moral abstraction, it also follows that they should have the right of access to those conditions that make such a choice a real physical, emotional, and intellectual possibility: the right to optimal need satisfaction. Indeed, given the enormous intellectual and emotional difficulties associated with moving from one morality to another, we should want our moral opponents to be in as good a shape as possible.

So consistency dictates that we must support, *in proportion* to our own commitment to the truth and superiority of our vision of the good, the right to optimal need satisfaction of strangers about whose moral beliefs we know nothing. To be victorious in bullying the weak and feeble is morally defeating. As with slaves, even if the weak say they agree, you can never be sure that they really do. Whatever personal gratification their agreement may bring in the short term, it will not be long-lasting. If a concern for virtue in the face of what is believed to be barbarity leads to the repression of the very preconditions for the optimal pursuit of virtue—the optimal need satisfaction of all of the potentially virtuous whatever their current beliefs—then the resulting bland conformity of action is a form of conceptual and emotional slavery. It is not the responsible moral choice that any morality should demand of its followers.

Thus far we have argued that to the degree that individuals take any vision of the good seriously, they have a duty to respect the right of all others who are deemed human to do their best to adopt the same vision. The idea of common human needs entails the right even of strangers to optimal need satisfaction.

Special Obligations and the Optimization of Need Satisfaction

So much for rights; what of duties or obligations? In practice, the right to optimal need satisfaction will entail not only acts of forbearance but also positive acts to make available the goods and services necessary for such decisions to be a material and psychological possibility. In short, we all have a responsibility, a duty, an obligation to help all humans to optimize their need satisfaction.

If this argument is accepted, it places an onerous responsibility on us all. The extent of dire needs throughout the world is staggering. How are individuals supposed to fulfill the duties specified, when they will naturally be preoccupied with satisfying the needs and wants of those whom they already know and for whom they feel a strong and explicit sense of responsibility (e.g., family and friends)?

To explore this question further, let us begin by hypothesizing a day at the beach. Suppose that the peaceful situation dramatically changes and a child is seen swimming for his life, caught by strong currents and being swept out to sea. Who is responsible for saving him—for respecting the need for survival that he himself is struggling to satisfy? If there is a lifeguard, the first response will no doubt be that it is he who has a "special responsibility" to do exactly this. He has voluntarily assumed his duty because it is stipulated in his contract of employment, which also guarantees certain rights for himself (e.g., to regular payment). But suppose he does nothing. Who else should act on the child's behalf? Would it make sense, for example, for everyone to shout, "We're not going to do anything until it is clear that his father and mother—who also have a special responsibility for his welfare—will do nothing"? Hardly. The child has a right to help not because of his contractual relationship with anyone else but because of his "dire need."[22] Everyone else who is in a position to intervene to satisfy his need for survival has a moral responsibility to do so—everyone, that is, who takes her vision of the good seriously.

But how is this responsibility to be apportioned? It should clearly not be on the basis of some fractionalization, where, for example, if there were two hundred swimmers present, each would share one two-hundredth of the responsibility. To the degree that each individual is in a position to satisfy the need in question—in this case through stopping the drowning—then each shares full responsibility for its occurrence. The only thing that can mitigate this responsibility is the fact that they cannot act without endangering their own basic need satisfaction (e.g., through being unable to swim) or that they honestly think that they will interfere with the success of others who are acting appropriately. This aside, any decision on whether the delay of onlookers is justifiable will depend on whether they wait too long for the needs of the child to be met. The fact that this may be difficult to determine is more a counsel for not taking any chances than it is for the avoidance of an undeniable duty to help. Goodin—on whom this analysis greatly depends—aptly makes the point: "The limit of this responsibility is, quite simply, the limit of the vulnerable agent's needs and of the responsible agent's capacity to act efficaciously—no more, but certainly no less."[23]

So responsibility for the drowning boy rests with all those on the beach. Yet if our theory is to be plausible, it must also be applicable to people in need whose distress *we do not directly witness and can do nothing directly to satisfy*. What are our practical obligations to strangers when weighed alongside our special duties toward those who for whatever reasons are "close" to us, or our duties toward strangers whom we are in a position to help directly? If need satisfaction begins at home, so to speak, then how far are we responsible for those who don't live there and with whom we have no direct contact?

The problem begins to resolve when it is accepted that it is not only agents but also agencies—social institutions of one sort or another—that can act to ensure need satisfaction, provided that they have adequate powers and material support. Individuals by themselves are clearly unable to stop the decline or encourage the improvement of the need satisfaction of persons with whom they have no contact. The same cannot be said of a collective that contains individuals who have the contact, along with the expertise and the resources, to intervene appropriately. It is through their support for such agencies—or through the policies that they support or oppose if they are members of such collectives—that individuals must discharge their moral responsibilities for the need satisfaction of strangers.[24]

So returning again to our example, many local citizens who do not themselves use the beach may and should recognize their responsibility to contribute to the protection of those who do. Thus they may collectively support the costs of a lifeguard—someone with special responsibilities for need satisfaction founded on his training and unique skills.

But why stop there and confine one's concern only to the beach round the corner, so to speak? All swimmers on all public beaches have the same need and therefore right to protection. It is this that morally justifies the strict duty to submit to taxation for such purposes. Otherwise, the moral irrationality or confusion of individual personalities will generate the "free rider" dilemma—it will be in the interest of all to enjoy the security a lifeguard provides but in the interests of none to pay for these services. The same argument applies to providing resources for, say, the local ambulance service, the nearby hospital, and all other agencies that might have to look after those who have been injured as the result of accidents. It is also the rationale behind preventive measures like the public provision of, say, swimming lessons and swimming pools. In other words, there is a strict duty on individuals to ensure they participate in the collective need satisfaction of strangers through their support for relevant institutional agencies.[25]

Such duties go to the heart of all rights-based justifications for the welfare state. Since, in a variety of national contexts, many of the institutions of the welfare state have shown themselves capable of considerable success in alleviating need, we have gone some way toward justifying the practicality of our emphasis on rights and duties. For the fact is that much higher than minimum levels of need satisfaction have been, and therefore can be, obtained. Equally, whatever their recorded abuses, there is no indication that state institutions of welfare must necessarily lead to a diminution in such satisfaction, especially as regards the basic need for autonomy. In practice, as well as in theory, we must always desire the optimum satisfaction that can be obtained for those whom we wish to do their best to pursue our vision of the good. That we might debate what this level practically entails and how it should be given effect does nothing to detract from the moral imperative of collectively helping others to reach the high levels of need satisfaction that we already know can be achieved.

Conclusion

We have distinguished needs from wants by reference to the preconditions for the avoidance of serious harm. These conditions can be regarded as goals that all humans should have in common if they are to be able to act in their objective interests. Human needs, therefore, are those levels of health and autonomy that should be—to the extent that they can be—achieved for all peoples now, without compromising the foreseeable levels at which they will be achieved by future generations. In the long term—if there is to be one—an awareness of the delicacy of the biosphere must go hand-in-hand with any feasible commitment to the optimization of need satisfaction. Taking rights seriously means doing the same for the environment.

Finally, we have argued that all individuals have a right to optimal need satisfaction. In the struggle to achieve it, participants must have an accurate understanding of the social and physical environments that they are attempting to improve, along with objective opportunities for change within these environments. Yet they also require the classic Greek virtues that MacIntyre has recently done so much to rehabilitate—reason, courage, truthfulness, and a willingness to sacrifice.[26] Ironically, some may think, successful political struggle will also entail the classic Christian virtues, particularly charity with respect to those with whom one disagrees and faith and hope that participation will contribute toward a more just distribution of material, intellectual, and emotional resources—even when it fails in the short term.

Notes

This chapter has been adapted from work first published in *A Theory of Human Need,* by Len Doyal and Ian Gough (London: Macmillan; New York: Guilford, 1991) and is reprinted with the permission of the authors, Macmillan Press Ltd, and Guilford Publications Inc.

1. J. Feinberg, *Social Philosophy* (Englewood Cliffs, N.J.: Prentice-Hall, 1973), 111; David Wiggins, "Claims of Need," in *Morality and Objectivity*, ed. Ted Honderich (London: Routledge, 1985), 153–59.

2. R. Goodin, *Reasons for Welfare* (Princeton, N.J.: Princeton University Press, 1988), 32–35.

3. R. Lindley, *Autonomy* (London: Macmillan, 1986), chap. 2.

4. M. Stacey, *The Sociology of Health and Healing* (London: Unwin Hyman, 1988), 169–72.

5. Len Doyal, "Health, Underdevelopment, and Traditional Medicine," *Holistic Medicine* 2, no. 1 (1987): 27–40.

6. J. Salmon, *Alternative Medicines* (London: Tavistock, 1984), 254–60.

7. T. Beauchamp and R. Faden, eds., *A Theory and History of Informed Consent* (New York: Oxford University Press, 1986), 241–56.

8. David Braybrooke, *Meeting Needs* (Princeton, N.J.: Princeton University Press, 1987), 48.

9. H. Entwistle, *Antonio Gramsci* (London: Routledge, 1979), parts 1, 2.

10. S. Grundy, *Curriculum: Product or Praxis?* (London: Falmer, 1987), chap. 3.

11. K. Fulford, *Moral Theory and Medical Practice* (Cambridge: Cambridge University Press, 1989), chaps. 8, 9.

12. G. Dworkin, *The Theory and Practice of Autonomy* (Cambridge: Cambridge University Press, 1988), chap. 5.

13. L. Haworth, *Autonomy* (New Haven: Yale University Press, 1986), chap. 6.

14. Isaiah Berlin, "Two Concepts of Liberty," in *Four Essays on Liberty* (New York: Oxford University Press, 1969), 118–72.

15. Len Doyal and R. Harris, *Empiricism, Explanation, and Rationality; An Introduction to the Philosophy of the Social Sciences* (London: Routledge, 1986), chap 5.

16. Len Doyal, "Medical Ethics and Moral Indeterminacy," *Journal of Law and Society* 17 (1990): 1.

17. K. Lederer, introduction to *Human Need*, ed. K. Lederer (Cambridge, Mass.: Oelgeschlager, Gunn & Hain, 1980).

18. Braybrooke, *Meeting Needs*, chaps. 2.3, 2.4; and C. Mallman and S. Marcus, "Logical Clarification in the Study of Needs," in *Human Needs*, ed. Lederer.

19. A. White, *Rights* (Oxford: Oxford University Press, 1984), 70.

20. R. Goodin, *Protecting the Vulnerable* (Chicago: University of Chicago Press, 1985), 151–53.

21. A. Gewirth, *Reason and Morality* (Chicago: University of Chicago Press, 1978), 240–48.

22. Goodin, *Protecting the Vulnerable*, 111.

23. Goodin, *Protecting the Vulnerable*, 135.

24. Gewirth, *Reason and Morality*, 312–19.

25. R. Plant, H. Lesser, and P. Taylor-Gooby, *Political Philosophy and Social Welfare* (London: Routledge, 1980), 93–96; A. Gewirth, *Human Rights* (Chicago: University of Chicago Press, 1982), 59–66.

26. Alasdair MacIntyre, *After Virtue* (London: Duckworth, 1983).

9

Is Redistribution to Help the Needy Unjust?

Gillian Brock

Is redistribution to help the needy unjust? According to an argument frequently pressed by libertarians,[1] redistribution to assist those in need is indeed unjust, since rights are thereby violated. One of the most well known advocates of such a position is Robert Nozick. Nozick proclaims, for instance, that "the state may not use its coercive apparatus for the purpose of getting some citizens to aid others," "redistribution is a serious matter indeed, involving as it does, the violation of people's rights," and "[t]axation of earnings from labor is on a par with forced labor."[2]

Nozick, along with many other libertarians, clearly believes that redistribution to assist the needy is unjust, and unjust because rights are thereby violated. Importantly, the rights that are apparently being violated are the rights to the freedom to do whatever we want with our wealth, income, and property more generally.[3] Those who maintain that their rights would be violated (if some of their property were to be redistributed to meet needs) frequently offer arguments for property rights that are labor based (that is to say, they frequently recognize labor as the crucial feature in generating rights to property).[4] As I briefly discuss, these labor-based arguments are far from unproblematic.

However, one of the central theses I argue for in this chapter is that even if we are sympathetic to libertarian arguments for property rights, we cannot get to libertarians' desired conclusion that any redistribution to meet needs violates the rights in question. As I argue in this chapter, to assume that others' needs may not affect the validity of property rights involves confusions about property rights. The kinds of cases under which property rights are justified and the nature of the right that is thereby accorded are not sufficient to render property rights immune from the sorts of claims others' needs can make on such rights. I begin by examining one of the most frequently invoked arguments for the defensibility of property rights in order to highlight some of the salient issues.

173

Some Preliminaries

Though not the best argument for property rights, probably the best known argument is one presented by Locke. The argument proceeds (roughly) from the claim that we have property rights in our bodies to the claim that we have property rights in the labor of our bodies and, therefore, in those things we mix our labor with, provided that what we appropriate will not be wasted and that we leave available enough and as good for others to appropriate suitably. The requirement of leaving available enough and as good for others is commonly referred to as "the Lockean proviso."

The weaknesses with Locke's argument are well documented. For instance, the notion that mixing one's labor gives rise to ownership rights is quite problematic. As Nozick points out, why should mixing one's labor with resources be a way of coming to own something?[5] Why isn't mixing one's labor just a way of losing something rather than a way of gaining anything? There are also problems with the Lockean proviso. Since one may not acquire goods so long as any person will be made worse off by not having enough and as good of the available resources, under conditions of scarce resources it appears that no acquisition can be justified. With scarce (especially nonrenewable) resources, every acquisition makes the pool of available resources smaller, which means each acquisition results in there not being as much as before. But of course, this would effectively mean that a great deal of acquisition is not, and never has been, justified. As Nozick argues, suppose that there is at some point a person, Z, for whom there is not enough or as good left to acquire, then the person, Y, whose acquisition resulted in this situation acquired unjustly.[6] But, similarly, X's acquisition then violated the proviso and so on back to the first acquisition, so the proviso cannot be met.

Although the weaknesses with Locke's argument have received much attention, what is overlooked, in my opinion, is that the argument attempts to capture the force of two central intuitions that seem right and that all adequate labor-based arguments for property rights must accommodate. The intuitions are, roughly:

I1. The efforts and actions on the part of the individual laborer can be an appropriate basis for desert.

I2. Whatever laborers deserve should not be such that it is unfair to others *(ceteris paribus)*.

It seems to me that these intuitions are both plausible and importantly right. (I2) is clearly an intuition central to moral theory: the inequitable effects on others must be taken into account when considering what is morally appropriate. Figuring out appropriate deserts in the case of labor is no exception. Inequitable effects on others are not only relevant but also integral to determining what is appropriately deserved. Indeed, then, let me emphasize this point once again: in order to be morally defensible, adequate arguments must recognize and accommodate the force of intuitions such as (I2).

Trying to explain why (I1) is in general plausible is trickier, although in this context (I1) is not in need of defense; in this chapter I take it as a point of departure that intuitions like (I1) have some force. Clearly, (I1) is hardly an intuition that really requires much defense to libertarians. Indeed, libertarians would typically be committed to principles far stronger than (I1), for instance, (I1a) and (I1b):

I1a. Individuals' laboring actions are an appropriate basis for desert in certain cases.

I1b. Among the deserts appropriate for laboring actions are rewards such as property rights.

Both (I1a) and (I1b) require some argument; neither is obviously true. And even if we can establish that (I1a) is true, it is not obvious that (I1b) is true too: even if labor is in certain cases an appropriate desert basis, why should the action be rewarded by granting something like property rights rather than being rewarded by (say) receiving a pat on the back, public recognition, or gratitude?

Clearly, intuitions like (I1a) and (I1b) require defense, but I will not dwell on this issue. Let me grant to my libertarian interlocutors the plausibility of intuitions such as (I1a) and (I1b). The question then arises: even if we grant that intuitions such as (I1a) and (I1b) are plausible, how do we get from granting that property rights may be appropriate deserts for labor to the view that redistribution to meet needs is impermissible? In the following section I show that even if we are quite sympathetic to the idea that the individual's laboring actions can give rise to property rights, we cannot get to the desired conclusion. In fact, as I argue, we have to recognize that sensitivity to others' needs must be built into any defensible account of property rights.

Why Must Property Rights Always Be Sensitive to Others' Needs?

In this section I develop a general argument for the thesis that people's being in a situation of need constrains and defines the limits of defensible property rights. Before I can give this general argument, I turn first to draw attention to an important general point about the nature of property rights. Though the point is widely recognized, as I argue, the implications of this point are not.

Rights to property are not impervious to, nor independent of, the conditions that justify them initially. Whatever conditions, provisos, or limitations constrain acquisitions when acquisitions are justified apply throughout the "life" of property rights. The constraints on legitimate initial acquisition play a *permanent role* in maintaining the legitimacy of property rights. Limitations inherent in titles may be invoked at any time.

One might suspect that this position, that is, the view that limitations on original acquisition permanently constrain the legitimacy of property rights, does not enjoy much support. Importantly for the dynamic of my argument, one might suspect that libertarians would be quite resistant to this thesis, but in fact they are not. Even Nozick recognizes the continuing force of constraints on initial acquisition, and, for his theory, this means the continuing force of the constraints provided by a modified Lockean proviso.[7] The passage below from Nozick is particularly illustrative and bears scrutiny. In this passage it is evident that Nozick not only believes that constraints on acquisition permanently constrain property rights but also acknowledges that others' predicament of need can powerfully affect the legitimacy of property rights.

> Each owner's title to his holding includes the historical shadow of the Lockean proviso on appropriation. . . . Once it is known that someone's ownership runs afoul of the Lockean proviso, there are stringent limits on what he may do with (what it is difficult any longer unreservedly to call) "his property." Thus a person may not appropriate the only water hole in a desert and charge what he will. Nor may he charge what he will if he possesses one, and unfortunately it happens that all the water holes in the desert dry up, except for his. This unfortunate circumstance, admittedly no fault of his, brings into operation the Lockean proviso and limits his property rights. Similarly, an owner's property right in the only island in an area does not allow him to order a castaway from a shipwreck off his island as a trespasser, for this would violate the Lockean proviso.[8]

In this passage Nozick acknowledges that the justifiability of property rights is always subject to "the shadow" of the Lockean proviso and that constraints provided by the Lockean proviso permanently affect the justifiability of retaining property rights. In addition, notice how Nozick recognizes that the predicament of others, especially their predicament of being in need, is quite relevant to circumscribing property rights (if only for a limited range of cases). In the examples it appears that one should recognize the force of others' needs in those cases where the property at issue is extremely scarce, necessary to sustain life, and currently owned by one person. Still, even in this form, the point is granted: others' being in a situation of need is exactly the sort of consideration identified as relevant to limiting property rights. In conditions of extreme scarcity, being needy and being potentially unable to meet a need other than through having access to certain property is exactly the sort of consideration that may limit property rights such that, as Nozick says, it is no longer even clear that we may properly refer to the property as "his property."[9]

Nozick's concessions at this point have a more far-reaching effect than is recognized (even by Nozick himself, for instance) in at least one obvious way. If Nozick's argument holds when one person monopolizes all the resources necessary for life, it retains its cogency whenever the goods necessary for life itself are monopolized by a few (or even many) who deny others access to these goods. In such cases, by Nozick's own standards, we have an unjust situation, unjust because we have a violation of the Lockean proviso. Many situations where there are needy people could hereby be accommodated. That is to say, there are many situations where it would (by Nozick's own standards) not only be permissible to redistribute property to assist the needy but where not to do so would be unjust because a violation of the Lockean proviso would have occurred.

At any rate, the primary point of this excursion into Nozick has been to show that even libertarians acknowledge that whatever constraints are imposed on justifiable initial acquisitions track property rights permanently. Indeed, all defensible accounts of property rights must acknowledge this, as others have argued.[10] Examination of Nozick's recognizing this point reveals something else of interest. Nozick acknowledges that people being in a situation of need in certain dire cases is exactly the sort of consideration relevant to limiting property rights. What I show next is that people being in a situation of need constrains property rights in a much wider range of cases than Nozick realizes. Indeed, all defensible accounts of property rights must recognize the pervasive constraining impact of others' needs on property rights in order to be defensible. A general argument for this point follows.

No *defensible* account of initial acquisition can endorse unconditional taking of unowned stuff. One cannot employ any means at all to get property, as in, say, a Hobbesian state of nature. Taking of unowned stuff or getting unowned things must be constrained at least by some sort of minimal respect for other people's liberties. For an account of property acquisition to be defensible, there must be at least some constraints on what counts as a permissible acquisition. From this quite general point, I move to a quite particular one.

Whether or not an initial acquisition is justified depends importantly on the scarcity of resources relative to those who need them. If one is alone on the philosophically proverbial desert island and, in order to sustain oneself, one appropriates many of the goodies on the desert island for one's own consumption, in the absence of this having any impact on anyone else, such appropriation appears perfectly acceptable.

But now assume there are several people on the island. Would it still be acceptable for one person to appropriate all the island's goods and exclude others from their use? In the absence of further information, clearly not. What it is acceptable to appropriate must now take into account the impact appropriation will have on others. In particular, a justified arrangement must be sensitive to whether the arrangement would be unfair to others. One person's appropriating all the goods and excluding others from them would completely undermine others' ability to sustain themselves, and so this cannot count as an equitable arrangement.[11] Indeed, it is not clear how any account of initial acquisition that maintains that some may seize and monopolize unowned goods and that therefore entails that others are obligated to perish can be a defensible account of initial acquisition. Such an account would be importantly unfair to others.[12] Such an account, then, would fail to accommodate (I2) acceptably. As highlighted above, not accommodating (I2) adequately is sufficient to disqualify an account of property acquisition from being defensible. And so, we see how others' situation of need constitutes an important constraint on determining whether initial acquisitions are justified.

Once the case is made that all acceptable accounts of *initial* acquisition must recognize the relevance of others' need in constraining defensible initial acquisition, we are home free, since the other crucial premise has already been argued for: constraints on initial acquisition play a permanent role in maintaining the defensibility of property rights. So, not only must all defensible initial acquisition take account of others' predicament of need, but this is a permanent feature of the property right. Whatever constraints are placed on initial acquisition must continue to be met if the property right is to retain its defensibility. Should the conditions that initially justified the property right no longer be met, the current defensibility of the property right may be called into question.

So, putting all the pieces together: since property rights are permanently tied to various constraints on initial acquisition, and since all initial property acquisition is subject to the constraints supplied by others' needs, it follows that property rights must be permanently sensitive to others' needs if they are to retain their defensibility.

The thesis I have argued for is that people's being in a situation of need is exactly the sort of consideration relevant to determining and circumscribing property rights. I have given a general argument as to why this must be the case. It may be objected that this general argument loses its force when others have worked to produce the scarce resource, when the scarce resource is not something stumbled upon "naturally occurring," like goodies on an island. I turn now to examine the impact of this kind of objection on the argument.

It is taken as a background assumption to the issues under discussion here that we are being sympathetic to the idea that laboring can in certain conditions deserve some benefit. The "but some have *labored*" objection has on its side our expressed sympathies. So, the question arises: Does the fact that some have labored to produce scarce resources mean that the laborers can ignore the needs of others? So, for instance, if a person had labored to produce a water hole, does the labor involved make it acceptable for the water hole owner to deny people access to the water hole? The laborer may deserve an appropriate reward for producing the water hole. What must be argued at this point for the objection to succeed, is that the most fitting (or even *a* fitting) reward for the labor is exclusive use of the water hole, that is, the right to banish all others from any use of the water hole under any conditions. Can this be a fitting reward for the labor?

When labor justifies a benefit or reward, what form the reward should take depends importantly on various factors. So, for instance, cultivating a small orchard does not justify owning all the fruits of a continent. Importantly, what counts as a fair reward also depends on the scarcity of various resources, especially the scarcity of resources necessary to meet basic needs; who needs access to these essential resources; and how fierce competition for such resources is. So, although the laborer has a justified claim to a suitable reward for her labor, it is not clear how an appropriate reward for the labor could be an *unconditional right* to the water hole, that is, the unconditional right to banish others from any use of the water hole. Why not?

The process of initial acquisition of property rights involves two important elements: "the unowned stuff" and "the taking of" or "the laboring to get" (the unowned stuff). I fully concede that the laboring to get can be an appropriate desert basis. However, what must be explained is not how the labor is to deserve something, but rather how the taking of unowned stuff is to be permissible. Any taking of unowned stuff that leaves others destitute cannot count as a permissible taking of unowned stuff on any account of defensible initial acquisition (labor-based or otherwise). Any acceptable criterion for defensible taking of unowned stuff must take into account who else needs access to that stuff. No account of legitimate initial acquisition (that had any pretensions to defensibility) could allow some to seize and monopolize property, thereby rendering others' survival impossible, no matter what sorts of appropriating activities usually give rise to property rights. And so, because constraints on initial acquisition permanently track property rights, no account of property rights, more generally, that had any pretensions to defensibility could allow some to have unconditional rights to property in cases where others' survival is not only endangered but rendered impossible.[13]

So, in response to the "but some have *labored*" objection, we have seen that laboring to produce the scarce resources may, in general, give one a strong justified claim to *some* reward, but what counts as an appropriate reward is highly subject to others' predicament. People's being in a situation of need is exactly the sort of consideration that can change the defensibility of property rights (and this seems to be the case whether those rights were acquired through labor or some other way). The "but some have *labored*" objection does not, then, have the sort of force objectors may think it has.[14]

Some Important Implications of the Argument

As I have argued, when property is redistributed to assist in certain cases of meeting others' needs, it is not necessarily an unjust interference with our rights, as libertarians insist. The kinds of cases under which property rights are justified and the nature of the rights that are thereby accorded are not sufficient to render property rights immune from the sorts of claims others' needs can make on such rights. As I argued, property rights are defensible only when certain conditions are met, and these rights retain their defensibility only while the conditions continue to be met. Indeed, the justifiability of retaining any property rights depends on accepting these inherent limitations. If property rights are only justified when they adequately take into account relevant conditions such as people's predicament of need, not only during the process of initial acquisition but all the while property rights retain their defensibility, then it is clear that others' needs already play a role in circumscribing the property rights that can defensibly be accorded. The property right is defensible and retains its defensibility only when it permanently takes account of relevant constraining conditions, such as others' need. So, far from people's needs constituting an unjust demand on others' property rights, accommodating others' needs plays a crucial role in the justification for having any defensible property rights at all.

Clearly, then, the libertarian thesis that any redistribution to meet needs is unjust is false. Redistribution to help those in need is not necessarily unjust. Quite the contrary: it is frequently a necessary condition for our retaining any defensible property rights at all. Those who claim defensible property rights must recognize a fundamental commitment to helping those in need. If only these conceptual points are conceded, the argument presented here does valuable work. After all, conceding these points flies in the face of crucial libertarian beliefs.

But let me try to go further. How far can the argument be pressed? How extensive is the range of needs for which redistribution is permissible? The argument works for people's most basic physical needs: adequate sustenance (food and water) and protection from the elements where necessary (minimal clothing and shelter), since these are clearly the sorts of resources at issue in the desert island thought experiments. But can the argument presented here justify redistribution to meet any other needs widely held to be basic, such as needs for health care and education? I gesture towards one line of argument that it can.

On one paraphrase of the main argument, taking resources is permissible so long as you leave enough for others to meet their own needs (that is, you leave enough for others to make their own way in meeting their own needs). So, your property rights are justified (initially and permanently) so long as you leave enough for others to meet their own needs. Perhaps this is unproblematically equivalent to, your property rights are justified (initially and permanently) so long as you leave enough for others to meet their own needs or provide the means (or necessary conditions) for others to meet their needs. In contemporary society the "leaving enough for others to meet their own needs" does not seem to be a viable option. So it seems that if property rights are to be defensible, we must supply the necessary conditions for others to make their own way in meeting their own needs. Since enjoying a certain minimal level of education and health is such a necessary condition for others to meet their needs in contemporary society, these are the sorts of needs for which redistribution is also justified.[15] Indeed, it seems that the argument presented here can be used to justify meeting a fairly robust range of needs: perhaps any and all those kinds of needs whose satisfaction is necessary for others to make their own way in meeting their own needs themselves.

Notes

This article originally appeared in *Analysis* 55, no. 1 (January 1995): 50–60. I would particularly like to thank Michael Ferejohn, Geoffrey Sayre-McCord, Peter Smith, and an anonymous reviewer for *Analysis* for helpful comments on earlier drafts of this chapter.

1. See, e.g., John Hospers, "The Nature of the State," *Personalist* 59, no. 4 (October 1978): 398–404; and Robert Nozick, *Anarchy, State, and Utopia* (New York: Basic Books, 1977).

2. See, e.g., Nozick, *Anarchy, State, and Utopia*. Quotations are from ix, 168, 169.

3. I use the more general term "property" to refer to all of this (wealth, income, earnings, holdings, etc.) from now on.

4. In fact, an appeal to some version of Locke's labor-based argument seems to be the point of departure for most libertarian justifications for property rights. See, e.g., Nozick, *Anarchy, State, and Utopia*, 167–82; and Hospers, "Nature of the State," 398–99.

5. Nozick, *Anarchy, State, and Utopia*, 174–75.

6. Nozick, *Anarchy, State, and Utopia*, 175–76.

7. Nozick modifies the Lockean proviso to something like this: "A process normally giving rise to a permanent bequeathable property right in a previously unowned thing will not do so if the position of others no longer at liberty to use the thing is thereby worsened" (*Anarchy, State, and Utopia*, 178). Nozick's modified proviso still faces the formidable problem of clarifying what constitutes worsening someone's position. My view is that granting property rights that would result in people's being made to suffer a loss with respect to their need satisfaction, or granting property rights that thereby mean that people are worse off with respect to the satisfaction of their needs, seems to be exactly the sort of case in which people's position is importantly worsened. I develop this argument and its implications more generally in this section.

8. Nozick, *Anarchy, State, and Utopia*, 180.

9. Though Nozick recognizes the kinds of cases outlined in the cited passage as running afoul of the Lockean proviso and so legitimately curtailing or overriding property rights, he does not believe that the scope of these kinds of cases is very large. He believes that the free operation of a market system will not in general run afoul of the Lockean proviso (*Anarchy, State, and Utopia*, 182). It seems likely that Nozick grossly underestimates the number and range of situations in which the free operation of a market system would actually run afoul of the Lockean proviso.

10. Lawrence Becker and Stephen Munzer, for instance, argue this in more detail. See Lawrence Becker, "Property and Social Welfare," in *Economic Justice,* ed. Kenneth Kipnis and Diana Meyers (Totowa, N.J.: Rowman & Allanheld, 1985), 71–86; and Stephen Munzer, *A Theory of Property* (New York: Cambridge University Press, 1990).

11. Even the fiercest libertarians acknowledge this (at least in principle). As Nozick concedes, it would not be acceptable to appropriate the only well with drinkable water or the only piece of land in the middle of the ocean if this would deny others exactly what would meet a fundamental need necessary to sustain life.

12. For those who claim 'hat no unfairness would be involved, the burden of proof is on them to show how this could be the case or to show how such accounts of property acquisition can be defensible.

13. In *The Right to Private Property* (Oxford: Clarendon Press, 1988), Jeremy Waldron makes a contractarian argument that closely parallels this part of the argument. My argument is more general than the one presented by Waldron and seeks to be persuasive to contractarians and noncontractarians alike. Waldron's argument would seem to have little grip with noncontractarians. I think there are other avertable sticking points for Waldron, e.g., Waldron's argument turns crucially on what could be rationally agreed to. What it can be rational to agree to can vary with different starting assumptions. So, for instance, if the risk of being destitute is sufficiently small, it might be rational (some might plausibly argue) to agree to certain kinds of Principles of Justified Acquisition that threaten and thwart others' needs, so long as one can be sure one will never be in such a situation.

14. I press the same general argument as the one presented in this section in my "Meeting Needs and Business Obligations: A Response to the Libertarian Skeptic,"

Journal of Business Ethics 15, no. 6 (June 1996): 695–702. (In that article I look at why businesses have obligations to help with needs of various kinds. The argument developed there is designed to be particularly devastating to libertarian views on businesses' social obligations.)

15. To state the obvious, most jobs require a minimal level of education, and minimal health care is required so that one is physically able to do one's job adequately.

Just how much education or health care does the argument justify? More generally, exactly how much assistance with needs does this argument justify? I think the "how much" question must ultimately be resolved in particular communities depending on resources, and this is as one should expect. As we saw in the desert island thought experiments, how much one should leave for others to meet their needs is very much determined by how scarce resources are, what others need, how fierce competition for resources is, and so forth. So, how much assistance one should offer with needs will be similarly variable.

10

From Liberty to Universal Welfare

James P. Sterba

Libertarians like to think of themselves as defenders of liberty. F. A. Hayek, for example, sees his work as restating an ideal of liberty for our times. "We are concerned," says Hayek, "with that condition of men in which coercion of some by others is reduced as much as possible in society."[1] Similarly, John Hospers believes that libertarianism is "a philosophy of personal liberty—the liberty of each person to live according to his own choices, provided that he does not attempt to coerce others and thus prevent them from living according to their choices."[2] And Robert Nozick claims that if a conception of justice goes beyond libertarian "side-constraints," it cannot avoid the prospect of continually interfering with people's lives.

Libertarians have interpreted their ideal of liberty in basically two different ways. Some libertarians, following Herbert Spencer, have (1) taken a right to liberty as basic and (2) derived all other rights from this right to liberty. Other libertarians, following John Locke, have (1) taken a set of rights, including typically a right to life and a right to property, as basic and (2) defined liberty as the absence of constraints in the exercise of these rights. Now both groups of libertarians regard liberty as the ultimate political ideal, but they do so for different reasons. For Spencerian libertarians, liberty is the ultimate political ideal because all other rights are derived from a right to liberty. For Lockean libertarians, liberty is the ultimate political ideal because liberty just is the absence of constraints in the exercise of people's fundamental rights.

One could, of course, develop the libertarian view in directions that libertarians are happy to go. For example, one could derive a range of nonpaternalistic policies, including the legalization of drugs, from a libertarian foundation. Unfortunately, developing libertarianism in such directions would do little to reconcile the differences between libertarians and welfare liberals over the provision of welfare and equal opportunity, given that libertarians think that their own ideal requires the rejection of rights to welfare and equal opportunity while welfare liberals endorse these rights as basic requirements of their ideals. Accordingly, I propose to develop the libertarian view in a direction that libertarians have yet to recognize by showing that the ideal requires the same rights to welfare and equal opportunity that are defended by welfare liberals.

Spencerian and Lockean Libertarians

Let us begin by considering the view of Spencerian libertarians, who take a right to liberty to be basic and define all other rights in terms of this right to liberty. According to this view, liberty is usually interpreted as being unconstrained by other persons from doing what one wants or is able to do. Interpreting liberty this way, libertarians like to limit constraints to positive acts (that is, acts of commission) that prevent people from doing what they otherwise want or are able to do. By contrast, welfare liberals and socialists interpret constraints to include, in addition, negative acts (acts of omission) that prevent people from doing what they otherwise want or are able to do. In fact, this is one way to understand the debate between defenders of "negative liberty" and defenders of "positive liberty." This is because defenders of negative liberty interpret constraints to include only positive acts of others that prevent people from doing what they otherwise want or are able to do, while defenders of positive liberty interpret constraints to include both positive and negative acts of others that prevent people from doing what they otherwise want or are able to do.

In order not to beg the question against libertarians, suppose we interpret constraints in the manner favored by libertarians to include only positive acts by others that prevent people from doing what they otherwise want or are able to do. Libertarians go on to characterize their political ideal as requiring that each person should have the greatest amount of liberty commensurate with the same liberty for all.[3] From this ideal, libertarians claim that a number of more specific requirements, in particular a right to life; a right to freedom of speech, press, and assembly; and a right to property can be derived.

Here it is important to observe that the libertarian's right to life is not a right to receive from others the goods and resources necessary for preserving one's life. It is not a right to welfare: it is simply a right not to be killed unjustly. Correspondingly, the libertarian's right to property is not a right to receive from others the goods and resources necessary to meet one's basic needs but, rather, a right to acquire goods and resources either by initial acquisitions or by voluntary agreements.

Of course, libertarians would allow that it would be nice of the rich to share their surplus goods and resources with the poor. Nevertheless, libertarians deny that government has a duty to provide for such needs. Some good things, such as the provision of welfare to the needy, are requirements of charity rather than justice, libertarians claim. Accordingly, failure to make such provisions is neither blameworthy nor punishable. As a consequence, libertarians contend that such acts of charity should not be coercively required. For this reason, libertarians are opposed to any coercively supported welfare program.

For a similar reason, libertarians are opposed to coercively supported equal opportunity programs. This is because the basic opportunities one has under a libertarian conception of justice are primarily a function of the property one controls, and, since unequal property distributions are taken to be justified under a libertarian conception of justice, unequal basic opportunities are also regarded as justified.

The same opposition to coercively supported welfare and equal opportunity programs characterizes Lockean libertarians, who take a set of rights, typically including a right to life and a right to property, as basic and then interpret liberty as being unconstrained by other persons from doing what one has a right to do. Understanding a right to life and a right to property the same way that Spencerians do, Lockean libertarians also reject both coercively supported welfare programs and equal opportunity programs as violations of liberty.

Spencerian Libertarians and the Problem of Conflict

To evaluate the libertarian view, let us begin with the ideal of liberty as defended by Spencerian libertarians and consider a typical conflict situation between the rich and the poor. In this situation, the rich have more than enough goods and resources to satisfy their basic needs.[4] By contrast, the poor lack the goods and resources to meet their most basic needs, even though they have tried all the means available to them that Spencerian libertarians regard as legitimate for acquiring such goods and resources. Under circumstances like these, libertarians usually maintain that the rich should have the liberty to use their goods and resources to satisfy their luxury needs if they so wish. Spencerian libertarians recognize that this liberty might well be enjoyed at the expense of the satisfaction of the most basic needs of the poor; they just think that liberty always has priority over other political ideals, and since they assume that the liberty of the poor is not at stake in such conflict situations, it is easy for them to conclude that the rich should not be required to sacrifice their liberty so that the basic needs of the poor may be met.

Of course, Spencerian libertarians allow that it would be nice of the rich to share their surplus goods and resources with the poor, just as Milton Friedman would allow that it would be nice of you to share the hundred dollars you found with your friends, and nice of the rich-islanded Robinson Crusoe to share his resources with the poor-islanded Robinson Crusoes. Nevertheless, according to Spencerian libertarians, such acts of charity cannot be required because the liberty of the poor is not thought to be at stake in such conflict situations.

In fact, however, the liberty of the poor is at stake in such conflict situations. What is at stake is the liberty of the poor not to be interfered with in taking from the surplus possessions of the rich what is necessary to satisfy their basic needs.[5]

Needless to say, Spencerian libertarians would want to deny that the poor have this liberty. But how could they justify such a denial? As this liberty of the poor has been specified, it is not a positive right to receive something but a negative right of noninterference. Nor will it do for Spencerian libertarians to appeal to a right to life or a right to property to rule out such a liberty, because on the Spencerian view, liberty is basic and all other rights are derived from a right to liberty. Clearly, what Spencerian libertarians must do is recognize the existence of such a liberty and then claim that it conflicts with other liberties of the rich. But when Spencerian libertarians see that this is the case, they are often genuinely surprised—one might even say rudely awakened—for they had not previously seen the conflict between the rich and the poor as a conflict of liberties.[6]

When the conflict between the rich and the poor is viewed as a conflict of liberties, either we can say that the rich should have the liberty not to be interfered with in using their surplus goods and resources for luxury purposes or we can say that the poor should have the liberty not to be interfered with in taking from the rich what they require to meet their basic needs. If we choose one liberty, we must reject the other. What needs to be determined, therefore, is which liberty is morally preferable: the liberty of the rich or the liberty of the poor.

Two Principles

In order to see that the liberty of the poor not to be interfered with in taking from the surplus resources of the rich what is required to meet their basic needs is morally preferable to the liberty of the rich not to be interfered with in using their surplus goods and resources for luxury purposes, we need to appeal to one of the most fundamental principles of morality, one that is common to all political perspectives. This is:

> The *"Ought" Implies "Can" Principle:* People are not morally required to do what they lack the power to do or what would involve so great a sacri-

fice that it would be unreasonable to ask them to perform such an action, and/or in the case of severe conflicts of interest, unreasonable to require them to perform such an action.[7]

For example, suppose I promised to attend a departmental meeting on Friday, but on Thursday I am involved in a serious car accident that leaves me in a coma. Surely, it is no longer the case that I ought to attend the meeting now that I lack the power to do so. Or suppose instead that on Thursday I develop a severe case of pneumonia for which I am hospitalized. Surely, I could legitimately claim that I cannot attend the meeting, on the grounds that the risk to my health involved in attending is a sacrifice that it would be unreasonable to ask me to bear. Or suppose the risk to my health from having pneumonia is not so serious that it would be unreasonable to ask me to attend the meeting (a supererogatory request), it might still be serious enough to be unreasonable to require my attendance at the meeting (a demand that is backed up by blame or coercion).

What is distinctive about this formulation of the "ought" implies "can" principle is that it claims that the requirements of morality cannot, all things considered, be unreasonable to ask, and/or in cases of severe conflict of interest, unreasonable to require people to abide by. The principle claims that reason and morality must be linked in an appropriate way, especially if we are going to be able justifiably to use blame or coercion to get people to abide by the requirements of morality. It should be noted, however, that although major figures in the history of philosophy and most philosophers today, including virtually all libertarian philosophers, accept this linkage between reason and morality, this linkage is not usually conceived to be part of the "ought" implies "can" principle.[8] Nevertheless, I claim that there are good reasons for associating this linkage with the principle, namely, our use of the word "can" as in the example just given and the natural progression from logical, physical, and psychological possibility found in the traditional "ought" implies "can" principle to the notion of moral possibility found in this formulation of the principle. In any case, the acceptability of this formulation of the "ought" implies "can" principle is determined by the virtually universal acceptance of its components and not by the manner in which I have proposed to join those components together.[9]

Now applying the "ought" implies "can" principle to the case at hand, it seems clear that the poor have it within their power willingly to relinquish such an important liberty as the liberty not to be interfered with in taking from the rich what they require to meet their basic needs. Nevertheless, it would be unreasonable to ask or require them to make so great a sacrifice. In the extreme case, it would involve asking or requiring the poor to sit back and starve to death. Of course, the poor may have no real alternative to relinquishing this liberty. To do anything else may involve worse consequences for themselves and their loved ones and may invite a painful death. Accordingly, we may expect that the poor would acquiesce, albeit unwillingly, to a political system that denies them the right to welfare supported by such a liberty, at the same time that we recognize that such a system imposes an unreasonable sacrifice upon the poor—a sacrifice that we cannot morally blame the poor for trying to evade.[10] Analogously, we might expect that a woman whose life was threatened would submit to a rapist's demands, at the same time that we recognize the utter unreasonableness of those demands.

By contrast, it would not be unreasonable to ask and require the rich to sacrifice the liberty to meet some of their luxury needs so that the poor can have the liberty to meet their basic needs.[11] Naturally, we might expect that the rich, for reasons of self-interest and past contribution, might be disinclined to make such a sacrifice. We might even suppose that the past contribution of the rich provides a good reason for not sacrificing their liberty to use their surplus for luxury purposes. Yet, unlike the poor, the rich could not claim that relinquishing such a liberty would involve so great a sacrifice that it would be unreasonable to ask and require them to make it; unlike the poor, the rich could be morally blameworthy for failing to make such a sacrifice.

Notice that by virtue of the "ought" implies "can" principle, this argument establishes that:

1. (a) Because it would be unreasonable to ask or require the poor to sacrifice the liberty not to be interfered with when taking from the surplus goods and resources of the rich what is necessary to meet their basic needs, (b) it is not the case that the poor are morally required to make such a sacrifice.

2. (a) Because it would not be unreasonable to ask and require the rich to sacrifice the liberty not to be interfered with when using their surplus goods and resources for luxury purposes, (b) it may be the case that the rich are morally required to make such a sacrifice.

What the argument does not establish is that it is the case that the rich are *morally required* to sacrifice (some of) their surplus so that the basic needs of the poor can be met. To establish that conclusion clearly, we need to appeal to a principle, which is, in fact, simply the contrapositive of the "ought" implies "can" principle. It is:

The Conflict Resolution Principle: What people are morally required to do is what is either reasonable to ask them to do, or in the case of severe conflicts of interest, reasonable to require them to do.

While the "ought" implies "can" principle claims that if any action is *not reasonable to ask or require* a person to do, all things considered, that action is *not morally required* for that person, all things considered [-R(A v Re) → -MRe], the conflict resolution principle claims that if any action is *morally required* for a person to do, all things considered, that action is *reasonable to ask or require* that person to do, all things considered [MRe → R(A v Re)].

This conflict resolution principle accords with the generally accepted view of morality as a system of reasons for resolving interpersonal conflicts of interest. Of course, morality is not limited to such a system of reasons. Most surely it also includes reasons of self-development. All that is being claimed by the principle is that moral resolutions of interpersonal conflicts of interest cannot be contrary to reason to ask everyone affected to accept or, in the case of severe interpersonal conflicts of interest, unreasonable to require everyone affected to accept. The reasons for the distinction between the two kinds of cases is that when interpersonal conflicts of interest are not severe, moral resolutions must still be reasonable to ask everyone affected to accept, but they need not be reasonable to *require* everyone affected to accept. This is because not all moral resolutions can be justifiably enforced; only moral resolutions of severe interpersonal conflicts of interest can and *should* be justifiably enforced. Furthermore, the reason why moral resolutions of severe interpersonal conflicts of interest should be enforced is that if the parties are simply asked but not required to abide by a moral resolution in such cases of conflict, then it is likely that the stronger party will violate the resolution, and that would be unreasonable to ask or require the weaker party to accept.[12]

When we apply the conflict resolution principle to our example of severe conflict between the rich and the poor, there are three possible moral resolutions:

I. a moral resolution that would require the rich to sacrifice the liberty not to be interfered with when using their surplus goods and resources for luxury purposes so that the poor can have the liberty not to be interfered with when taking from the surplus resources of the rich what is necessary to meet their basic needs

II. a moral resolution that would require the poor to sacrifice the liberty not to be interfered with when taking from the surplus goods and resources of the rich what is necessary to meet their basic needs so that the rich can have the liberty not to be interfered with when using their surplus resources for luxury purposes

III. a moral resolution that would require the rich and the poor to accept the results of a power struggle in which both the rich and the poor are at liberty to appropriate and use the surplus goods and resources of the rich

Applying our previous discussion of the "ought" implies "can" principle to these three possible moral resolutions, it is clear that (1a) (it would be unreasonable to ask or require the poor . . .) rules out (II), but (2a) (it would not be unreasonable to ask and require the rich . . .) does not rule out (I). But what about (III)? Some libertarians have contended that (III) is the proper resolution of severe conflicts of interest between the rich and the poor.[13] But a resolution, like (III), that sanctions the results of a power struggle between the rich and the poor is a resolution that, by and large, favors the rich over the poor. So all things considered, it would be no more reasonable to require the poor to accept (III) than it would be to require them to accept (II). This means that only (I) satisfies the conflict resolution principle by being a resolution that is reasonable to require everyone affected to accept. Consequently, if we assume that however else we specify the requirements of morality, they cannot violate the "ought" implies "can" principle or the conflict resolution principle, it follows that despite what Spencerian libertarians claim, the basic right to liberty endorsed by them, as determined by a weighing of the relevant competing liberties according to these two principles, actually favors the liberty of the poor over the liberty of the rich.[14]

Yet couldn't Spencerian libertarians object to this conclusion, claiming that it would be unreasonable to require the rich to sacrifice the liberty to meet some of their luxury needs so that the poor could have the liberty to meet their basic needs? As has been pointed out, libertarians don't usually see the situation as a conflict of liberties, but suppose they did. How plausible would such an objection be? Not very plausible at all.

Consider: What are Spencerian libertarians going to say about the poor? Isn't it clearly unreasonable to require the poor to sacrifice the liberty to meet their basic needs so that the rich can have the liberty to meet their luxury needs? Isn't it clearly unreasonable to require the poor to sit back and starve to death? If it is, then there is no resolution of this conflict that would be reasonable to require both the rich and the poor to accept. But that would mean that libertarians could not be putting forth a moral resolution, because according to the conflict resolution principle, a moral resolution resolves severe conflicts of interest in ways that it would be reasonable to require everyone affected to accept. Therefore, as long as libertarians think of themselves as putting forth a moral resolution for cases of severe conflict of interest, they cannot allow that it would be unreasonable *both* to require the rich to sacrifice the liberty to meet some of their luxury needs in order to benefit the poor and to require the poor to sacrifice the liberty to meet their basic needs in order to benefit the rich. But I submit that if one of these requirements is to be judged reasonable, then, by any neutral assessment, it must be the requirement that the rich sacrifice the liberty to meet some of their luxury needs so that the poor can have the liberty to meet their basic needs. There is no other plausible resolution if libertarians intend to be putting forth a moral resolution.[15]

It should also be noted that this case for restricting the liberty of the rich depends upon the willingness of the poor to take advantage of whatever opportunities are available to them to engage in mutually beneficial work, so that failure of the poor to take advantage of such opportunities would normally cancel or at least significantly reduce the obligation of the rich to restrict their own liberty for the benefit of the poor.[16] In addition, the poor would be required to return the equivalent of any surplus possessions they have taken from the rich once they are able to do so and still satisfy their basic needs. Nor would the poor be required to keep the liberty to which they are entitled. They could give up part of it, or all of it, or risk losing it on the chance of gaining a greater share of liberties or other social goods.[17] Consequently, the case for restricting the liberty of the rich for the benefit of the poor is neither unconditional nor inalienable.

Of course, there will be cases in which the poor fail to satisfy their basic needs, not because of any direct restriction of liberty on the part of the rich, but because the poor are in such dire need that they are unable even to attempt to take from the rich what they require to meet their basic needs. In such cases, the rich would not be performing any act of commission that would prevent the poor from taking what they require. Yet, even in such cases, the rich would normally be performing acts of commission that would prevent other persons from taking part in the rich's own surplus possessions and using it to aid the poor. And when assessed from a moral point of view, restricting the liberty of these allies or agents of the poor would not be morally justified for the very same reason that restricting the liberty of the poor to meet their own basic needs would not be morally justified: It would not be reasonable to require all of those affected to accept such a restriction of liberty.

The Benefit of the Poor

Nevertheless, Spencerian libertarians might respond that even assuming a right to welfare could be morally justified on the basis of the liberty of the poor not to be interfered with when taking from the rich in order to meet their basic needs and the liberty of third parties not to be interfered with when taking from the rich to provide for the basic needs of the poor, the poor still would be better off without the enforcement of such a right.[18] For example, it might be argued that when people are not forced through taxation to support a right to welfare, they are both more productive, since they are able to keep more of what they produce, and more charitable, since they tend to give more freely to those in need when they are not forced to do so. As a result, so the argument goes, the poor would benefit more from the increased charity of a libertarian society than they would from the guaranteed minimum of a welfare state.

Yet surely it is difficult to comprehend how the poor could be better off in a libertarian society, assuming, as seems likely, that they would experience a considerable loss of self-respect once they had to depend upon the uncertainties of charity for the satisfaction of their basic needs without the protection of a guaranteed minimum. It is also difficult to comprehend how people who are presently so opposed to a guaranteed minimum would turn out to be so charitable to the poor in a libertarian society.

Moreover, in a libertarian society, providing for the needs of the poor would involve an impossible coordination problem. For if the duty to help the poor is at best supererogatory, as libertarians claim, then no one can legitimately force anyone who does not consent to provide help. The will of the majority on this issue could not legitimately be imposed upon dissenters.[19] Assuming then that providing for the needs of the poor requires coordinated action on a broad front, such coordination could not be achieved in a libertarian society because it would first require a near unanimous agreement of all its members.[20]

Nevertheless, it might still be argued that the greater productivity of the more talented people in a libertarian society would provide increased employment opportunities and increased voluntary welfare assistance that would benefit the poor more than a guaranteed minimum would in a welfare state. But this simply could not occur. For if the more talented members of a society provided sufficient employment opportunities and voluntary welfare assistance to enable the poor to meet their basic needs, then the conditions for invoking a right to a guaranteed minimum in a welfare state would not arise, since the poor are first required to take advantage of whatever employment opportunities and voluntary welfare assistance are available to them before they can legitimately invoke such a right. Consequently, when *sufficient* employment opportunities and voluntary welfare assistance obtain, there would be no practical difference in this regard between a libertarian society and a welfare state, since neither would justify invoking a right to a guaranteed minimum. Only when *insufficient* employment opportunities and voluntary welfare assistance obtain would there be a practical difference between a libertarian society and a welfare state, and then it would clearly benefit the poor to be able to invoke the right to a guaranteed minimum in a welfare state. Consequently, given the conditional nature of the right to welfare and the practical possibility— and in most cases, the actuality—of insufficient employment opportunities and voluntary welfare assistance obtaining, there is no reason to think that the poor would be better off without the enforcement of such a right.[21]

In brief, if a right to liberty is taken to be basic, then, contrary to what Spencerian libertarians claim, not only would a right to welfare be morally required but also such a right would clearly benefit the poor.

Lockean Libertarians and the Problem of Conflict

Let us now consider whether these same conclusions can be established against Lockean libertarians, who take a set of rights, typically including a right to life and a right to property, as basic and then interpret liberty as being unconstrained by other persons from doing what one has a right to do. According to this view, a right to life is understood as a right not to be killed unjustly, and a right to property is understood as a right to acquire goods and resources either by initial acquisition or by voluntary agreement. In order to evaluate this view, we must determine what is entailed by these rights.

Presumably, a right to life understood as a right not to be killed unjustly would not be violated by defensive measures designed to protect one's person from life-threatening attacks.[22] Yet would this right be violated when the rich prevent the poor from taking what they require to satisfy their basic needs? Obviously, as a consequence of such preventive actions, poor people sometimes do starve to death. Have the rich, then, in contributing to this result, killed the poor, or have they simply let them die; and, if they have killed the poor, have they done so unjustly?

Sometimes the rich, in preventing the poor from taking what they require to meet their basic needs, would not in fact be killing the poor but would only be causing them to be physically or mentally debilitated. Yet since such preventive acts involve resisting the life-preserving activities of the poor, when the poor do die as a consequence of such acts, it seems clear that the rich would be killing the poor, whether intentionally or unintentionally.[23]

Of course, libertarians would want to argue that such killing is simply a consequence of the legitimate exercise of property rights and, hence, not unjust. But to understand why libertarians are mistaken in this regard, let us appeal again to those fundamental principles of morality, the "ought" implies "can" principle and the conflict resolution principle. In this context, these principles can be used to assess two opposing accounts of property rights. According to the first account, a right to property is not conditional upon whether other persons have sufficient opportunities and resources to satisfy their basic needs. This view holds that the initial acquisition and voluntary agreement of some can leave others, through no fault of their own, dependent upon charity for the satisfaction of their most basic needs. By contrast, according to the second account, initial acquisition and voluntary agreement can confer title of property on all goods and resources except those surplus goods and resources of the rich that are required to satisfy the basic needs of those poor who through no fault of their own lack opportunities and resources to satisfy their own basic needs.

Recall that there are two interpretations of the basic right to liberty on which the Spencerian view is grounded: one interpretation ignores the liberty of the poor not to be interfered with when taking from the surplus possessions of the rich what they require to meet their basic needs; the other gives that liberty priority over the liberty of the rich not to be interfered with when using their surplus for luxury purposes. Here too there are two interpretations of the right to property. The first regards the right to property as *not* conditional upon the resources and opportunities available to others, and the second regards the right to property as conditional upon the resources and opportunities available to others. And just as in the case of the Spencerian view, here we need to appeal to those fundamental principles of morality, the "ought" implies "can" principle and the conflict resolution principle, to decide which interpretation is morally acceptable.

It is clear that only the unconditional interpretation of property rights would generally justify the killing of the poor as a legitimate exercise of the property rights of the rich. Yet it would be unreasonable to require the poor to accept anything other than some version of the conditional interpretation of property rights. Moreover, according to the conditional interpretation, it does not matter whether the poor would actually die or would only be physically or mentally debilitated as a result of such acts of prevention. Either result would preclude property rights from arising. Of course, the poor may have no real alternative to acquiescing to a political system modeled after the unconditional interpretation of property rights, even though such a system imposes an unreasonable sacrifice upon them—a sacrifice that we could not blame them for trying to evade. At the same time, although the rich may be disinclined to do so, it would not be unreasonable to require them to accept a political system modeled after the conditional interpretation of property rights—the interpretation favored by the poor. Consequently, if we assume that, however else we specify the requirements of morality, they cannot violate the "ought" implies "can" principle and the conflict resolution principle, it follows that, despite what Lockean libertarians claim, the right to life and the right to property endorsed by them actually support a right to welfare.

Now it might be objected that the right to welfare that this argument establishes from libertarian premises is not the same as the right to welfare endorsed by welfare liberals and socialists. This is correct. We could mark this difference by referring to the right that this argument establishes as "a negative welfare right" and by referring to the right endorsed by welfare liberals and socialists as "a positive welfare right." The significance of this difference is that a person's negative welfare right can be violated only when other people through acts of commission interfere with its exercise, whereas a person's positive welfare right can be violated not only by such acts of commission but by acts of omission as well. Nonetheless, this difference will have little practical import, for in recognizing the legitimacy of negative welfare rights, libertarians will come to see that virtually any use of their surplus possessions is likely to violate the negative welfare rights of the poor by preventing the poor from rightfully appropriating (some part of) their surplus goods and resources. So in order to ensure that they will not be engaging in such wrongful actions, it will be incumbent on them to set up institutions guaranteeing adequate positive welfare rights for the poor. Only then will they be able to use legitimately any remaining surplus possessions to meet their own nonbasic needs. Furthermore, in the absence of adequate positive welfare rights, the poor, either acting by themselves or through their allies or agents, would have some discretion in determining when and how to exercise their negative welfare rights.[24] In order not to be subject to that discretion, libertarians will tend to favor the only morally legitimate way of preventing the exercise of such rights: they will set up institutions guaranteeing adequate positive welfare rights that will then take precedence over the exercise of negative welfare rights. For these reasons, recognizing the negative welfare rights of the poor will ultimately lead libertarians to endorse the same sort of welfare institutions favored by welfare liberals and socialists.[25]

Distant Peoples and Future Generations

Now it is possible that libertarians convinced to some extent by the above argument might want to accept a right to welfare for members of one's own society but then deny that this right extends to distant peoples and future generations. Since it is only recently that philosophers have begun to discuss the question of what rights distant peoples and future generations might legitimately claim against us, a generally acceptable way of discussing the question has yet to be developed. Some philosophers have even attempted to answer the question, or at least part of it, by arguing that talk about the rights of future generations is conceptually incoherent and thus analogous to talk about square circles. Thus Richard De George writes:

> The argument in favor of the principle that only existing entities have rights is straightforward and simple: Nonexistent entities by definition do not exist. What does not exist cannot be subject or bearer of anything. Hence, it cannot be the subject or bearer of rights.[26]

Accordingly, the key question that must be answered first is this: Can we meaningfully speak of distant peoples and future generations as having rights against us or of our having corresponding obligations to them?

Answering this question with respect to distant peoples is much easier than answering it with respect to future generations. Few philosophers have thought that the mere fact that people are at a distance from us precludes our having any obligations to them or their having any rights against us. Some philosophers, however, have argued that our ignorance of the specific membership of the class of distant peoples does rule out these moral relationships. Yet this cannot be right, given that in other contexts we recognize obligations to indeterminate classes of people, such as a police officer's obligation to help people in distress or the obligation of food producers not to harm those who consume their products.

Yet others have argued that while there may be valid moral claims respecting the welfare of distant peoples, such claims cannot be rights because they fail to hold against determinate individuals and groups.[27] But in what sense do such claims fail to hold against determinate individuals and groups? Surely all would agree that existing laws rarely specify the determinate individuals and groups against whom such claims hold. But morality is frequently determinate where existing laws are not. And at least there seems to be no conceptual impossibility to claiming that distant peoples have rights against us and that we have corresponding obligations to them.

Of course, before distant peoples can be said to have rights against us, we must be capable of acting across the distance that separates us. Yet as long as this condition is met—as it typically is for people living in most technologically advanced societies—it would certainly seem possible for distant peoples to have rights against us and for us to have corresponding obligations to them.

By contrast, answering the above question with respect to future generations is much more difficult and has been the subject of considerable debate among contemporary philosophers.

One issue concerns the referent of the term "future generations." Most philosophers seem to agree that the class of future generations is not "the class of all persons who simply *could* come into existence." But there is some disagreement concerning whether we should refer to the class of future generations as "the class of persons who will definitely come into existence, assuming that there are such" or as "the class of persons we can reasonably expect to come into existence." The first approach is more existential, specifying the class of future generations in terms of what will exist; the second approach is more epistemological, specifying the class of future generations in terms of our knowledge. Fortunately, there does not appear to be any practical moral significance to the choice of either approach.

Another issue relevant to whether we can meaningfully speak of future generations as having rights against us or our having obligations to them concerns whether it is logically coherent to speak of future generations as having rights now. Of course, no one who finds talk about rights to be generally meaningful should question whether we can coherently claim that future generations *will* have rights at some point in the future (specifically, when they come into existence and are no longer *future* generations). But what is questioned, since it is of considerable practical significance, is whether we can coherently claim that future generations have rights *now* when they don't yet exist.

Let us suppose, for example, that we continue to use up the earth's resources at present or even greater rates, and, as a result, it turns out that the most pessimistic forecasts for the twenty-second century are realized.[28] This means that future generations will face widespread famine, depleted resources, insufficient new technology to handle the crisis, and a drastic decline in the quality of life for nearly everyone. If this were to happen, could persons living in the twenty-second century legitimately claim that we in the twentieth century violated their rights by not restraining our consumption of the world's resources? Surely it would be odd to say that we violated their rights over one hundred years before they existed. But what exactly is the oddness?

Is it that future generations generally have no way of claiming their rights against existing generations? While this does make the recognition and enforcement of rights much more difficult (future generations would need strong advocates in the existing generations), it does not make it impossible for there to be such rights. After all, it is quite obvious that the recognition and enforcement of the rights of distant peoples is a difficult task as well.

Or is it that we don't believe that rights can legitimately exercise their influence over long durations of time? But if we can foresee and control at least some of the effects our actions will have on the ability of future generations to satisfy their basic needs, why should we not be responsible for those same effects? And if we are responsible for them, why should not future generations have a right that we take them into account?

Perhaps what troubles us is that future generations don't exist when their rights are said to demand action. But how else could persons have a right to benefit from the effects our actions will have in the distant future if they did not exist just when those effects would be felt? Our contemporaries cannot legitimately make the same demand, for they will not be around to experience those effects. Only future generations could have a right that the effects our actions will have in the distant future contribute to their well-being. Nor need we assume that in order for persons to have rights, they must exist when their rights demand action. Thus, to say that future generations have rights against existing generations, we can simply mean that there are enforceable requirements upon existing generations that would benefit or prevent harm to future generations.

Most likely what really bothers us is that we cannot know for sure what effects our actions will have on future generations. For example, we may at some cost to ourselves conserve resources that will be valueless to future generations who may develop different technologies. Or, because we regard them as useless, we may destroy or deplete resources that future generations will find to be essential to their well-being. Nevertheless, we should not allow such possibilities to blind us to the necessity for a social policy in this regard. After all, whatever we do will have its effect on future generations. The best approach, therefore, is to use the knowledge that we presently have and assume that future generations will also require those basic resources we now find to be valuable. If it turns out that future generations require different resources to meet their basic needs, at least we will not be blamable for acting on the basis of the knowledge we have.[29]

Notice too that present existence could not be a logical requirement for having rights now, for the simple reason that past people don't presently exist in our society, yet we continue to respect their rights, for example, through the enforcement of the terms of their wills. So if past people, who do not presently exist, can have rights against us, it should be possible for future people, who don't presently exist but who will exist in the future, to presently have rights against us. Hence, there is nothing logically incoherent in the possibility of future generations presently having rights against us.

Now once it is recognized that we can meaningfully speak of distant peoples and future generations as having rights against us and us as having corresponding obligations to them, there is no reason not to extend the argument for a right to welfare grounded on libertarian premises that I have developed in this chapter to distant peoples and future generations as well as to the members of our own society. This is because the argument is perfectly general and applies whenever serious conflicts of liberty arise between those who can have rights against us and us who can have corresponding obligations to them.

A Right to Equal Opportunity

Now it is possible that libertarians convinced to some extent by the above arguments might want to accept a right to welfare but then deny that there is a right to equal opportunity. Such a stance, however, is plausible only if we unjustifiably restrict the class of morally legitimate claimants to those within a given (affluent) society, for only then would a right to equal opportunity require something different from a right not to be discriminated against in filling roles and positions in society that follows from a right to welfare.[30] To see why this is the case, consider what is required by a right to welfare when the class of morally legitimate claimants is not unjustifiably restricted but is taken to include both distant peoples and future generations.

At present the worldwide supply of goods and resources is probably sufficient to meet the normal costs of satisfying the basic nutritional needs of all existing persons. According to former U.S. secretary of agriculture Bob Bergland, "[f]or the past 20 years, if the available world food supply had been evenly divided and distributed, each person would have received more than the minimum number of calories."[31] Other authorities have made similar assessments of the available world food supply.[32]

Accordingly, the adoption of a policy of supporting a right to welfare for all existing persons would necessitate significant changes, especially in developed countries. For example, the large percentage of the U.S. population whose food consumption clearly exceeds even an adequately adjusted poverty index may have to alter their eating habits substantially. In particular, they may have to reduce their consumption of beef and pork in order to make more grain available for direct human consumption. (Currently, 37 percent of worldwide production of grain and 70 percent of U.S. production is fed to animals.)[33]

Of course, it may be possible simply to produce more grain to feed people in need rather than redirecting the grain already produced from animal consumption to human consumption. But in order for this to be possible, we would have to have the capacity to increase grain production by around 30 percent (the amount currently fed to animals), and it is not clear that this capacity presently exists, given that the world grain harvest has grown more slowly than population since 1984 and has not grown at all since 1990.[34]

Moreover, there is reason to expect that as China with its population of 1.2 billion continues its rapid industrialization, it will soon, like other densely populated countries that have industrialized before it (namely, Japan, South Korea, and Taiwan) become a significant importer of grain. Japan, South Korea, and Taiwan have all moved from being largely self-sufficient to importing around 70 percent of the grain they consume, and Japan has become the world's largest importer of grain. So if China develops similarly, its demand for grain will tend to absorb whatever additional capacity there is in worldwide grain production.[35]

Yet even if there is still further capacity to increase grain production, someone would have to pay to actualize it. Obviously, the malnourished cannot pay for it or they would have already done so; the well-nourished would have to pay. Indeed, the well-nourished would have to divert some of the income they would have used to meet their nonbasic needs to pay for the increased grain production. And if the nonbasic needs that the well-nourished choose not to meet are their nonbasic needs for the pleasures of eating beef and pork, the resulting reduced demand for beef and pork would thereby lead to cutbacks in the amount of grain directed into beef and pork production. Of course, the well-nourished could cut back on their satisfaction of other nonbasic needs instead, and so not directly affect the production of beef and pork. But the negative impact of such cutbacks on the production of other nonbasic goods could still impact negatively on the production of beef and pork.

Nevertheless, whatever its exact impact on the production of beef and pork, there clearly is a need for redistribution here—the satisfaction of at least some of the nonbasic needs of the more advantaged in developed countries would have to be forgone if the basic nutritional needs of all those in developing and underdeveloped countries are to be met. Of course, meeting the long-term basic nutritional needs of these societies will require other kinds of aid, including appropriate technology and training and the removal of trade barriers favoring developed societies.[36] In addition, raising the standard of living in developing and underdeveloped countries will require a substantial increase in the consumption of energy and other resources. But such an increase would have to be matched by a substantial decrease in the consumption of these goods in developed countries; otherwise, global ecological disaster would result from increased global warming, ozone depletion, and acid rain, lowering virtually everyone's standard of living.[37] For example, some type of mutually beneficial arrangement needs to be negotiated with China, which, with 50 percent of the world's coal resources, plans to double its use of coal within the next two decades and is currently burning 85 percent of its coal without any pollution controls whatsoever.[38]

Furthermore, once the basic nutritional needs of future generations are taken into account, the satisfaction of the nonbasic needs of the more advantaged in developed countries would have to be further restricted in order to preserve the fertility of cropland and other food-related natural resources for the use of future generations. Obviously, the only assured way to guarantee the energy and resources necessary for the satisfaction of the basic needs of future generations is to set aside resources that would otherwise be used to satisfy the nonbasic needs of existing generations.

Once basic needs other than nutritional needs are taken into account as well, still further restrictions would be required. For example, it has been estimated that presently a North American uses about fifty times more goods and resources than a person living in India. This means that in terms of resource consumption the North American continent's population alone consumes as much as 12.5 billion.[39] So unless we assume that basic goods and resources, such as arable land, iron, coal, oil, and so forth, are in unlimited supply, this unequal consumption would have to be radically altered in order for the basic needs of distant peoples and future generations to be met.[40] Accordingly, recognizing a right to welfare applicable both to distant peoples and to future generations would lead to a state of affairs in which few resources are available for directly meeting nonbasic needs, and this significantly affects the right to equal opportunity that people can be guaranteed.[41]

Now the form of equal opportunity that John Rawls defends in *A Theory of Justice* requires that persons who have the same natural assets and the same willingness to use them have an equal chance to occupy roles and positions in society commensurate with their natural assets.[42] So construed, equal opportunity provides two sorts of benefits. It benefits society as a whole by helping to ensure that the most talented people will fill the most responsible roles and positions in society. It benefits individuals by ensuring that they will not be discriminated against with respect to filling the roles and positions in society for which they are qualified, thereby giving them a fair chance of securing whatever benefits attach to those roles and positions in society.

I have argued, however, that once it is recognized that the class of morally legitimate claimants includes distant peoples and future generations, then guaranteeing a right to welfare to all morally legitimate claimants would lead to a state of affairs in which few resources are available for directly meeting nonbasic needs, although such needs may still be met indirectly though the satisfaction of basic needs. As a consequence, there normally won't be greater benefits attaching to certain roles and positions in society, since people can expect only to have their basic needs directly met in whatever roles and positions they happen to occupy. Of course, we will still want the most talented people occupying the most responsible roles and positions in society; it is just that occupying those roles and positions will normally not secure greater benefits to those who occupy them. Therefore, to ensure that the most talented people occupy roles and positions that are commensurate with their abilities, we will need to do something like the following. First, borrowing an idea from socialist justice, we will need to make the roles and positions people occupy as intrinsically rewarding as possible. Second, we will need to convince the more talented that they have a moral responsibility to the less talented and to society as a whole to use their talents to the fullest. Consequently, the equal opportunity that will be guaranteed to everyone in society will, for the most part, be a fair means of ensuring that everyone's basic needs are met rather than a means of providing differential rewards or of directly serving to meet nonbasic needs.

Accordingly, my practical reconciliation argument fails to guarantee a right to equal opportunity that provides greater benefits to the talented, enabling them to directly meet nonbasic as well as basic needs. But the failure to guarantee this sort of equal opportunity is no objection to my argument, given that having this sort of equal opportunity is incompatible with the more fundamental requirement of meeting everyone's basic needs. On this account, both libertarians and welfare liberals would come to endorse the same right to equal opportunity—an equal right, compatible with a right to welfare, not to be discriminated against in filling roles and positions in society.

In brief, what I have argued is that a libertarian conception of justice supports the same rights to welfare and equal opportunity as those endorsed by a welfare liberal conception of justice.

Libertarian Objections

In his book *Individuals and Their Rights*, Tibor Machan criticizes the preceding argument that a libertarian ideal of liberty leads to a right to welfare, accepting its theoretical thrust but denying its practical significance.[43] He appreciates the force of the argument enough to grant that if the type of conflict cases that we have described between the rich and the poor actually obtained, the poor would have a right to welfare. But he denies that such cases—in which the poor have done all that they legitimately can to satisfy their basic needs in a libertarian society—actually obtain. "Normally," he writes, "persons do not lack the opportunities and resources to satisfy their basic needs."[44]

But this response virtually concedes everything that the preceding argument intended to establish, for the poor's right to welfare is not claimed to be unconditional. Rather, it is said to be conditional principally upon the poor's doing all that they legitimately can to meet their own basic needs. So it follows that only when the poor lack sufficient opportunity to satisfy their own basic needs would their right to welfare have any practical moral force. Accordingly, on libertarian grounds, Machan has conceded the legitimacy of just the kind of right to welfare that the preceding argument hoped to establish.

The only difference that remains is a practical one. Machan thinks that virtually all of the poor have sufficient opportunities and resources to satisfy their basic needs and that, therefore, a right to welfare has no practical moral force. In contrast, I think that many of the poor do not have sufficient opportunities and resources to satisfy their basic needs and that, therefore, a right to welfare has considerable practical moral force.

But isn't this practical disagreement resolvable? Who could deny that most of the 1.2 billion people who are currently living in conditions of absolute poverty "lack the opportunities and resources to satisfy their basic needs"?[45] And even within our own country, it is estimated that some 32 million Americans live below the official poverty index and that one-fifth of American children are growing up in poverty.[46] Surely, it is impossible to deny that many of these Americans also "lack the opportunities and resources to satisfy their basic needs." Given the impossibility of reasonably denying these factual claims, Machan would have to concede that the right to welfare, which he grants can be theoretically established on libertarian premises, also has practical moral force.[47]

Recently, however, Machan, seeking to undercut the practical force of my argument, has contended that when we compare economic systems to determine which produce more poverty, "no one can seriously dispute that the near-libertarian systems have fared much better than those going in the opposite direction, including the welfare state."[48] Here one would think that Machan has the United States in mind as a "near-libertarian system" because earlier in the same paragraph he claims, "America is still the freest of societies, with many of its legal principles giving expression to classical liberal, near-libertarian ideas."[49] Yet apparently this is not what Machan thinks, since in a footnote to the same text he says:

> It is notable that the statistics that Sterba cites [in my above response to Machan's critique] are drawn from societies, including the United States of America, which are far from libertarian in their legal construction and are far closer to the welfare state, if not to outright socialism.[50]

Obviously, then, Machan is surprisingly unclear as to whether he wants to call the United States a near-libertarian state, a welfare state, or a socialist state. Yet, whichever of these designations is most appropriate, what is clear is that the poor do less well in the United States than they do in the welfare liberal or socialist states of Western Europe such as Germany, Sweden, and Switzerland.[51] For example, 22.4 percent of children live below the poverty line in the U.S. as compared to 4.9 percent in Germany, 5 percent in Sweden, and 7.8 percent in Switzerland, and the United States shares with Italy the highest infant mortality rate of the major industrialized nations. The United States also ranks sixty-seventh among all nations in the percentage of national income received by the poorest 20 percent of its population, ranking the absolute lowest among industrialized nations.[52] Accordingly, the success that welfare liberal and socialist states have had, especially in Western Europe, in coming close to truly meeting the basic needs of their deserving poor should give us good reason to doubt what Machan proclaims is the superior practical effectiveness of "near-libertarian states" in dealing with poverty.

Douglas Rasmussen has developed another libertarian challenge to the previous argument that begins by conceding what Machan denied—that the poor lack the opportunity to satisfy their basic needs.[53] Rasmussen distinguishes two ways that this can occur. In one case, only a few of the poor lack the opportunity to satisfy their basic needs. Here, Rasmussen contends that libertarian property rights still apply even though the poor who are in need morally ought to take from the surplus property of the rich what they need for survival. Since libertarian property rights still apply, Rasmussen contends that the poor who do take from the legal property of the rich can be arrested and tried for their actions, but what their punishment should be, Rasmussen contends, should simply be left up to judges to decide.[54] Rasmussen also rejects the suggestion that the law should make an exception for the poor in such cases on the grounds that one can never have perfect symmetry between what is moral and what the law requires.[55]

But why should the question of punishment simply be left up to judges to decide? If the judicial proceedings determine what is assumed in this case—that the poor morally ought to take from the legal property of the rich what they need for survival—then it is difficult to see on what grounds a judge could inflict punishment. Surely, if it would be unreasonable to require the poor to do anything contrary to meeting their basic needs at minimal cost to the rich, it would be equally unreasonable to punish the poor for actually doing just that—meeting their basic needs at minimal cost to the rich.

Nor will it do to claim that we cannot expect symmetry between what morality requires and what the law requires in this case. Of course, there is no denying that sometimes the law can justifiably require us to do what is morally wrong. In such cases, opposing the law, even when what it requires is immoral, would do more harm than good. This can occur when there is a bona fide disagreement over whether what the law requires is morally wrong (for example, the *Roe v. Wade* decision), with those in favor of the law justifiably thinking that it is morally right and those against the law justifiably thinking that it is morally wrong. When this occurs, failing to obey the law, even when what it requires is immoral, could, by undermining the legal system, do more harm than good. However, in our case of severe conflict of interest between the rich and the poor, nothing of the sort obtains. In our case, it is judged that the poor morally ought to take from the legal property of the rich and that no other moral imperative favoring the rich overrides this moral imperative favoring the poor. So it is clear in this case that there are no grounds for upholding any asymmetry between what morality and the law require. Accordingly, the law in this case should be changed to favor the poor.

However, Rasmussen distinguishes another case in which many of the poor lack the opportunity to satisfy their basic needs.[56] In this case, so many of the poor lack the opportunity to satisfy their basic needs that Rasmussen claims that libertarian property rights no longer apply. Here Rasmussen contends that morality requires that the poor should take what they need for survival from the legal property of the rich and that the rich should not refuse assistance. Still Rasmussen contends that the poor have no right to assistance in this case, nor the rich presumably any corresponding obligation to help the poor, because "the situation cannot be judged in social and political terms."[57]

But why cannot the situation be judged in social and political terms? If we know what the moral directives of the rich and the poor are in this case, as Rasmussen admits that we do, why would we not be justified in setting up a legal system or altering an existing legal system so that the poor would have a guaranteed right to welfare? Now it may be that Rasmussen is imagining a situation where it is not possible for the basic needs of everyone to be met. Such situations are truly lifeboat cases. But while such cases are difficult to resolve (maybe only a chance mechanism would offer a reasonable resolution), they surely do not represent the typical conflict situation between the rich and the poor. For in such situations, it is recognized that it is possible to meet everyone's basic needs, and what is at issue is whether (some of) the nonbasic or luxury needs of the rich should be sacrificed so that everyone's basic needs can be met. So when dealing with typical conflict situations between the rich and the poor, there is no justification for not securing a legal system that reflects the moral directives in these cases.

In sum, both Machan's and Rasmussen's objections to grounding a right to welfare on libertarian premises have been answered. Machan's attempt to grant the theoretical validity of a libertarian right to welfare but then deny its practical validity fails once we recognize that there are many poor who lack the opportunities to satisfy their basic needs. Rasmussen's attempt to grant that there are poor who lack the opportunity to meet their basic needs but then deny that the poor have any right to welfare fails once we recognize that the moral directives that Rasmussen grants apply to the rich and the poor in severe conflict of interest cases provide ample justification for a right to welfare.

More recently, different objections to my attempt to derive a right to welfare from libertarian premises have been raised by John Hospers.[58] First, Hospers contends that I am committed to distributing welfare too broadly, to the undeserving poor as well as to the deserving poor. Second, Hospers contends that the taxes on the wealthy that I defend, in effect, commit me to killing the goose that lays the golden egg, because the poor would be worse off under a tax-supported welfare system than they would be in a completely libertarian society.

In response to the first objection Hospers raises, I have in a number of places made it clear that I am defending a right to welfare only for the deserving poor, that is, the poor who have exhausted all of their legitimate opportunities for meeting their basic needs. Hospers's second objection, however, questions whether even the deserving poor would be better off demanding welfare, even if they have a right to it. Hospers cites the example of Ernst Mahler, an entrepreneurial genius who employed more than one hundred thousand and produced newsprint and tissue products tnat are now used by more than two billion people. Hospers suggests that requiring Mahler to contribute to a welfare system for the deserving poor would not only "decrease his own wealth but that of countless other people."

In response to this objection, I contend that if the more talented members of a society provided sufficient employment opportunities and voluntary welfare assistance to enable the poor to meet their basic needs, then the conditions for invoking a right to welfare would not arise, since the poor are first required to take advantage of whatever employment opportunities and voluntary welfare assistance are available to them before they can legitimately invoke such a right. Consequently, when *sufficient* employment opportunities and voluntary welfare assistance obtain, there would be no practical difference in this regard between a libertarian society and a welfare or social state, since neither would justify invoking a right to welfare. Only when *insufficient* employment opportunities and voluntary welfare assistance obtain would there be a practical difference between a libertarian society and a welfare or socialist state, and then it would clearly benefit the poor to be able to invoke the right to welfare. Consequently, given the practical possibility, and in most cases the actuality, of insufficient employment opportunities and voluntary welfare assistance obtaining, there is no reason to think that the poor would be better off without the enforcement of such a right.

Now one might think that once the rich realize that the poor should have the liberty not to be interfered with when taking from the surplus possessions of the rich what they require to satisfy their basic needs, they should stop producing any surplus whatsoever. This appears to be what Hospers is suggesting by citing the example of Ernst Mahler. Yet it would be in the interest of the rich to stop producing a surplus only if (a) they did not enjoy producing a surplus, (b) their recognition of the rightful claims of the poor would exhaust their surplus, and (c) the poor would never be in a position to be obligated to repay what they appropriate from the rich. Fortunately for the poor, not all of these conditions are likely to obtain.[59] But suppose they all did. Wouldn't the poor be justified in appropriating, or threatening to appropriate, even the nonsurplus possessions of those who can produce more in order to get them to do so?[60] Surely this would not be an unreasonable imposition on those who can produce more, because it would not be unreasonable to require them to be a bit more productive when the alternative is requiring the poor to forgo meeting their basic needs. Surely if we have no alternative, requiring those who can produce more to be a bit more productive is less of an imposition than requiring the poor to forgo meeting their basic needs.

This is an important conclusion in our assessment of the libertarian ideal, because it shows that ultimately the right of the poor to appropriate what they require to meet their basic needs does not depend, as many have thought, upon the talented having sufficient self-interested incentives to produce a surplus. All that is necessary is that the talented can produce a surplus and that the (deserving) poor cannot meet their basic needs in any other way.

It might be objected, however, that if the talented can be required to produce a surplus so that the (deserving) poor can meet their basic needs, then the poor should be required to sterilize themselves as a condition for receiving that surplus. What the objection rightly points to is the need for the poor, and everyone else as well, to take steps to control population growth. What the objection wrongly maintains is that the poor would have a greater obligation to limit their procreation than the rich would have to limit theirs. Surely population can be brought under control by a uniform policy that imposes the same requirements on both rich and poor. There is no need or justification for a population policy that comes down harder on the poor.

Eric Mack raises still another objection to my libertarian argument for welfare.[61] Mack allows that my appeal to the "ought" implies "can" principles does show that in severe conflict of interest situations the rich do not have a right to their surplus. What Mack denies, however, is that I have shown that the poor in such situations have a right to the surplus of the rich. Mack contends that in these conflict situations neither the rich nor the poor have a right to the surplus of the rich. Instead, he thinks that both the rich and the poor are at liberty to appropriate and use the surplus if they can. Thus, what obtains in these conflict of interest situations, according to Mack, is a Hobbesian state of nature, a war of all against all.

There are two problems with Mack's analysis of these conflict situations between the rich and the poor. The first problem is that Mack's analysis denies the existence of property rights to a surplus whenever severe conflicts of interest between the rich and the poor obtain, without recognizing any alternative (welfare) rights as applicable in those circumstances. This means that property rights to a surplus would be justified only in those rare cases in which they equally served the interest of both the rich and the poor. In all other cases, no property rights to a surplus would be justified. But surely this is not the real-world justification of property rights that libertarians had promised.

The second problem with Mack's analysis is even more serious. It is that while Mack accepts the "ought" implies "can" principle, his own proposed moral resolution of severe conflict of interest situations violates that very principle. This is because his moral resolution of such situations requires the poor to accept the results of a power struggle in which both the rich and the poor are at liberty to appropriate and use the surplus resources of the rich insofar as they are able to do so. But obviously such a resolution favors the rich over the poor. Consequently, it would be no more reasonable to require the poor to accept this resolution than it would be reasonable to require them to accept the resolution that Mack concedes fails to satisfy the "ought" implies "can" principle—the resolution that secures for the rich property rights to their surplus. This implies that for severe conflict of interest situations only a resolution that guarantees the poor a right to welfare would satisfy the "ought" implies "can" principle.

Moreover, this is just the sort of resolution that the contrapositive of the "ought" implies "can" principle, which I call the conflict resolution principle, requires. This principle requires that moral resolutions of severe conflicts of interest must be reasonable to require everyone affected to accept. So in the severe conflict of interest situation we are considering, only a moral resolution that guarantees the poor a right to welfare would be reasonable for both the rich and the poor to accept. Thus, for such conflict situations, only a moral resolution that guarantees the poor a right to welfare would satisfy both the "ought" implies "can" principle and its contrapositive, the conflict resolution principle.

In sum, what I have argued is that a libertarian conception of justice supports the practical requirements that are usually associated with a welfare liberal conception of justice, namely, a right to welfare and a right to equal opportunity. I have also attempted to show that recent work done by libertarians Tibor Machan, Douglas Rasmussen, John Hospers, and Eric Mack neither undercuts nor is incompatible with this argument for reconciling these two conceptions of justice.[62]

Notes

1. F. A. Hayek, *The Constitution of Liberty* (Chicago: University of Chicago Press, 1960), 11.

2. John Hospers, *Libertarianism* (Los Angeles: Nash, 1971), 5.

3. See John Hospers, "The Libertarian Manifesto," in *Morality in Practice*, ed. James P. Sterba, 5th ed. (Belmont, Calif.: Wadsworth, 1997), 21.

4. Basic needs, if not satisfied, lead to significant lacks or deficiencies with respect to a standard of mental and physical well-being. Thus, a person's needs for food, shelter, medical care, protection, companionship, and self-development are, at least in part, needs of this sort. For a discussion of basic needs, see my *How to Make People Just*, (Totowa, N.J.: Rowman & Littlefield, 1988), 45–48.

5. It is not being assumed here that the surplus possessions of the rich are either

justifiably or unjustifiably possessed by the rich. Moreover, according to Spencerian libertarians, it is an assessment of the liberties involved that determines whether the possession is justifiable.

6. See Hospers, *Libertarianism*, chap. 7; and Tibor Machan, *Human Rights and Human Liberties* (Chicago: Nelson-Hall, 1975), 231 ff.

7. I first appealed to this interpretation of the "ought" implies "can" principle to bring libertarians around to the practical requirements of welfare liberalism in an expanded version of an article entitled "Neo-Libertarianism," which appeared in the fall of 1979 in my edited volume, *Justice: Alternative Political Perspectives* (Belmont, Calif.: Wadsworth, 1979), 172–86. In 1982, T. M. Scanlon, in "Contractualism and Utilitarianism" (in *Utilitarianism and Beyond*, ed. Amartya Sen and Bernard Williams [Cambridge: Cambridge University Press, 1982], 103–28), appealed to much the same standard to arbitrate the debate between contractarians and utilitarians. In my judgment, however, this standard embedded in the "ought" implies "can" principle can be more effectively used in the debate with libertarians than in the debate with utilitarians, because the sacrifices that libertarians standardly seek to impose on the less advantaged are more outrageous and, hence, more easily shown to be contrary to reason.

8. This linkage between morality and reason is expressed by the belief that (true) morality and (right) reason cannot conflict. Some supporters of this linkage have developed separate theories of rationality and reasonableness, contending, for example, that, while egoists are rational, those who are committed to morality are both rational and reasonable. On this interpretation, morality is rationally permissible but not rationally required, since egoism is also rationally permissible. Other supporters of the linkage between reason and morality reject the idea of separate theories of rationality and reasonableness, contending that morality is not just rationally permissible but also rationally required and that egoism is rationally impermissible. But despite their disagreement over whether there is a separate theory of rationality distinct from a theory of reasonableness, both groups link morality with a notion of reasonableness that incorporates a certain degree of altruism. For further discussion of these issues, see, e.g., James P. Sterba, *Justice for Here and Now* (Cambridge: Cambridge University Press, 1998), chap. 2.

9. I am indebted to Alasdair MacIntyre for helping me make this point clearer.

10. See James P. Sterba, "Is There a Rationale for Punishment?" *American Journal of Jurisprudence* 29 (1984): 29–43.

11. By the liberty of the rich to meet their luxury needs, I continue to mean the liberty of the rich not to be interfered with when using their surplus possessions for luxury purposes. Similarly, by the liberty of the poor to meet their basic needs, I continue to mean the liberty of the poor not to be interfered with when taking from the surplus possessions of the rich what they require to meet their basic needs.

12. My thanks to Tara Smith for helping me to clarify the argument in this paragraph.

13. See, e.g., Eric Mack, "Individualism, Rights, and the Open Society," in *The Libertarian Alternative*, ed. Tibor Machan (Chicago: Nelson-Hall, 1974), 21–37.

14. Since the conflict resolution principle is the contrapositive of the "ought"

implies "can" principle, whatever logically follows from the one principle logically follows from the other. Nevertheless, by first appealing to one principle and then the other, as I have here, I maintain that the conclusions that I derive can be seen to follow more clearly.

15. For an analogous resolution, consider the following report of a former slave: "[I]t is all right for us poor colored people to appropriate whatever the white folks' blessings the Lord put in our way." Julius Lester, *To Be a Slave* (New York: Dial Books, 1968), 102.

16. The employment opportunities offered to the poor must be honorable and supportive of self-respect. To do otherwise would be to offer the poor the opportunity to meet some of their basic needs at the cost of denying some of their other basic needs.

17. The poor cannot, however, give up their liberty to which their children are entitled.

18. See Hospers, "The Libertarian Manifesto."

19. Sometimes advocates of libertarianism inconsistently contend that the duty to help others is supererogatory but that a majority of a society could justifiably enforce such a duty on everyone. See Theodore Benditt, "The Demands of Justice," in *Economic Justice*, ed. Diana Meyers and Kenneth Kipnis (Totowa, N.J.: Rowman & Allanheld, 1985), 108–20.

20. Sometimes advocates of libertarianism focus on the coordination problems that arise in welfare and socialist states concerning the provision of welfare and ignore the far more serious coordination problems that would arise in a night-watchman state. See Burton Leiser, "Vagrancy, Loitering, and Economic Justice," in *Economic Justice,* ed. Meyers and Kipnis, 149–60.

21. It is true, of course, that if the rich could retain the resources that are used in a welfare state for meeting the basic needs of the poor, they might have the option of using those resources to increase employment opportunities beyond what obtains in any given welfare state, but this particular way of increasing employment opportunities does not seem to be the most effective way of meeting the basic needs of the poor, and it would not at all serve to meet the basic needs of those who cannot work.

22. See James P. Sterba, "Moral Approaches to Nuclear Strategy: A Critical Evaluation," *Canadian Journal of Philosophy* 12, special issue (1986): 75–109.

23. Although in this case the rich would be blameworthy for bringing about the death of (i.e., killing) the poor, it is not clear to me that they can properly be called "killers."

24. When the poor are acting collectively in conjunction with their agents and allies to exercise their negative welfare rights, they will want, in turn, to institute adequate positive welfare rights to secure a proper distribution of the goods and resources they are acquiring.

25. It is important to see how moral and pragmatic considerations are combined in this argument from negative welfare rights to positive welfare rights, as this will become particularly relevant when we turn to a consideration of distant peoples and future generations. What needs to be seen is that the moral consideration is primary and the pragmatic consideration secondary. The moral consideration is that until positive

welfare rights for the poor are guaranteed, any use by the rich of their surplus posses-sions to meet their nonbasic needs is likely to violate the negative welfare rights of the poor by preventing the poor from appropriating (some part of) the surplus goods and resources of the rich. The pragmatic consideration is that, in the absence of positive welfare rights, the rich would have to put up with the discretion of the poor, either act-ing by themselves or through their allies or agents, in choosing when and how to exer-cise their negative welfare rights. Now, obviously, distant peoples who are separated from the rich by significant distances will be able to exercise their negative welfare rights only either by negotiating the distances involved or by having allies or agents in the right place, willing to act on their behalf. And with respect to future generations, their rights can be exercised only if they too have allies and agents in the right place and time, willing to act on their behalf. So unless distant peoples are good at negotiat-ing distances or unless distant peoples and future generations have ample allies and agents in the right place and time, the pragmatic consideration leading the rich to endorse positive welfare rights will diminish in importance in their regard. Fortunate-ly, the moral consideration alone is sufficient to carry the argument here and elsewhere: libertarians should endorse positive welfare rights because it is the only way that they can be assured of not violating the negative welfare right of the poor by preventing the poor from appropriating (some part of) the surplus goods and resources of the rich.

26.   Richard De George, "Do We Owe the Future Anything?" in *Law and the Eco-logical Challenge* (Buffalo, N.Y.: W. S. Hein, 1978), 2: 180–90.

27.   Rex Martin, *Rawls and Rights* (Lawrence: University of Kansas Press, 1984), chap. 2.

28.   Anita Gordon and David Suzuki, *It's a Matter of Survival* (Cambridge: Harvard University Press, 1990). See also Donella H. Meadows et al., *The Limits to Growth*, 2d ed. (New York: New American Library, 1974), chaps. 3, 4.

29.   For a somewhat opposing view, see M. P. Golding, "Obligations to Future Gen-erations," *Monist* 56 (1972): 85–99.

30.   Moreover, libertarians have not restricted the class of morally legitimate claimants in this fashion. After all, the fundamental rights recognized by libertarians are universal rights, that is, rights possessed by all people, not just those who live in certain places or at certain times. Of course, to claim that these rights are universal rights does not mean that they are universally recognized. Obviously, the fundamental rights that flow from the libertarian ideal have not been universally recognized. Rather, to claim that they are universal rights, despite their spotty recognition, implies only that they ought to be recognized at all times and in all places by people who have or could have had good reasons to recognize these rights, whether or not they actually did or do so. Nor need these universal rights be unconditional. This is particularly true in the case of the right to welfare, which, I have argued, is conditional on people's doing all that they legitimately can to provide for themselves. In addition, this right is conditional on there being sufficient goods and resources available so that everyone's welfare needs can be met. So where people do not do all that they can to provide for themselves or where there are not sufficient goods and resources available, people simply do not have a right to welfare.

Yet even though libertarians have claimed that the rights they defend are universal rights in the manner I have just explained, it may be that they are simply mistaken in this regard. Even when universal rights are stripped of any claim to being universally recognized or unconditional, still it might be argued that there are no such rights, that is, that there are no rights that all people ought to recognize. But how would one argue for such a view? One couldn't argue from the failure of people to recognize such rights, because we have already said that such recognition is not necessary. Nor could one argue that not everyone ought to recognize such rights because some lack the capacity to do so. This is because "ought" implies "can" here, so that the obligation to recognize certain rights only applies to those who actually have (or have had at some point) the capacity to do so. Thus, the existence of universal rights is not ruled out by the existence of individuals who have never had the capacity to recognize such rights. It would be ruled out only by the existence of individuals who could recognize these rights but for whom it would be correct to say that they ought, all things considered, not to do so. But we have just seen that even a minimal libertarian moral ideal supports a universal right to welfare. And as I have argued, when "ought" is understood prudentially rather than morally, a non-question-begging conception of rationality favors morality over prudence. (See Sterba, *Justice for Here and Now*, chap. 2). So for those capable of recognizing universal rights, it simply is not possible to argue that they, all things considered, ought not to do so.

31. Bob Bergland, "Attacking the Problem of World Hunger," *National Forum* 69 (1979): 4.

32. Bread for the World Institute, *Hunger 1995: Fifth Annual Report on the State of World Hunger* (Silver Spring, Md.: Bread for the World Institute, 1994), 10; Ruth Sivard, *World Military and Social Expenditures* (Washington, D.C.: World Priorities, 1993), 28; Frances Moore Lappé, *World Hunger* (New York: Grove Press, 1986), 9.

33. Lester Brown, Christopher Flavin, and Hal Kane, *Vital Signs 1996* (New York: W. W. Norton, 1996), 34–35; Jeremy Rifkin, *Beyond Beef* (New York: Penguin, 1992), 1.

34. Lester Brown, *State of the World 1996* (New York: Norton, 1996), 10; Lester Brown, *State of the World 1992* (New York: Norton, 1992), 79.

35. Lester Brown, *Who Will Feed China?* (New York: Norton, 1995). For reasons for thinking that the additional capacity for grain production worldwide is quite limited, see 104 ff.

36. Henry Shue, *Basic Rights* (Princeton, N.J.: Princeton University Press, 1980), chap. 7.

37. For a discussion of these causal connections, see Cheryl Silver, *One Earth, One Future* (Washington, D.C.: National Academy Press, 1990); Bill McKibben, *The End of Nature* (New York: Anchor Books, 1989); Jeremy Leggett, ed., *Global Warming* (New York: Oxford University Press, 1990); and Lester Brown, ed., *The World Watch Reader* (New York: Nelson, 1991).

38. Charles Park Jr., ed., *Earth Resources* (Washington D.C.: Voice of America, 1980), chap. 13; Lester Brown, *State of the World 1992* (New York: Norton, 1992), chap. 7; Brown, *World Watch Reader*, 268.

39. G. Tyler Miller Jr. *Living with the Environment* (Belmont, Calif.: Wadsworth, 1990), 20. See also Janet Besecker and Phil Elder, "Lifeboat Ethics: A Reply to Hardin," in *Readings in Ecology, Energy, and Human Society*, ed. William Burch (New York: Harper & Row, 1977), 229. For higher and lower estimates of the impact of North Americans, see Holmes Rolston III, "Feeding People versus Saving Nature?" in *World Hunger and Morality*, 2d ed. (Englewood Cliffs, N.J.: Prentice-Hall, 1966), 259–60; Paul Ehrlich, Anne Ehrlich, and Gretchen Daily, *The Stork and the Plow* (New York: Grosset/Putnam, 1995), 26.

40. Successes in meeting the most basic needs of the poor in particular regions of developing countries (e.g., the Indian state of Kerala) should not blind us to the growing numbers of people living in conditions of absolute poverty (1.2 billion by a recent estimate) and how difficult it will be to meet the basic needs of all these people in a sustainable way that will allow future generations to have their basic needs met as well, especially when we reflect on the fact that the way we in the developed world are living is not sustainable at all!

41. In *How to Make People Just*, I argued similarly that "[f]or all practical purposes the argument from the welfare rights of distant peoples and future generations is sufficient to show that . . . there will be very few resources left over for the satisfaction of nonbasic needs" (109–10). I then went on to advance a rather complicated argument that depended on a claim of symmetry between a right not to be born and a right to be born (but not on the claim that the fetus is a person) to arrive at the conclusion that in some thoroughly just, and hence nonsexist, world that is also underpopulated (obviously not the real world we live in), abortion and even contraception may be morally impermissible in certain circumstances. Derek Parfit and others have challenged this argument in print ("A Reply to Sterba," *Philosophy and Public Affairs* 16 [1987]: 193–94), but Parfit later conceded in correspondence that he now thinks that the argument works. After searching in vain for a mistake in it, I also think the argument works. But I also see more clearly now that the argument does little to support my case for equality, since under present conditions it justifies both abortion and contraception. So I have not used it here. My initial argument buttressed by the new considerations that I have brought to bear here is more than sufficient to establish the conclusion I want.

42. John Rawls, *A Theory of Justice* (Cambridge: Harvard University Press, 1971), chap. 2.

43. Tibor Machan, *Individuals and Their Rights* (La Salle, Wisc.: Open Court, 1989), 100-111.

44. Machan, *Individuals and Their Rights,* 107.

45. Alan Durning, "Life on the Brink," *World Watch* 3 (1990): 24.

46. Durning, "Life on the Brink," 29.

47. Machan also sketches another line of argument that unfortunately proceeds from premises that contradict his line of argument that I have discussed here. The line of argument that I have discussed here turns on Machan's claim that "normally, persons do not lack the opportunities and resources to satisfy their basic needs." Machan's second line of argument, by contrast, concedes that many of the poor lack the opportunities and resources to satisfy their basic needs but then contends that this lack is the

result of political oppression in the absence of libertarian institutions. See Machan, *Individuals and Their Rights*, 109. See also Machan's contribution to James P. Sterba et al., *Morality and Social Justice: Point and Counterpoint* (Lanham, Md.: Rowman & Littlefield, 1994), 59–106, where Machan develops this second line of argument in more detail. For my response to this line of argument, see "Comments by James P. Sterba," in *Morality and Social Justice*, 110–13.

48. Tibor Machan, "The Nonexistence of Welfare Rights" (new expanded version), in *Liberty for the Twenty-first Century*, ed. Tibor Machan and Douglas Rasmussen, Social, Political, and Legal Philosophy Series, ed. James P. Sterba (Lanham, Md.: Rowman & Littlefield, 1995), 218–20.

49. Machan, "The Nonexistence of Welfare Rights."

50. Machan, "The Nonexistence of Welfare Rights."

51. Richard Rose and Rei Shiratori, eds., *The Welfare State East and West* (Oxford: Oxford University Press, 1986). In fact, the living standards of poor children in Switzerland, Sweden, Finland, Denmark, Belgium, Norway, Luxembourg, Germany, the Netherlands, Austria, Canada, France, Italy, the United Kingdom, and Australia are all better than they are in the United States. See James Carville, *We're Right, They're Wrong* (New York: Random House, 1996), 31–32.

52. Michael Wolff, *Where We Stand* (New York: Bantam Books, 1992), 23, 115; George Kurian, *The New Book of Work Rankings*, 3d ed. (New York: Facts on File, 1990), 73; *New York Times*, 17 April 1995.

53. Douglas Rasmussen, "Individual Rights and Human Flourishing," *Public Affairs Quarterly* 3 (1989): 89–103. See also Douglas Rasmussen and Douglas Den Uyl, *Liberty and Nature* (La Salle, Wisc.: Open Court, 1991), chaps. 2–4.

54. Rasmussen, "Individual Rights and Human Flourishing," 98.

55. Rasmussen, "Individual Rights and Human Flourishing," 99.

56. Rasmussen, "Individual Rights and Human Flourishing," 100.

57. Rasmussen, "Individual Rights and Human Flourishing," 101.

58. John Hospers, "Some Unquestioned Assumptions," *Journal of Social Philosophy* 22 (1991): 42–51.

59. Although given what I have said about the welfare rights of distant peoples and future generations, it would seem that (b) and (c) are unlikely to obtain.

60. Actually, the possessions in question are not truly nonsurplus, since those who have them could relatively easily produce a surplus.

61. Eric Mack, "Libertarianism Untamed," *Journal of Social Philosophy* 22 (1991): 64–72.

62. But what, you might ask, is my response to the defenses of libertarianism provided by the examples from Friedman and Nozick? My response to Friedman's defense should be obvious. When basic needs are at stake, the poor can have a claim against the rich, and poor Robinson Crusoes can have a claim against rich Robinson Crusoes. My response to Nozick's defense of libertarianism is that it seems to apply only to political ideals that require an absolute equality of income. Since a welfare liberal conception of justice is not committed to an absolute equality of income, the inequalities of income generated in Nozick's example would be objectionable only if they deprived

people of something to which they had a right, such as welfare or equal opportunity. And whether people are so deprived depends on to what uses the Wilt Chamberlains or Michael Jordans of the world put their greater income. Thus, it is perfectly conceivable that those who have legitimately acquired greater income may use it in ways that do not violate the rights of others.

11

Responsibility for Needs

John Baker and Charles Jones

Egalitarians believe, among other things, that everyone's basic needs ought to be satisfied. In this chapter we take belief in that principle (or something like it) for granted. The question we are concerned with is who is responsible for ensuring that the principle is honored. A widely held view is that, as far as possible, responsibility for needs should be shouldered by individuals themselves and that those who are incapable of satisfying their own needs should be looked after by the local communities to which they belong. We criticize this view and argue that every person has a strong degree of responsibility to act collectively to ensure that everyone's basic needs are satisfied. This defense of global collective action is not in our view constitutive of egalitarianism, but the two ideas have a long association that we are happy to endorse.

We begin, in section 1, by considering the obviously mistaken view that each person should satisfy their own needs, arguing that any plausible approach must give a major role to collective responsibility. In section 2 we devise a more complicated principle in the same spirit. The revised principle combines the idea of giving each person a genuinely equal opportunity for satisfying their own needs with the aim of devolving collective responsibility to local communities. We proceed to discuss each part of the principle in turn. We argue that genuinely equal opportunity presupposes wide-ranging collective responsibilities (section 2); that the case for individual responsibility can be grossly exaggerated (section 3); and that global, collective responsibility for needs is unavoidable (section 4). We conclude in section 5 by recognizing the place of devolved responsibility within a just global order. For the most part, we assume a working understanding of the idea of a basic need, although occasionally we make use of specific ideas. For simplicity, we use the term "need" throughout to refer to basic needs.

1. "Each Person Should Satisfy Their Own Needs"

Our starting point is a simple view that no one could seriously hold but that provides a good basis for what follows: the view that each person should be responsible for satisfying their own needs. The most obvious reason why no one could seriously hold this view is that some people are quite clearly incapable of satisfying their own needs. Examples are young children and people with serious physical or mental impairments (although we will return to the issue of impairment in a moment). Again, some needs are intrinsically social, such as the needs for love and companionship. No one could satisfy these needs literally by themselves. A third reason is that some needs are for specialized services that no one seriously expects people to provide for themselves, even though it is logically possible for them to do so, such as needs for education and medical care.

There is a deeper reason why the view is untenable. It is that every act of satisfying a need "by oneself" takes place within a structure of choice that is socially constructed and maintained. For example, if I can "satisfy my own needs" by getting a job, getting paid, going into the supermarket, and buying food, this is only because of a set of institutions that are created and sustained by others. My capacity to get a job results from a certain upbringing within a certain family lodged within a wider array of family structures and from an education that was available within a certain kind of educational system. My skills are in demand because of the existence of a certain kind of economy and of certain economically effective preferences. The financial transactions between my employer, my bank, and the supermarket depend on a specific set of social conventions, laws, and relationships. And so on.

These objections to the simple view are not trivial. A very substantial proportion of humanity at any one time is either young or living with a serious impairment. Intrinsically social needs and needs for specialized services make up a large proportion of our most urgent needs on any account of what these are. And a very large proportion of the cases in which people are not currently satisfying their own needs are cases in which the social structures in which people find themselves provide them with no feasible opportunity for doing so.

This last point is brought home very forcefully by proponents of the "social model of disability."[1] These writers point out that for at least a large proportion of cases, disability is a matter of the difference between the ways social structures are adapted to the capacities of able-bodied people and the ways they fail to be adapted to people with physical and mental impairments. A stock example is the existence of stairs, which are an indispensable, socially constructed means for most people to get from one floor of a building to another. People who use stairs are not really satisfying their own mobility needs;

they are using more widely provided means for satisfying these needs than those provided to people in wheelchairs.

Similarly, in a capitalist economy the basic means for satisfying most people's material needs are provided by the labor market. That some people are able to access this market successfully is not simply a fact about them but also about the social system within which they operate. Without the labor market they would be as needy as any other unemployed person. It is therefore quite misleading to describe them simply as satisfying their own needs: there is no such thing as a "self-made man."

A natural response to these obvious considerations is to seek to define a more complicated principle that preserves the spirit of the simple view in a more realistic form. In section 2 we spell out this more complicated view and begin to assess its strength.

2. A More Complicated View

Consider the following three-part principle:

A. Social structures should be organized to ensure as far as possible that individuals have an equal and real opportunity to satisfy their own basic needs; that is, they are equally enabled to satisfy these needs.

B. Insofar as people do have such an opportunity/ability, they should be responsible for satisfying their own needs.

C. Such responsibility for satisfying basic needs as it remains impossible to devolve onto individuals should be shouldered by people attached to them by kinship, religion, ethnicity, nationality, or other forms of communal attachment, not by strangers.

The principle modifies the simple view in three important ways. First, it recognizes that people can satisfy their own needs only to a limited extent. They can make a greater or lesser contribution to satisfying their needs but cannot in general take full responsibility for doing so. Second, it recognizes that the degree to which people are able to take responsibility for their needs is a consequence of social policy. Social structures can enable or disable individuals in their efforts to satisfy their needs. Third, it specifies who should be responsible for that contribution to need satisfaction that remains outside individual abilities. In the spirit of the simple view, it seeks to devolve this responsibility to those most closely connected to each individual.

The new principle has been formulated to preserve the spirit of the simple view in a form that is at least plausible and therefore to articulate what we take to be a widely held view about responsibility for needs. Parts A and B are meant to capture what might be called the idea of equal opportunity for the satisfaction of needs, while part C is intended to express the idea of local responsibility for needs. In this and the next two sections, we discuss each part of the principle in turn.

Perhaps the most controversial aspect of part A of the revised principle is the understanding of equal opportunity it involves, namely, a strong conception in which equality of opportunity is defined in terms of capability rather than the absence of certain formal constraints.[2] Why shouldn't the principle be defined in more conventional terms? The answer is that in this context only a strong conception of equal opportunity will suffice because of the connection between responsibility and capability. Broadly speaking, no one can be held responsible for actions that are outside their control. The spirit of the principle is to maximize the extent to which each individual is responsible for satisfying their own needs. It follows that we should maximize the extent to which each individual is capable of doing so. Quite how to interpret the idea of maximizing the degree to which each individual has some good or quality is a common problem in political philosophy that is answered differently by utilitarians and egalitarians. The egalitarian answer is to ensure, as far as possible, an equal distribution of the good in question at the highest possible level. For this reason, part A endorses the greatest possible equality of capability for satisfying one's own needs.[3]

On this understanding of equal opportunity, it is clear that part A is an enormously radical principle, since providing a social framework in which individuals can indeed take a large degree of responsibility for satisfying their own basic needs would arguably require very substantial changes to existing social structures. Within broadly market-based economies the only way most individuals are able to provide for their material needs is through employment. So if we are committed to ensuring that every individual is, as far as possible, able to satisfy their own needs, we must be committed to a policy of full employment, where full employment is defined in terms of guaranteeing a job to every person capable of doing one, with a level of pay at least adequate for meeting their material needs at market prices. It should be noted, in keeping with the social model of disability introduced earlier, that a much larger proportion of people are capable of employment than is often imagined. It should also be noted that any feasible policy of full employment has correspondingly radical implications for education and training, since the capacity of individuals to take up available employment depends on their learned skills. Another wideranging implication concerns the treatment of what Kittay calls "dependency workers," those whose work consists in the care of others.[4] Much of this work is currently unpaid work performed by women. Part A implies that dependency work should be paid for so that dependency workers are themselves able to take responsibility for their own needs.

Material needs are not the only basic needs. If, as seems incontrovertible, people also have a basic need for rest and relaxation, for satisfying and supportive relationships, and for cultural activities and many other "leisure pursuits" in the broad sense of the term, part A also entails that employment should not be so time-consuming or exhausting or isolating as to make it impossible for people to satisfy these other needs. It may be too controversial to maintain that satisfying work is itself a basic need, but work that is so soul-destroying or personally destructive as to interfere with someone's ability to cope would be contrary to the principle as well.

Clearly it cannot be the responsibility of each individual to ensure that she or he lives in the kind of full-employment economy just described, with everything this entails about education and training, the care of dependents, and the nature of work. These are by their nature collective responsibilities. Thus, part A of the principle, though it is specifically designed to create a framework within which individuals can be held responsible for their own needs, entails wide-ranging collective responsibilities for the framework itself.

Given these radical implications, and taking other social objectives into account, many people may prefer to reject part A or to adopt it in only a qualified form. Nothing we have said prevents them from doing so. What we do maintain is that part A defines the limits within which individuals can be held responsible for satisfying their needs: the weaker the principle, the narrower the range of individual responsibility. Insofar as collectives are unable or unwilling to endorse part A and to maintain the framework it entails, they cannot go on to hold individuals responsible for needs they are incapable of satisfying but must exercise direct, collective responsibility of the type associated with social welfare or basic income schemes. Thus, with or without part A, there is a substantial degree of collective responsibility. How this responsibility should be distributed is the business of part C of the principle, which we discuss below.

3. Individual Responsibility

Part B of the principle insists that individuals should be held responsible for satisfying their own needs to whatever extent part A makes possible. This is an attractive position in societies gripped by a revolt against a "culture of dependency" and subscribing to an ideology of self-reliance. In section 5 below, we try to identify the merits of these ideas. In this section, however, we argue that their merits can be grossly exaggerated. Inevitably, our discussion is connected to broader discussions about the use of markets versus collective provision, because markets constitute the strongest model for exercising individual responsibility for needs.

According to part B, individuals who have a genuine opportunity to satisfy their own needs should be held responsible for doing so. If they fail, it is not the business of the rest of us to intervene. The first argument against such a strict policy of individual responsibility is that it may be counterproductive. Suppose, for example, that Smith's failure to satisfy his own needs occurs like this: instead of prudently taking a job and spending his income on food, clothes, and so on, Smith irresponsibly squanders his income on drugs and becomes addicted. He loses his job, and under the pressure of material need and drug dependency, unaided by any collective intervention, he begins to steal from shops and houses. We arrest Smith and put him in jail. Smith is now completely dependent, and the collective cost of our policy of personal responsibility (in terms of crime, policing, and detention, as well as Smith's lost productivity) is far greater than if we had intervened earlier under a more qualified policy. This hypothetical example bears only a superficial relationship to real problems of drug addiction, since in the majority of cases drug users do not start from a position of equal capability. But it does make the obvious point that the policy of strict personal responsibility can easily backfire. It might be replied that the example succeeds only because we have been unable to impose on Smith the full cost of his irresponsibility. But how much more can he pay? When we have exhausted his own capabilities, we must foot the bill ourselves.

A second problem with individualizing responsibility arises from well-known ways in which coordinated collective action can be preferable to uncoordinated individual action. A classic example is the choice between individual and public transportation as a means for satisfying people's mobility needs. It is now widely recognized that reliance on individual transportation in the form of cars is simply untenable in modern cities. Only a collective solution in the form of an efficient public transportation system has even a hope of solving this particular problem and many like it.[5] A different type of problem occurs in cases of "public goods," where the effect of some people providing a good for themselves is inevitably to provide the good cost-free to others. A standard example is the need for a healthy environment. I cannot satisfy my need for clean air without satisfying it for you, too. As classically demonstrated by Olson, uncoordinated individual action is likely to be suboptimal because no one is likely to find it worth their while to shoulder the entire cost of providing such a good (of ensuring, to pursue the example, that no one pollutes the environment). The optimal arrangement, in which everyone contributes their fair share to providing the good, requires coordinated action.[6]

Another set of problems occurs in relation to monopolies such as water providers. Uncoordinated action by individuals to satisfy their needs for drinking water by purchasing from the monopoly supplier is less efficient than a cooperative solution.[7] This list is not exhaustive, but it illustrates some relatively uncontentious ways in which the doctrine of strict individual responsibility can be seriously inefficient.[8]

A rather different line of attack on maximizing individual responsibility is that this can undermine social solidarity. One of the key ties that bind communities together is collective provision for needs.[9] It may be technically feasible to provide education or health care on an individualized basis, but it may make for a stronger sense of community to provide them collectively. In the case of education, collective provision or at least collective control also creates the possibility for certain common, core elements that can be used, benignly or otherwise, to foster social solidarity.

All of the arguments so far take needs for granted, without asking how needs are generated or defined. Human beings as a natural species need water and oxygen and various nutrients, but many of our needs do not arise so simply. They are in various ways generated by, or defined in terms of, the type of society we live in. For example, we have not always needed to be literate and numerate, but these are now basic needs by any account. The kind of clothing, food, and shelter we need depends not just on our biology but on what is necessary to function and to maintain self-respect in particular social structures. These facts are established by collective action, even if it is often unintended. That is to say, our collective action in defining and reproducing the kind of society we live in has consequences for each individual living in it in terms of what they need. The doctrine of strict individual responsibility says that although we collectively generate individual needs, we should hold individuals responsible for satisfying them. It would seem more in keeping with the idea of responsibility itself to recognize that, like other actions, our collective action in generating needs entails a certain level of responsibility for satisfying them.

There is, finally, a certain harshness and inhumanity in the doctrine of strict individual responsibility. It entails that accident victims who have no insurance should be left on the street; that smokers, alcoholics, and drug addicts who freely start their habits should be offered no help; that people who make unwise choices of education or employment should not have a second chance; that the person who swims too far from shore should be allowed to drown. These are dramatic but genuine cases of the conflict between responsibility and humanity. No one is logically compelled to choose humanity; but it would be ironic, to say the least, for humanity to have no bearing on whether to come to the aid of people in need, despite their need being of their own making.

Generosity, fellow-feeling, compassion, and decency call on us to respond to need regardless of its provenance, and their call is not silenced, even if it is sometimes overridden, by other moral principles.[10]

Our conclusion is not that there is no room for individual responsibility but that it should not be exaggerated. The doctrine that individuals should be held responsible for satisfying their needs to the extent to which they are genuinely able to do so, attractive as it seems, can be counterproductive and inefficient, can work against social solidarity, ignores the social generation of needs, and is ultimately inhumane. Collective responsibility is often better, even where individual responsibility is possible.[11]

4. Local Responsibility

We have come a long way from the simple view that individuals should be responsible for satisfying their own needs. We noted to begin with that there are many needs that individuals simply cannot satisfy on their own and that satisfying virtually any need depends on a socially established framework. We constructed a principle that took these facts into account by aiming to maximize the degree to which individuals could be held responsible for satisfying their needs and found that this presupposed an appropriate framework that it would take considerable collective action to establish. Insofar as we are collectively unwilling or unable to provide such a framework, we are correspondingly unable to devolve responsibility for needs onto individuals themselves. Even within such a framework, we argued, there were a number of reasons why it would be unacceptable to push individual responsibility to its limits. Taking all of these points together provides a strong case for a substantial degree of collective responsibility for needs.

Part C of the principle set out above attempts to deal with this collective responsibility in the spirit of the original simple view, by trying as far as possible to confine collective responsibility to the people most closely related to individuals in need. According to this doctrine of local responsibility, it is the job of family, friends, compatriots, and other communities to shoulder collective responsibilities for need, not the job of strangers. In this section we argue that local responsibility is too limited a view and that responsibility for needs is unavoidably global.

Some of the arguments against local responsibility are simply extensions of the arguments against individual responsibility. Providing an economic framework in which local communities have the capacity to take responsibility for needs is itself a global project because we live in a global economy. Like strict individual responsibility, strict local responsibility is potentially counterproductive, inefficient, and inhumane. But there are other arguments more specific to the idea of local responsibility.

A very basic argument against limiting responsibilities to local groups is that such limits seem to contradict the widely acknowledged principle that every person is due equal consideration. If responsibility is tied to comembership in a nation, religion, or ethnic group, those outside the group appear to be the victims of ethical demotion for no good reason. If the basic needs of everyone are accorded the same weight, why should the burden of satisfying those needs fall only upon some subset of humanity, thereby excusing others from responsibility?

One answer to that question is to insist that confining obligations in this manner is perfectly compatible with equal consideration: local responsibility is simply the best way to ensure that everyone's needs are in fact met. Since this is an empirical claim, it raises the question of what would really happen if needs were met only by people near and dear to one another. The answer is that hundreds of millions of human beings would have unmet basic needs, for those near and dear to them would lack the means to meet those needs. This argument is especially important for those who place a significant value on caring for particular others such as family members, since it reminds us that caring for others requires resources that can be provided only through global action. Otherwise, many people simply would not be cared for at all.[12] Allocating responsibilities to particular groups would be acceptable, then, only if each of those groups possessed in equal measure the capacity realistically to fulfill those responsibilities. To put it another way, part C has its own analogue to part A, namely, a requirement that local groups are equally able to satisfy their members' needs.

Another common objection to global responsibility is based on the special relationships of friends and families. There are some needs, such as those for companionship and love mentioned earlier, that it is literally impossible for strangers to satisfy. Our needs for friendship or familial love must be met by people who are attached to us in special ways. And the importance of these needs is undeniable, given the value of intimacy in a fulfilling human life. This is an element of local responsibility we are happy to endorse, while remembering as always that the ability to carry out these responsibilities depends on adequate resources.

What we reject is the way part C attempts to generalize these relations of intimacy. In saying that needs should not be met by strangers but by people related by ties of group solidarity, it ignores the fact that religious, ethnic, or national groups are themselves composed largely and inevitably of strangers. Since the normative force of our special ties to our friends and family depends on the role of intimacy in a meaningful life, it cannot be transferred to these groups of anonymous strangers among whom intimacy is simply not possible (or is possible only with a small minority of other members). Hence part C of the principle embodies a false dichotomy between strangers and group members, and the real choice is between two sets of strangers. The appeal of special responsibilities to compatriots, coreligionists, and the like is significantly weakened once its rationale is distinguished from the sorts of reasons used to defend special concern for family members.

The proponent of part C of the principle might still object to global responsibility by claiming that we are constitutionally incapable of sympathizing with every other human being.[13] Consequently, the only practical way to meet needs is to assign responsibilities to comembers of national, ethnic, religious, or other such groups, where sympathy is sufficiently strong to underpin individual motivation. But this objection underestimates our capacities for sympathetic identification, for we can and do sympathize with the suffering of faraway people who lack the means to satisfy their basic needs. We can recognize that our own condition could have been one of severe deprivation, and this provides the basis for taking an interest in others. Of course, we cannot feel the same level of sympathy for every needy person; nevertheless, we can identify with the plight of the needy and understand that each instance is potentially as sympathy-generating as any other. Once we see that everyone is entitled to our concern, we have grounds for supporting institutions whose purpose is to meet the basic needs of everyone, near and far. And where sympathy within some community does seem to be locked within its own boundaries, we may reasonably attempt to extend those limits by helping its members to imagine themselves in other people's shoes.

A related point often made by defenders of special, local responsibilities is that acceptance of such responsibilities and the sacrifices they entail is contingent upon mutual feelings of solidarity between group members. These sentiments presuppose some basis of identification such as shared nationality.[14] There are two reasons to be skeptical about this claim. First, we have already seen that a sense of solidarity with all human beings is perfectly possible, especially where it is based on acknowledging the fundamental needs we all share. And second, even if nationalist feelings do facilitate redistribution, this does not show that they are necessary for achieving it. The supposed fact that special sentiments help welfare states to function within their limited spheres of concern does not justify neglecting the needs of nonnationals.

One final point: Defending global responsibility with respect to human needs does not amount to denying local responsibility in other respects. For instance, once basic needs are protected everywhere, it is perfectly acceptable for the obligation to protect cultural, religious, and other community values to be restricted mainly to fellow members of those communities.

In this section we have argued that the requirement of equal concern for all human beings suggests the prima facie plausibility of global responsibility for meeting needs; that such concern would support limiting responsibilities to group members only where each group had roughly equal resources; that, apart from family and friends, those with whom we share various sorts of group membership are strangers, and therefore the ethical appeal of closeness in relationships does not support special concern for fellow nationals or compatriots; that, contrary to what is sometimes believed, human beings are able to sympathize with the suffering of faraway others; and that, while nationalist and patriotic sentiments may increase the reliability of redistributive regimes of institutionalized care (welfare states), this provides no reason for confining concern within national communities. The upshot of this section is that responsibility for needs is unavoidably global.[15]

5. The Benefits of Devolved Responsibility

We have argued for a substantial degree of global, collective responsibility for satisfying basic needs. This does not mean that every need should be the responsibility of some global state but that global responsibility is a major and unavoidable factor in a just world order. There is also a strong case for devolved responsibility, and we wish to conclude by reviewing some of its benefits.

The first reason for enabling individuals and communities to satisfy their own needs and expecting them to do so is simple efficiency. Individuals and local communities are in general the best judges of their own needs and in general can be counted on to have strong motivations for satisfying them. Given appropriate background institutions and an egalitarian distribution of relevant resources, it will therefore often be more efficient to provide individuals or communities with the opportunity to identify and satisfy their own needs than to try to do so for them.

A second argument for devolved responsibility is the point discussed above that some needs, such as those for companionship and love, can be satisfied only through intimate relationships. In these cases, devolved responsibility is a necessary feature of the kind of need involved, although ensuring that people have enough resources to be able to carry out their responsibilities remains a global issue.

A third argument is based on considerations of power and vulnerability. Insofar as the satisfaction of my needs becomes the responsibility of some wider collective, that collective possesses effective power to define my needs and to provide or withhold the means for satisfying them. By contrast, if I am personally responsible for my needs and capable of meeting them, I am free to define them and to satisfy them. If our view in this chapter is correct, collective power is to a large degree unavoidable and the problem can be addressed only by developing strongly democratic structures with appropriate guarantees for minorities. But there remains a case for individual responsibility where it is feasible.

A related reason for devolved responsibility is that in general, and again against an appropriate background, individuals tend to achieve satisfactions of self-realization and self-worth if they are able to identify and satisfy their own needs as distinct from relying on others to do so. Similarly, self-reliant communities can also develop a sense of efficacy and self-respect. The image behind the criticism of the "nanny state" taps a real egalitarian concern about dominance, subordination, and self-respect. What is wrong with the current use of this image is that oppressed individuals and communities are expected to "stand on their own two feet" without access to the resources enabling them to do so. That is why we have argued that any defensible principle of individual or local responsibility has to be located within a framework of equal capability.

A final reason for devolved responsibility has to do with disagreements about needs. Individuals and cultures have very different conceptions of human well-being, and these conceptions generate differences in their lists of basic needs. If you disagree about whether something even counts as one of my basic needs, it may be unreasonable for me to expect you to take responsibility for ensuring its satisfaction. A more appropriate solution is to ensure that I have the opportunity to satisfy the alleged need myself or through a local communal effort. Devolved responsibility is a way to avoid imposing one definition of need on everyone.[16]

So there are genuine reasons for devolving responsibility for needs onto individuals and local communities. None of these reasons, however, provides a strong argument against our collective responsibility for (1) providing background institutions that ensure people the genuine opportunity—that is, the ability—to satisfy their own needs, (2) ensuring that those who are tied by communal attachments to people in need are themselves able to act to satisfy those needs, (3) providing a safety net for those who irresponsibly fail to satisfy their own needs, and (4) recognizing that considerations of prudence, efficiency, and solidarity may call for the assumption of global collective responsibility for needs even when it is possible in principle for them to be satisfied in other ways.

We end this chapter as we began, with the principle that in a just world, everyone's basic needs would be satisfied. Although we endorse this as an egalitarian principle, it has a wider appeal as well. What we hope to have shown is that the principle entails a strong, global, collective responsibility for ensuring its implementation. We cannot pretend that we care about people's needs and expect to do nothing to meet them.

Notes

1. Examples are John Swain et al., eds., *Disabling Barriers—Enabling Environments* (London: Sage, 1993); Len Barton, ed., *Disability and Society* (London: Longman, 1996); and Jane Campbell and Mike Oliver, *Disability Politics: Understanding Our Past, Changing Our Future* (London: Routledge, 1996).

2. For the articulation and defense of ideas along similar lines, see G. A. Cohen, "On the Currency of Egalitarian Justice," *Ethics* 99 (1989): 906–44; and Amartya Sen, *Inequality Reexamined* (Oxford: Oxford University Press, 1992).

3. More precisely, egalitarians are likely to endorse some form of qualified leximin principle under which we seek first to maximize the capability of the least capable, then of the next least, and so on, subject to intuitive constraints about the degree to which large reductions of greater capability can be sacrificed for small improvements of lesser capability. (For a parallel discussion, see Philippe Van Parijs, *Real Freedom for All* [Oxford: Oxford University Press, 1995], 25 and n.) For the purposes of this chapter, it will suffice to stick to the general idea of ensuring, as far as possible, an equal capability to satisfy one's needs.

4. See Eva Feder Kittay, "Human Dependency and Rawlsian Equality," in *Feminists Rethink the Self*, ed. Diana T. Meyers (Boulder, Colo.: Westview Press, 1997), 219–66.

5. For a relevant exposition, see Brian Barry, *The Liberal Theory of Justice* (Oxford: Oxford University Press, 1973), chap. 11.

6. Mancur Olson, *The Logic of Collective Action*, 2d ed. (Cambridge: Harvard University Press, 1971).

7. See John E. Roemer, *Free to Lose* (London: Radius, 1988), 149–52, for a brief exposition of this and other inefficiencies in the market.

8. For further discussion, see Brian Barry and Russell Hardin, eds., *Rational Man and Irrational Society?* (London: Sage, 1982), part 1.

9. Michael Walzer, *Spheres of Justice* (Oxford: Blackwell, 1985), chap. 3; R. H. Tawney, *Equality* (London: George Allen & Unwin, 1964); Richard Norman, "Equality, Needs, and Basic Income," in *Arguing for Basic Income*, ed. Philippe Van Parijs (London: Verso, 1992), 141–52.

10. For similar arguments, see Richard Arneson, "Opportunities versus Outcomes in Distributive Justice Norms," (1993); and Marc Fleurbaey, "Equal Opportunity or Equal Social Outcome?" *Economics and Philosophy* 11 (1995): 25–55, esp. 38–44.

11. The foregoing discussion subsumes what might be considered two distinct categories, namely, cooperation between responsible individuals and intervention on behalf of the irresponsible. Although the distinction is relevant to our problem, it is not

central, since the doctrine of individualized responsibility is incompatible with both of these ideas.

12. See Marilyn Friedman, *What Are Friends For? Feminist Perspectives on Personal Relationships and Moral Theory* (Ithaca, N.Y.: Cornell University Press, 1993), 75.

13. An example of this objection may be found in George Fletcher, *Loyalty: An Essay on the Morality of Relationships* (Oxford: Oxford University Press, 1993), 21.

14. See David Miller, *On Nationality* (Oxford: Clarendon Press, 1995), 90–96.

15. For an elaboration of these and related arguments, see Charles Jones, *Global Justice* (Oxford: Oxford University Press, forthcoming).

16. For a discussion of how this problem about needs fits into a wider conception of economic equality, see John Baker, "An Egalitarian Case for Basic Income," in *Arguing for Basic Income*, ed. Van Parijs, 101–27.

Index

About the Contributors

JOHN BAKER teaches political theory and equality studies in the Politics Department and Equality Studies Centre at University College Dublin, National University of Ireland, Dublin. He is the author of *Arguing for Equality*. He is currently working on collaborative projects in equality studies.

DAVID BRAYBROOKE holds the Centennial Commission Chair in the Liberal Arts at the University of Texas at Austin, where he is professor of government and professor of philosophy. He is McCulloch Professor of Philosophy and Politics Emeritus, Dalhousie University. Among his recent books, some with collaborators, have been *Philosophy of Social Science* (1987), *Meeting Needs* (1987), *Logic on the Track of Social Change* (1995), *Social Rules* (1996), and *Moral Objectives, Rules, and the Forms of Social Change* (1998).

GILLIAN BROCK is a senior lecturer in philosophy at the University of Auckland, New Zealand. She writes mainly on issues in ethics, social and political philosophy, and applied ethics. Much of her recent work has focused on the role human needs can play in moral and political theory, and particularly on our responsibilities to meet needs. She has published several articles in this area.

DAVID COPP is professor of philosophy at the University of California, Davis. He writes mainly in moral and political philosophy and is the author of *Morality, Normativity, and Society* (1995), a book on the foundations of morality. He is an associate editor of *Ethics*.

LEN DOYAL is professor of medical ethics at St. Bartholomew's and the Royal London School of Medicine and Dentistry, Queen Mary and Westfield College, University of London, and an Honorary Consultant to the Royal Hospitals Trust in East London. He is author (with Roger Harris) of *Empiricism, Explanation, and Rationality: An Introduction to the Philosophy of the Social Sciences* and (with Ian Gough) *A Theory of Human Need*. He edited the ethical and legal guidelines of the Royal College of Surgeons in the United Kingdom and writes widely on ethicolegal issues concerning the practice of clinical medicine.

HARRY G. FRANKFURT is professor of philosophy at Princeton University. He is the author of *Demons, Dreamers, and Madmen: The Defense of Reason in Descartes's Meditations* and *The Importance of What We Care About.* He is a former president of the American Philosophical Association (Eastern Division) and a Fellow of the American Academy of Arts and Sciences. His work is currently devoted mainly to topics in moral philosophy and in philosophical anthropology.

ROBERT E. GOODIN is professor of philosophy at the Research School of Social Sciences, Australian National University. His books straddle political theory, public policy, and applied ethics. They include *Political Theory and Public Policy* (1982), *Protecting the Vulnerable* (1985), *Reasons for Welfare* (1988), *No Smoking: Ethical Issues* (1989), *Motivating Political Morality* (1992), *Green Political Theory* (1992), *Utilitarianism as a Public Philosophy* (1995), and (with David Schmidtz) *Social Welfare as an Individual Responsibility: For and Against* (1998).

CHARLES JONES is Boole Fellow and lecturer in philosophy at University College, Cork, Ireland. His first book, *Global Justice,* will be published by Oxford University Press in 1999. He is currently editing (with Desmond M. Clarke) a book of philosophical essays entitled *National Identities in a Changing Europe.*

MARTHA NUSSBAUM is Ernst Freund Professor of Law and Ethics at the University of Chicago, with appointments in the Department of Philosophy, the Law School, and the Divinity School. She is the author of, among others, *The Fragility of Goodness; Love's Knowledge; The Therapy of Desire; Poetic Justice;* and *Cultivating Humanity.* Her 1998 Seeley Lectures at Cambridge University are entitled "Feminist Internationalism."

ONORA O'NEILL is principal of Newnham College, Cambridge. She has published widely in ethics, political philosophy, and Kant studies. Recent books include *Constructions of Reason: Explorations of Kant's Practical Philosophy* and *Towards Justice and Virtue: A Constructive Account of Practical Reasoning.*

JAMES P. STERBA is professor of philosophy at the University of Notre Dame, where he teaches moral and political philosophy. He has written more than 150 articles and published 16 books, including *How to Make People Just; Contemporary Ethics; Feminist Philosophies; Earth Ethics;* and *Morality in Practice.* His latest book is *Justice for Here and Now.* He is past president of the American Section of the International Society for Social and Legal Philosophy, Concerned Philosophers for Peace, and the North American Society for Social Philosophy. He has lectured widely in the United States and Europe and the Far East.

DAVID WIGGINS has been Wykeham Professor of Logic in the University of Oxford since 1993. Previously, he was professor of philosophy at Birkbeck College, London. He is the author of *Sameness and Substance* (1980; 2d ed., 1999) and *Needs, Values, Truth* (1987; 3d ed., 1998).